Sociocracy For All

MANY VOICES ONE SONG

Shared power with sociocracy

Ted J. Rau & Jerry Koch-Gonzalez

Sociocracy For All
Amherst, MA USA
sociocracyforall.org

Sociocracy For All

120 Pulpit Hill Road, Unit 8
Amherst MA, 01002
United States of America
info@sociocracyforall.org

Published by Sociocracy For All. Sociocracy For All is a project of Institute for Peaceable Communities (IPC), an incorporated 501(c)(3) non-profit organization in Massachusetts, USA.

Rau, Ted J. Many Voices One Song. Shared power with sociocracy/Ted J. Rau, and Jerry Koch-Gonzalez.
    Includes bibliographical references, diagrams, index.
    ISBN 978-1-949183-00-9

Cover and graphic design: Julian Howell, United Kingdom.

What I want in my life
is compassion,
a flow between myself and others
based on mutual giving from the heart.

(Marshall Rosenberg)

Short table of contents

Detailed table of contents

Preface

We all know what deep connection feels like. We know it when we talk to a good friend who truly sees us. We all know what deep belonging feels like – when we enter a group and we tap into knowing deep inside that these are our people. We all know what it feels like to be known and trusted, and to matter to the people around us and they to us.

In every community of people, may it be at work, with friends, neighbors or family, it is connection that nurtures people. When we work alongside each other, care for each other and make decisions together.

How can we have more of that? How can we be aligned with our need for connection wherever we go, in our workplaces, neighborhoods, towns, clubs, faith groups, associations and in our families? We think that sociocracy can contribute to a more connected, integrated life. The principles behind sociocracy are not new. They are common sense. People have cooperated for as long as humanity exists. And still, we see a need to collect and describe tools and good practices so we can get more skilled with our interactions in organizations.

Human interactions are complex and have simultaneous layers that we need to tend to as we cooperate. What are we doing and how are we doing it? Who and what do we depend on? How do we divide our labor in the best way? Who decides, how do we decide, and how do we talk about these decisions? It all boils down to how we relate to our work and how we relate to each other.

> the more I live the more I think
> two people together is a miracle.
>
> (Adrienne Rich)

Sociocracy is one of many systems that provide guidance in the process of relating to each other, in the context of organizations. Other systems focus on how we relate to each other in interpersonal relationships or in our relationship to our environment. Each of them attempting to integrate where we are separated, to aid where we struggle, and to broaden our minds where we are stuck.

What does it take to lead a more integrated life, to form a more connected society, to create communities with more sense of belonging and harmony? We think there are three ingredients.

- We need tools and systems that support listening, participation, agency and a way to link our minds and hearts to work toward a shared goal.
- We need practice. We need to unlearn the messages that have harmed us, and to re-tell each other the stories that reunite us. Regular practice changes the fabric between us. It strengthens our skills and carries real change into the world.

- We need hope. Hope comes with the confidence that we are agents that can change the world. Hope that together, we can create systems that serve people close to us and in the larger community, without doing harm somewhere else.

In organizations, we come together to achieve a shared aim. In singing together, every voice contributes, even though they might not be singing the same tune. We each sing our part and together, it sounds more beautiful than what any individual can accomplish alone. Hence the book title *"Many voices one song"*!

Ted and Jerry

Acknowledgements

We are deeply grateful to the legacy of everyone contributing to the wonderful set of tools that we know as sociocracy. Above all, this is Gerard Endenburg who developed the sociocratic circle method and the many people in The Sociocracy Group, like Annewiek Reijmer, who advanced and spread sociocracy for decades. Marshall Rosenberg, who developed the theory and practice of Non-Violent Communication, and Gerard Endenburg are like hidden co-authors of this book. We are also grateful for John Buck and Sharon Villines who brought sociocracy to the English-speaking world and who supported us in publishing this book.

Many people in different places are now working on sociocracy. We enjoy our heartfelt connections with quite a few of them. They have each shaped our thinking with their unique perspective. Among them are John Schinnerer, Francine Proux-Kenzle, Sheella Mierson, Linda Cote-Small, Gina Price, Diana Leafe-Christian. We are grateful for our connection with James Priest and Lili David, with Barbara Strauch, with Rakesh RootsMan, Pierre Houben, John MacNamara, Marcia Carlson, Kent Smith, Ruth Andrade, Tanya Stergiou, Peter Richtsteig. We have received support from Vincent Van Der Lubbe and Leif Hanack, Eric Tolson, Laureen Golden, Daniel King, Martyn Griffin and many members of Sociocracy For All. A special thank you goes to the book circle that supported the editing process for this book: Elle Vallance, Stephanie Nestlerode, John Root. Gloria Zmolek, Allyn Steffen, Jesse Marshall, Mukunda Das, Randall Johnson, Simon Copsey, Harris Kaloudis, Parveen Sherif, Julya Rose, Ben Roberts, John Buck, Frederic Laloux, Richard Longman, Georges Romme, Jan Höglund, Jutta Eckstein and Stephane Brodu helped us improve this book. Julian Howell, with his knowledge of design and sociocracy made the design clear and simple – he came up with the way this book represents double-linking. Edwin M John's vision and the neighborhood parliaments have a place in our hearts.

We are grateful for the many organizations, communities and the individuals we have worked with. The biggest inspiration in our lives are the people we train all over the world, as we spend hour after hour in video calls exploring details of human organizations and interactions together. Many of our training participants are now peers in our membership organization, Sociocracy For All, and they continue to be a source of companionship, connection, and learning.

Thanks also to our personal network: Gina Simm, Jennifer Ladd, Darla Stabler, Nancy Bair, Greg Bates, Sophia Rau, Helena Rau, Jochen Rau. The place we call home, Pioneer Valley Cohousing community, provided not only practice ground for sociocracy but was also where we met.

This book is just the beginning, and just a small piece of a collective journey into a collaborative future. May it do good in the world!

Glossary

agenda	an ordered plan of topics to talk about during a meeting; will include desired outcome and estimated duration; consented to by the group before the beginning of the meeting; can be adjusted during the meeting
aim	a description of what an organization/a circle is doing, for example "keeping website current and posting new content on social media"
backlog	a list of topics that the circle intends to talk about in the future
circle	a group of members of an organization working together; has defined membership, defined aim and domain.
consent	method of decision-making; a decision on a proposal is made when no one in the circle has an objection
delegate	(representative) a circle member who reports from their circle to the parent circle; full member of the circle and the parent circle
domain	the area of authority where a circle has full authority to act, including both policy making and operational activities
facilitator	circle role; moderator of circle meetings
general circle (GC)	a circle made up of two members of each of its child circles; serves for flow of information and coordination among circles
helping circle	a temporary circle formed by a circle; can be a subset of the circle or have other members; often formed to accomplish a defined set of tasks to support the parent circle
lead-do-measure	an iterative process of planning, carrying out the plan , measuring and evaluating the success of the action performed
leader	circle role; the leader (1) oversees the operations of the circle (2) reports to the circle from the parent circle (3) is a full member of the parent circle

linking	the concept of connecting two circles by having members be part of two directly related circles for flow of information and influence between the circles
logbook	a repository for the knowledge base and policies of an organization
minutes	meeting notes; final when consented to by all circle members/attendees
mission	the overall strategy an organization chooses to reach its vision. Comparable to Board of Directors.
mission circle (MC)	the circle that translates the mission of the organization into the aims; holds the organization true to its mission
NVC	non-violent communication: a communication framework for understanding how it affects our feelings whether we perceive our needs as met or unmet
objection	a formal concern that approving and carrying out a proposal would negatively affect how a circle can achieve its aim
operations	the tasks performed to achieve the aim of the circle
policy	general decisions on how operations are being performed; can be governance, workflow, definition of roles, strategy
proposal	a suggested piece of policy brought to a circle for decision
range of tolerance	what a given circle member can work with; includes personal preference and whatever member does not object to
role	a cluster of defined tasks and authority; a member can be selected to fill a role and will perform the tasks with the given authority in the role;
circle role	role that enables the circle to function in general
operational role	role that is created to cover a certain set of tasks
round	a conversation format; every group member will speak in a selected order, with no (or limited) talking out of order
secretary	circle role; the secretary takes notes during the meeting, prepares and publishes meeting minutes and interprets decisions in case of ambiguities in wording
selections	(elections) a format to choose which member will fill what role
sub-circle	a circle that is formed by another (parent) circle
term	the duration of how long a policy is in effect or how long a role is filled before new (s)elections
vision	a defined statement about ideal conditions that the organization commits to working toward

Alternative terminology

Self-management	**sociocracy** | Dynamic Governance | Dynamic Self-Governance **meeting minutes** | meeting notes **policy** | guidelines | agreements **draft agenda** | **agenda proposal** **needs statement** | background | driver statement **performance review** | role improvement review **aim** | **desired outcome** | objective
Circle structure	**mission circle (MC)** | top circle | board | advisory board | council of elders **general circle (GC)** | coordination circle | hub | management team **department circles** | main circles | core circles | division circles **parent circle** | super-circle | higher circle | more broad/abstract circle **child circle | sub-circle** | lower circle | more concrete/specific circle
Roles	**facilitator** | moderator **secretary** | note-taker | circle administrator **delegate** | representative | bottom-up link | up link **leader** | coordinator | lead link | top-down link | down link **circle role** | process role | structural role | functional role **operational role** | content role

1: Equivalent alternatives to the terminology used in the book

Chapter 1

Sociocracy: Why, What and Who?

Sociocracy is a set of tools and principles that ensure shared power. How does one share power?

The assumption of sociocracy is that sharing power requires a plan. Power is everywhere all the time, and it does not appear or disappear – someone will be holding it. We have to be *intentional* about how we want to distribute it. Power is like water: it will go *somewhere* and it tends to accumulate in clusters: the more power a group has, the more resources they will have to aggregate more power. The only way to counterbalance the concentration of power is intentionality and thoughtful implementation.

Power, like water, is neither good nor bad. In huge clusters and used against the people, power will be highly destructive. Used to serve the people and the earth, distributed to places where it can work toward meeting the needs of the people and the earth, power is constructive, creative, and nourishing like an irrigation system.

One can think of a sociocratic organization as a complicated irrigation system, empowering each team to have the agency and resources they need to flourish and contribute toward the organization's mission. We avoid large clusters of power, and we make sure there is flow. Water that is allowed to flow will stay fresh and will reach all the places in the garden, nourishing each plant to flourish. Sociocratic organizations nourish and empower each team to have the agency to flourish and contribute toward the organization's mission.

Power does not have only one source. In that respect, power is different from an irrigation system. *All* members of the organization feed their own agency and resources into the organization, in each team. *Everyone contributes their power and relies on each other's power.* From there, power, and with it, resources, gets distributed into the whole and gets channeled to where the group wants to put their energy. Sociocratic organizations keep everyone's own agency and power intact and support people to make changes bigger than they could have made alone.

In order to achieve this, our sociocratic organizations differ from organizations with aggregated, centralized hierarchical power in two ways:

- We distribute power more evenly. Those who come with less agency get support to step into more agency. Those who come with more sense of agency contribute toward the whole without diminishing anyone else's power. Teams doing work together are empowered to contribute.

1

- We let power flow. Flow means the distribution of power needs to be adjusted and potentially changed over time. The sociocratic organization is adaptable and resilient.

Building a system that distributes power by empowering everyone requires thought and intentionality. That is what sociocracy is: the design principles for distributing power in a way that flows with life.

1.1 The values under sociocracy

What kind of world do we want to live in? The way we answer this question is: We want to live in a world where people support each other, consider each other and help each other meet needs. A collaborative world.

1.1.1 Organizations are living systems

Organizations are designed in a way that fosters our connection with each other and with ourselves, both within and outside of the organization. To effectively create connections, organizations need to be life-serving and all-embracing. *Life-serving* means that we want to foster organizations that work for everyone in the organization and hold care for everyone affected by the organization. No one and nothing can be ignored if we want to honor connection.

We want to support living organizations. Living systems can be on any kind of scale: a cell is a living system as it creates a membrane, forms an identity and interacts as a whole with its outside. Organizations are living systems: they interact with their outside (clients, students, consumers, investors), and their members on the inside interact as and information, goods, and energy are being exchanged. A system that does not let the organization breathe like a living system will constrain and muffle its unique expression of life. Living systems have characteristics that we want to be aware of:

- Living systems form a whole and can act as a whole. For example, a human body is a complex system of smaller complex systems, but it is perceived and acts as a whole.
- Living systems are interdependent with their context. There are no isolated systems. However, many people in Western cultures have been conditioned to think individualistically, as if we were separate from our context and could ignore our impact on the world around us.
- Living systems are interactive and open (within limits). An organism that does not interact with its outside will not be able to survive. Organisms provide a (permeable) "membrane" between their inside and their outside. This is the basis of identity and capacity to act.
- Within a system, parts are interdependent, which means they rely on each other to meet their needs. This is both true for parts of a cell and it is true for a society.
- Living systems are dynamic, they are not static. They change over time as they adapt and change constantly. Living systems can learn and heal. They are resilient.
- Living systems are inherently ordered, in their own way. A forest, for example, has an order. So does an organization – living systems are defined by the fact that they create more order than is present in the entropy of their surrounding. Organizations do exactly that: organize to exchange information and resources to meet needs.

What helps organizations to survive and thrive? What helps people in an organization to survive and thrive? What values does sociocracy embody? The urge to boil something down to only a small set of values is likely to leave out aspects of consideration that would have been meaningful for values and needs of other people. That said, here is what is important to *us*:

- Clarity: clarity comes along with predictability, safety. We want organizations where we know what to expect, who is doing what etc.
- Choice: we want to be in choice about what we do, and not act out of submission to or rebellion against, authority.
- To matter: to know that what we think and feel matters to those around us.
- Agency: to know that what we are doing has a positive impact.
- Learning: we want to experience learning and discovery about each other, ourselves, and about how the world works.
- Connection, belonging, equivalence & resilience: when we experience ourselves as one person within a well-connected organization, it can increase our sense of belonging. Connection and belonging are essential needs for all human beings. A decentralized, tight-knit community is more resilient, than a loose system or a rigid hierarchical system.

1.1.2 Principles

Applied to self-governance, each of these values translates into principles that guide self-governance.

- Equivalence: no one ignored. The essential principle underlying sociocracy. (Definition in figure 3.) We try to consider everyone affected in everything we do; no individual or group is disregarded.
- Distributed leadership: Decentralized systems are less vulnerable and therefore more resilient than centralized monocultures. We distribute leadership wherever we can.
- Seek the win-win: Every situation will be approached assuming that there is a solution that is mutually beneficial. Scarcity thinking (*"when you get what you want, it means I get less"*) is not accurate. There are countless examples of how synergy can make an exchange mutually beneficial.
- Open to emergence: Acceptance of not knowing and letting go of an attachment to an outcome. The less ego is involved, the easier it is for a solution to present itself. In complex systems, we cannot predict what will happen. No one person will have access to the absolute truth or the perfect idea. Considering everyone's input is key.
- Feedback-rich environments: Feedback and evaluation are the basis of learning. We want organizations to implement many occasions for meaningful evaluation. We rely on data as often as possible to evaluate our work, trying to be as true to data as possible when we interpret and make meaning of that data. Like any living system, we work with reality, and the principle of empiricism ensures we tie our interpretations to actual observations and not wishful thinking or expectations.
- Decisions by few, input from many: while we want to hear as much information as possible, this does not mean decisions have to be made in large groups. On the contrary: we can gather more feedback if we separate input and decision making.

- Omni-directional flow of information: we try to get information from as many sources as possible. More information is always positive.
- Transparency is important because it allows us to access data, and understand and learn. Transparency also levels the playing field because it gives everyone the same access to information. Power dynamics are not played out over access to information.
- *Good enough for now* and *safe enough to try* are the two key slogans of sociocracy. They mean that we can act on an idea that is not perfect. The key to this principle is that it allows for agency, flow and learning instead of keeping us static.
- Intentionality: when we do things with intentionality, we have agency. We are in choice over what we do.
- Tensions point to lack of clarity: when there is tension, it is not because someone is to blame but because there is lack of clarity on domains, about roles or about someone's needs. Tensions are typically a sign that we do not yet understand what is going on. Tensions are an invitation to explore. We don't want connection and creativity to be shut down by conflict avoidance or moralistic judgment ("right and wrong" thinking).
- Effectiveness: we want to know that what we are doing works, is useful, and matters.

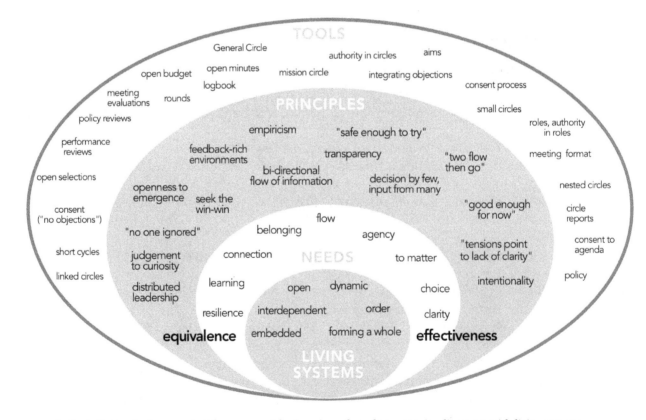

2: Tools that embody our principles; our most basic universal needs are met in alignment with living systems

This book describes a collection of tools that may help in carrying out the principles we have named. To use tools with integrity, we use them with the intention of the principles behind them. A hammer can be used to build or to destroy. Both are important, tools and principles, practice and intent. We are wedded to values and principles, not to using tools in a rigid way.

This manual focuses on specific tools because we see that this is what the movement needs right now. However, throughout this book, there will be references to principles with the most salient principles being *effectiveness* and *equivalence*.

1.1.3   Effectiveness and equivalence

We define equivalence as "everyone's needs matter", regardless of that person's role or status. Everyone's voice has equal value, but not everyone's voice has equal influence. By equivalence we do not mean sameness. Every person is equal to others and every person is unique. When the needs present in a context are known, we collectively decide how to most effectively meet those needs within whatever limitations are also present.

e·quiv·a·lence

i'kwivələns/
noun

the condition of being equal or equivalent in value, worth, function etc.

Synomyns:
equality, sameness, interchangeability, comparability, correspondence

3: Definition of equivalence

Honoring everyone's needs is wonderful, but what do we actually do? If we spend too much time talking, our work is not getting done and needs are going unmet. Inefficient process ultimately disregard needs, like the need to contribute to our clients, our students, or our community. *What sociocracy does is to create integration between the commitment to action/agency/forward motion and the promise to hold everyone's needs in consideration at all times.*

Mutual reinforcement between equivalence and effectiveness is what makes sociocracy so different. Sociocracy breaks down the many binary principles that do not serve us: *individual vs. group, workers vs. management, us vs. them.* In the end, we are all one, and sociocracy supports us in reuniting *and staying* connected, in working, in deciding, and in growing together.

Sociocracy overcomes the misconception that effectiveness has to be at the expense of equivalence and that more equivalence has to slow down an organization. Sociocratic tools harvest hearing people's needs in a way that increases effectiveness. An effective organization will be more successful at creating a place where all can contribute to meet needs. We are not creating a balance between two opposite ends, we are transforming it to a both-and: *both* effectiveness *and* equivalence.

e·ffec·tive·ness

iˈfektivnəs/
noun

The degree to which something is successful in producing a desired result.

4: Definition of effectiveness

1.1.4   What sociocracy feels like: Flow

In Sociocracy For All, we get requests from people who would like to witness sociocratic meetings to see what they feel like. As we welcome visitors whenever possible, we have a standard response to their request: Be aware that in a sociocratic meeting one might not see anything amazing. Good governance is invisible. Good governance means getting everything out of the way that distracts us. Distracting feelings can be generated when our needs for connection, integrity or shared reality are not met. That means we want to create a context of clarity for our work, for emotional safety amongst all team members and for process. What exists then is flow. Flow happens when a group is fully and creatively immersed in their process. Governance as a tool blends into the background and in the foreground is content. Good governance is therefore invisible. It only serves to create the conditions where we can be productive together.

1.2   The paradox of teaching self-governance

In self-governance, we want groups to decide for themselves how to govern themselves. Isn't it ironic to tell people how to *self*-govern themselves? That is a concern we deal with on a daily basis. How can we be helpful and share our experiences without imposing a fixed system? The following pages describe what we do with this paradox of teaching self-governance.

1.2.1   Design-principles vs. tools

To us, running organizations in alignment with principles is more important than a particular strategy. For example, running an organization where all needs are considered is more important than performing a consent round 'by the book' – even this book! The consent round is only a *tool* to ensure the principle of equivalence. If readers can find a better way to live the principle of equivalence than what we are presenting here (without compromising effectiveness), do it. In that case, please share so others can benefit as well! To us, sociocracy is a mindset: the mindset that all needs matter, always. The needs of those who we serve, the needs of those who work together, the needs of all interdependent life on the planet, and the needs of the generations to come.

Why write a book full of tools if only the basic principles count? There are four reasons:

- Building skills. We notice that most people ask for a 'boxed set' of good practices. Finding the right tools and combining them seems daunting for people who are new to shared power –

not because it is so hard to do, but because most of us lack experience.

- Let's not reinvent the wheel. If people are in organizations because the organization's mission is dear to their heart then developing a governance system is not at the center of their attention. In that spirit, this book is our *offer* to share everything we know about shared power and how to do it. It's what we do and we have a lot of experience with governance.
- We deeply care about equivalence. Having no system or just a vague system means there is a lot of space between the lines that will be filled by daily life in organizations. Like the water analogy: power will flow somewhere. Without being intentional about equivalence, power will flow back into the hands of a few.
- We write in detail. The reason we do that is because we hear frequent requests for practical information. Oftentimes, we offer several tools to choose from. We do not mean this book to be prescriptive. If we understand the principles and the tools, we will be more able to use them and to adjust them to our context and the specific moment.

1.2.2 Take what seems helpful – but the more the better

Sociocracy is *not* an all-or-nothing approach. Readers can use as few or many features and tools as they want and they can change their minds over time. No one owns the individual tools. People do what they do. There is no right and wrong. There are only more and less effective tools for managing and governing ourselves. In this spirit, here is what we want.

- We want readers to understand the design principles.
- We want to offer readers practical guidance in how to put the principles into practice.
- We want to empower readers to tailor the tools to their organization's needs.

The good practices in sociocracy fit very well together and mutually reinforce each other. For example, double-linking (see section 2.4 on page 45) makes a circle structure more transparent. Decisions in smaller groups make it easier to operate on consent decision making. Any area left out will be filled in otherwise, and sometimes by practices that do not effectively support equivalence. We recommend taking all that seems useful, and to keep the eyes open for signs indicating that the governance method might have areas that need improvement.

1.2.3 Change anything you want – by consent

We have devoted this time in our lives to spreading sociocracy because we are convinced that it is an excellent set of principles and tools, and we have picked the tools that we are describing in this book based on years of experience, observing different tools and techniques and their impact. Governance is a highly complex construct. If one makes a change in one spot, one might shift the balance in a different place. For that reason, we recommend to stay as close as possible to the basic tools and to use as many of them as possible. The tools one uses can easily be adapted – as long as one measures the success of your adaptation. As practitioners gain experience, they can be more flexible with the tools.

Consent is the default decision-making method in sociocracy. Consent means that if I make a proposal to the group, my proposal will be approved if no one in the group has an objection to it. Consent will be addressed deeply in this manual but this description might suffice for now.

By consent, a group can decide to do anything. We often jokingly say, you want a dictator for your organization? We can decide that by consent. (We recommend that the dictator role have a term end, however!) Groups can decide by consent to vote. Groups decide what their governance system looks like at all times. The only thing one cannot do is ignore reasoned objections.

So let's say a group decides to use only the organizational structure from sociocracy and to combine it with majority rule as your decision-method. That is allowed – because it is your decision. Here is the catch: We have talked to countless organizations. When they struggle around governance, it is always for either or both of these reasons: (1) They have gaps in their implementation, or (2) They have not invested enough resources in education.

So we hereby say it: we want groups to take full ownership of your own governance system. *And* we want to give them the most exhaustive and accurate and experience-based information we can possibly give because we think this is an excellent set of principles and most tweaks we have seen were detrimental.

Soci·o·cra·cy

/soʊsiˈɑː/krəsi
socio - cracy

like in *socio*-logy, like in demo-*cracy*

5: How to pronounce sociocracy

1.3   Sociocracy in context

1.3.1   Brief history

Beginnings

The term "sociocracy" was brought into common use by the French philosopher Auguste Comte in the 1850's. The word began to take its current meaning in the 1940's in a Quaker school in the Netherlands.

The founders of that school, Kees Boeke and Betty Cadbury were Quakers, educators, and peace activists. Boeke saw sociocracy as a form of governance that presumes equality of individuals. This equality is not expressed with the "one man, one vote" law of democracy, but rather by a group of individuals (the circle) reasoning together until a decision is reached that is satisfactory to each one of them. To make sociocratic ideals operational, Boeke used a system of circles to organize decision making within a large organization. Members of each circle were responsible for decisions within their domain. Each circle elected representatives to a "higher" circle. Use of representatives maintained the efficiency of a hierarchy while maintaining basic equivalence of the members of the organization. The school was unique in that the teachers and the students participated in decision making about the running of the school.

One of the students in that school, Gerard Endenburg, went on to study engineering. He further developed and applied Boeke's principles in the company he took over from his parents, the electrical engineering company Endenburg Elektrotechniek. He articulated the four basic principles as we now know them. This resulted in a formal organizational method, named the *"Sociocratische Kringorganisatie Methode"* (SCM: the Sociocratic Circle Method).

Gerard Endenburg intended sociocracy to be a method that includes and invites people to show up in their organizations as co-responsible whole human beings. Sociocracy was brought to the United States primarily by John Buck, co-author with Sharon Villines of the 2007 book on sociocracy, *We The People: Consenting to a Deeper Democracy.* Jerry Koch-Gonzalez studied and worked with John, and Ted J. Rau has done the same with Jerry.

As time passes since the early days of sociocracy, variations in its application have emerged, most notably Holacracy and Sociocracy 3.0. An exploration of the similarities and differences in the variations of sociocracy is beyond the scope of this book. The sociocratic lineage of Sociocracy For All is "classical" sociocracy - meaning directly from Gerard Endenburg and the Sociocratic Circle Method that he and others developed.

In this book we have tried to only use and coin jargon where it supports clarity. How true "Many Voices One Song" is to classical sociocracy will be a matter of debate. We do not intend with this book to start another variation, and we view any fragmentation of the movement around circle-based power with some sadness and skepticism. Our intent is to be Sociocracy For All, which – for us – means that we support any effort to spread sociocracy and sociocracy-related education and application.

Dynamic Governance

In the USA, sociocracy is also known as Dynamic Governance or Dynamic Self-Governance. These names were chosen to emphasize the dynamic nature of sociocracy and because the word sociocracy generated negative reactions. To some people, the word sociocracy sounded like socialism, implying the loss of individual freedom. To others, the word sociocracy sounded like another oppressive power-over "-cracy". And for even others, sociocracy was just a strange word that was hard to pronounce.

In using the original term, Sociocracy For All acknowledges the international nature of the sociocratic movement.

The spread of sociocracy

Sociocracy originated in the Netherlands, which also explains a bigger density of sociocratic organizations there. It has since spread slowly in all sectors.

Cohousing communities and ecovillages have been early adopters of sociocracy in Europe and in North and South America. The combination of sociocracy being grounded in community and equal voice had a special appeal in intentional communities. Different from consensus, sociocracy balances the needs of a group with that of the individual which is essential to keep a community sane. Intentional communities were (and many still are) grappling with their own governance, but they are places where:

- There is not the endless see-saw of power or domination by majority rule.
- Accountability is to the whole, not only to the supervisor.
- Leadership is distributed.
- No one can be ignored.

These traits made these communities a good breeding ground for sociocracy. A big contribution there came from individuals who were, and have been, promoting sociocracy and were themselves deeply rooted in intentional communities. Driving the spread of sociocracy was also the conviction that if they, living together with some sense of shared purpose, cannot work through miscommunications and struggles, then there is no hope for those who aren't living together, do not have a shared purpose, and have enemy images of each other. Some wanted to prove that working toward a common aim in a community while maintaining harmony *can* be done. Others simply wanted to reduce the time spent in meetings. The authors of this book live in an intentional community.

Up to this day, those are two possible entry-ways into sociocracy. Some people want a system that is more aligned with their values of an egalitarian, more just society. Others value and appreciate sociocracy for the clarity, effectiveness and transparency it brings to their companies and organizations. Early adopters were independent schools, agile and value-based organizations, people interested in non-violent communication (NVC).

Because people have different priorities that they see in sociocracy, their responses will be very different. We would like to honor the variety of experiences by just making a list of original quotes of people stating what sociocracy means to them.

"What does sociocracy mean to you?"

"All voices are heard and valued."

"Attention to everyone, helping everyone gain their voice, and rational dealing with policy proposals, helps make everyone a more responsible member."

"Sociocracy makes it less likely that things are swept under the rug because objections are encouraged and sought out."

"Sociocracy is about collective learning and adapting to circumstances."

"It allows more voices in the decision-making process and therefore more transparency in decision-making for the whole organization. "

"It empowers its members."

"It taps into groups' collective intelligence."

"As curiosity is the beginning of intelligence, Sociocracy is the beginning of effective collaboration."

6: Voices from our training participants

1.3.2 Ally movements

Sociocracy is not the only movement that supports life-serving collaboration. There are other movements that we call the ally movements, in which, organically, sociocracy has been growing in the last years:

- Permaculture design as a way to approach stewardship with the flora and fauna (especially the social aspect of permaculture, "people care")
- Non-violent communication as a way to communicate (for the shared value that *everyone's needs matter*)
- Agile software development (focus on short cycles with continuous improvement, empiricism and semi-autonomous teams)
- The cooperative movement (shared value: shared ownership and equal voice for every worker), along with the new-economy movement

More allies are (in no particular order) the transition movement, lean, circular economy, social justice, solidarity economy, workplace democracy, participatory democracy, commoning, community-controlled energy, responsive organizations, mindfulness movement, alternative currencies, inclusive workplace, restorative justice, platform cooperativism, conscious capitalism, democratic schools, anthroposophy, and Montessori education. No one person has the key to everything, and no one movement will always be able to meet all our needs for new systems for all areas of our life. Together, however, these movements, systems and mindsets are potent game changers in how our societies operate.

It is wonderful to see how people take what they know, combine it with sociocracy, and make it into something better. The individuals we have worked and been in contact with have typically been from one of the above movements. There are sociocratic elder care facilities, homeschooling groups, consulting companies, community organizations, restaurants, and summer camps for families. The most touching experience for us has been to hear how tens of thousands of children in India change their immediate situation through their neighborhood-based parliaments and elect leaders using the sociocratic election process.

We, the authors of this book, are in the lucky position of beneficiaries. We have learned an incredible amount about all those movements through our students who often pointed out to us how sociocratic values applied in their particular situation. There are people implementing sociocracy in families, relationships, dance associations, and faith-based groups. The mindset behind sociocracy dovetails with a vision so much bigger than governance: a world based on integration and cooperation.

1.4   How to use this manual

Governance is tricky to teach. The biggest challenge is that one has to know everything at the same time. Practitioners have to know the meeting format, all processes, understand consent, know what a helping circle is, how to do a round, be aware of feedback, have emotional literacy and needs consciousness and more at once – oh, and be aware of operational roles! Sociocratic governance works best if practitioners master it all. How can we achieve that? We tried to write this book so readers can browse through the book, reading sections at a time. That is the reason why there is some repetition in the book, as we strive to keep each section more or less comprehensive.

We compare it to learning how to swim. We can talk a lot about how to shape your hand for the perfect breaststroke or the line your arms have to form when doing a crawl stroke. But if we are struggling to stay afloat, that is irrelevant information because it is too detailed. If we forget our feet while focusing on our breathing we might still go down. The first step is to stay above the water. Then make your strokes more efficient, work on breathing, better form and so on. If you ever learned to swim and you were taught explicitly, you might remember that moving through water seemed impossible at first. Then, after practice, practice, practice, something clicks. We get the hang of it.

So, we are swimming teachers. We want readers to stay above the water without anxiety. If you are a beginner whose goal it is to stay above water, you are holding a book in your hands that gives you a level of detail that is probably too much for now. If we could wave a magic wand, we would want readers to read it twice and practice in between. Then read it again six months later. It will be an entirely different book by then because more experienced learners will take in the information very differently.

When teaching our daughters to swim, I would often take them on my back to give them a sense of swimming, feeling the movements in their body. I was hoping that the different elements might make more sense to them after experiencing them together. That's what *Sociocracy For All* does in online training. We figuratively throw teams of people into a pool and safely carry them through initial meetings, letting go more and more as they are able to stay afloat by themselves.

That is not the case for this book. Some people have an easy time applying what they read to real-life contexts. For many, it will be hard, and we encourage readers to get help. Much of this book makes sense once one has first-hand experience. If this does not correspond to how you prefer to learn, we can work with you in finding different ways to learn, or we can refer you to a coach. (See links to resources in section 7.1 in the appendix.)

1.4.1   Online resources

We wish we could offer readers case studies from organizations in all phases, from all sectors, in different languages. We wish we could offer sample by-laws or governance agreements and organizational structures for every sociocratic organization that exists or should exist. We are working on it. We strive to make any piece of information we produce or get a hold of public because we want all information that would be helpful to others, to be accessible to everyone.

Online content

sociocracyforall.org/resources

- case studies
- organizational structures of real, existing organizations
- printables (incl. high-resolution templates from this manual)
- articles on particular topics
- videos

sociocracyforall.org/events

- webinars on individual topics
- training opportunities, including online facilitation training, open self-study options

sociocracyforall.org/sofa

- ways to connect with other practitioners, trainers and developers in our membership organization

7: Sociocracy For All's online content

Sociocracy For All is about accessibility. We believe that sociocracy skills and knowledge have to be a common good – accessible for *all*. We know that online content in a limited number of languages is not accessible to everyone, but it is the best we can do. Online content allows for new content to be added and updated, and there have been numerous collaborative translation projects.

We invite readers to reach out if they have resources to share or if they would like to cooperate or translate to create content. We can also often connect people who are interested with someone from the same industry or region to work with.

1.4.2   How to give us feedback on this book

Feedback is a big topic in sociocracy. We talk about feedback loops. We plan something, carry it out, and evaluate how well our product has worked. There is a lot of data to consider and readers have a huge part in helping us understand how this book could be improved in the next round.

What do you want to see in the next edition?

On the website www.manyvoicesonesong.com, readers can give us feedback on this book. That would be our preferred way of receiving feedback. Readers will find the following questions – we say it now so readers can think about it as they read through the next chapters. (Of course, the survey is subject to change as we learn about what we can improve about the survey!) We invite readers to fill out the survey at any time. Thank you in advance!

Feedback on this manual
www.manyvoicesonesong.com

First contact with sociocracy
How did you hear about sociocracy?
Did you buy a copy or did you get a copy from someone/used?
Did you get an e-book?

Your context
Did you know about sociocracy before getting this book?
Is this a professional interest, or outside of (paid) work?
Do you use sociocracy in an organziation you are a part of?

What were your hopes around this book?
Curious what sociocracy was
Applying sociocracy and want to get better
Considering to apply sociocracy

Did this book meet your expectation?
Tell us what helped you.
Tell us what you think is missing and needed.

8: Give us feedback about this book at www.manyvoicesonesong.com

Chapter 2

Organizational Structure

In every organization, we need to integrate effectiveness and equivalence. The organizational design principles at work here are as simple as they are effective:

- Empower every workgroup (circle) by giving it as much authority as possible. Any circle can form its own sub-circles.
- Nest every circle with other related circles to keep communication lines short.
- At the center of the circle structure, have a circle for information sharing and support to avoid silos or disconnected compartments.
- Circles are linked with each other by two people to ensure feedback and good flow of information.

These design principles are the foundation for every circle structure, from the beginning on. Some organizations start out as full-fledged organizations, some start out as a group of friends working together. All organizations will go through similar stages as they differentiate and mature. A sociocratic organization can be as small as three people, or as large as ten-thousands of people. Like fractals, the principles that guide how we organize our work are the same on every level of the organization. Like in a living organism, every part of the system is autonomous but interdependent.

Since the organizational structure in sociocracy is decentralized, the system can grow and adapt on its own. New branches can be formed following the same mechanisms, like a tree that forms buds in the right place when the right time comes. Growth (and de-growth) is smooth and follows the demand and intention of the organization.

2.1 The circle

We call work teams "circles". They are the heart of every organization. A circle is a group of people who work together and decide together how the work is being done. Circles are a way to "package" related parcels of work and to focus attention easily and maximally, while still keeping the pieces of the whole connected. The difference between non-sociocratic committees and circles is that circles have more authority and the requirement to be connected to the other circles. Circles are never floating around, they are always linked to another related circle. An ideal circle structure will represent the idea of "a place for everything, and everything in its place". Since the circle structure is also dynamic, we have order without having rigidity. We can grow, adapt, and be nimble.

The members of the circles are workers *and* they are policy-makers. Sociocracy translates to "those who associate together govern together". The circle members are the experts of the work they do, and they have the skills and knowledge to govern *how* their work is being done. Policy is made as workers see fit in order to make their work together easier and more successful.

On an organizational level, decision-making power is distributed with the work: Whatever circle is performing the work in one area of responsibility makes the decisions for that area. For example, the group of people that takes care of membership matters in an organization decides *how* this is being done.

As clusters of tasks get more complex, we divide up the tasks and form what we call sub-circles. Like in a fractal structure, there can be sub-sub-circles formed by any sub-circle.

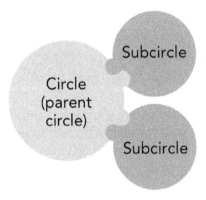

9: A circle with two sub-circles

We make as many decisions as possible on the most specific level of the organization. That means if a decision can be made in a sub-sub-circle, then there is no need for approval anywhere else. Any circle will be dealing with the specific decisions for their level. Power is always as decentralized as possible: Power is configured in a healthy way, and every circle is empowered to act.

Distributed power has many advantages. A system with distributed power will be resilient, fast and nimble. Every circle is part of a network of related domains. The support system for every circle is baked into the circle system. If one circle struggles, there will be a circle around it that can help the circle get back on track.

Since the do-ers are the decision-makers, we have authority and power to act. No one has to wait for anyone's approval.

> Imagine a customer has a request for a change in a recipe for a Pastry Circle in a bakery restaurant. Let's say, a loyal customer is allergic to hazelnut and is asking whether there could be chocolate croissants without hazelnut. The request is in the domain of Pastry Circle. Pastry circle will consider this request. Let's assume they decide to change their recipe. They do not have to ask anyone for permission, they just change it.

In addition, workers will have a high level of buy-in and intrinsic motivation because they are taking full responsibility. No one will be forced to do anything they do not see the need to be doing because

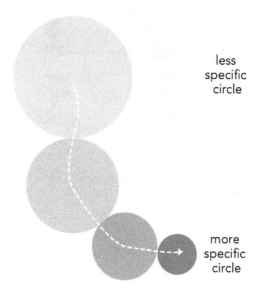

less
specific
circle

more
specific
circle

10: Drive the power to the most specific circle possible

everyone in the circle decides together what and how it is being done. Again, in our example, if someone sees harm in making puff pastry for the Pastry Circle or the entire bakery, the group of workers in that area will be able to address this. No policy *in their own domain* can be forced onto them.

We think of it as a living organism where each system (respiratory system, circulatory system, nervous system, etc.) is autonomous in that it responds to needs in its own system. The respiratory system does not have to ask permission from the circulatory system. Every system (every circle) takes care of their own needs. On the other hand, however, the systems are interdependent: if the muscular system requires more oxygen, this will affect the respiratory system. One system over-ruling the other systems does not sound healthy. Circles in a sociocratic organization work the same way: they are semi-autonomous because they have full authority over their domain, but they also are part of a whole system that needs to respond to each other's needs.

2.2 Empowering the circle: aims, domains and members

What do we need to make something happen? We need to have a clear understanding of *what* it is we are getting together to do; the aim is the invitation. We need the authority and resources to get it done (domain), and we need to be clear who is a part of the effort (members). Sociocracy provides clarity on all three of those aspects as shown in diagram 11.

2.2.1 Aims

People can only work together effectively if they are clear about what they want to do together. Aims describe and guide the work. Collaboration requires explicit and specific sharing of ideas and resources to fulfill the aim.

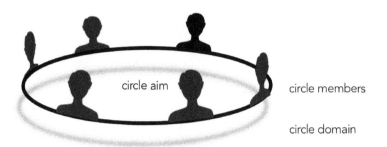

11: A circle: members, aim and domain

What is an aim?

The written "purpose" of the circle is our aim. The more specific and clear your aims are, the easier your decision making will be. A clearly stated aim will stimulate focused action, producing tangible and measurable outcomes. A few examples for aims are *"producing and selling baked goods in Amherst Massachusetts, brewing gluten-free beer and selling it online, providing an online platform to increase connection between people in neighborhoods in Mexico city"*.

What is the difference between aims and vision/mission?

How is the aim different from visions or missions? In an aim, we define what it is we are doing. Aims are what we need to do to get us closer to fulfilling our mission, and working toward our vision. Someone wants to end homelessness? If that is the mission, then the vision might be a world with adequate shelter for every human being. Visions and missions are helpful to create a set of shared values, but it is more important to define the aims of the organization. The mission informs the aims, but the aims will be the backdrop for every policy decision one makes in the organization (see section 3.2.4).

It is not enough to only define the vision and mission. Organizations with the same mission and vision might have very different aims. The mission of "ending homelessness" can be accomplished by different aims which are the strategies we are using, as shown in 12. On the flipside, we might have very different visions and still be able to get behind the same aim. (To some extent, this is probably true more often than we realize!) For example, for volunteers at a vegetarian soup kitchen, the motivation might be health, or environmental or ethical concerns. The same strategy can be in support of very different needs.

The more homogenous an organization is in terms of vision/mission/aim, the easier decision making will be. If an organization is more diverse in its views and perspectives, then we need more clarity on our vision/mission and aims. Here are some more examples of missions.

- *"to end hunger"*
- *"to provide educational opportunities for children from working-class families"*
- *"to provide role models for young men in the UK."*

We phrase missions as *to*-infinitives. Aims tend to be expressed in *-ing* forms, or whatever their counterpart might be in your language. One can also try the fill-in-the-blank statement for a specific

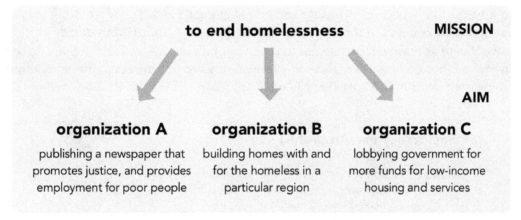

12: Example: same mission "to end homelessness", different aims

Vision, mission, aim

We are dreaming of a world where it is true that _____

We work to _____ by _____

VISION / MISSION / AIM

13: Vision, mission, aims

organization in figure 13. Another example would be "I wish this world was a world with nutritious and fresh food for everyone. Our mission is to provide healthy and fresh food in Madison County and we intend to begin by baking and selling baked goods at a storefront in Huntsville". Our mission is our overall strategy to get closer to our vision. Aims describe in a simple way what needs doing to stay true to our mission – the action strategy that we hope will contribute to fulfilling the mission.

Let's look at Sociocracy For All (SoFA), the organization to which the authors of this book belong. As shown in Box 14, The vision is an inspirational place where we want to be. The mission is our contribution of how to get there. In SoFA's case, it is about making knowledge accessible. We want

14: Sociocracy For All vision and mission

to live in a world that works for everyone (no one is ignored) and we are guessing that making sociocracy accessible is a way to contribute to a world where everyone is considered.

What we choose as reasonable strategies to *act* on our mission are the aims. If SoFA decides that something we are not doing yet is a good way to work toward our mission, another aim might be added. The current aims of SoFA are listed in table 15.

Sociocracy For All (SoFA)

AIMS
1. Spreading sociocracy with accessible, educational and inspirational materials about sociocracy (articles, videos, webinars, social media).

2. Supporting training by supporting trainers' learning and advertising trainings.

3. Networking and supporting the sociocracy world; more specifically practitioners, SoFA members, regional and language-oriented groups.

(as of June 2018)

15: Sociocracy For All aims

Begin with the aim in mind

Define the aim as early in an organization's life as possible. What is the organization *actually* going to do? Clearly state what the product or service is, who the audience is, how the product will be delivered, and what the exchange will be (for example, product or service in exchange for money) in a way that is understandable. If it is clear what the aim is and how it is distinct from the aim of other organizations or circles, the organization is ready to start working. Everything members do in the organization, they will do to carry out that aim.

An informal way to understand what an aim is is to imagine being at a party. If someone asks *"So, what do you do?"*, most people want to hear the aim of your organization (or circle). *"I make gluten-free beer and we sell it in an online shop"* would be a satisfactory answer. If we say *"Oh, I end homelessness"* or *"I support the cooperative movement"*, it will most likely provoke further questions. Those are missions. An aim has to be something anyone understands because it is concrete.

Every circle within your organization will have its own aim that will be a more specific sub-aim than the organization's overall aim. How we define the aim determines the nature of the product or service. We can see how an aim breaks into sub-aims in table 16.

If we want to build a housing community, we need clarity on our aim. In order to be specific in our aim, we will have to make a few decisions:

- Does this project include housing only or also businesses or an education program?
- Nice neighborhood or social change demonstration project? Level of ecological focus?
- Density level: one building, clustered, or dispersed?

Example: aims in a training organization

Circle	Aim
Whole organization	Educating people in Massachusetts about permaculture design.
Circle A	Training workshop leaders.
Circle B	Maintaining and developing a website that includes advertising local training opportunities.
Circle C	Delivering permaculture design courses. Developing and improving workshop curriculum and training materials.

16: Organization aim and circle aims

- Location: Urban? Rural? North or south of the city?
- Balance between priority of affordability and amenities?
- Expected unit/house price?
- What forms of governance and decision making?

For example, if a group is planning to build a cohousing community in Toronto, it is helpful to narrow down *where* the community might be built. If some of the founding members can only live in the northern part of the city, while others cannot work with that, it is wiser to split up early and each group pursues their aim. How we answer those questions will change who our customers (potential home buyers) are. If these aims are not agreed upon, it will be hard to move forward as a group. It might be painful but in the long run, it is better to split groups and have clarity about shared aims than to suffer. If we do not define whether we want to form a rural or an urban community, your Site Search Circle will probably be in a deadlock situation: every site will be either rural or urban, and for each one, someone in the group will object and we won't be able to settle anywhere. Think of the aim as the invitation: this is what we are doing; and if you like what we are doing, please join us. The more specific the invitation is in the beginning, the less disappointment and friction there will be in the future.

Aims can change over time

There might be adjustments on the level of aims from time to time. This is true for the organizational level and for the individual circles.

We might change the overall aim. A year and a half after SoFA was founded, we realized that networking among people who were practicing and sharing sociocracy was a key contribution SoFA was making to the spread of sociocracy. It was then that we added the last aim in figure 15 on page 20 to our list of aims. We might also add or dissolve circles or change the aims of an existing circle. For example, this handbook was made by a Manual Circle within the organization Sociocracy For All (SoFA). Now that the handbook is published, the Manual Circle will dissolve or become dormant until the next edition will be worked on. Instead of a Manual Circle, there might be a Manual Distribution Circle to manage orders and shipping or Translation Circles to make this handbook available in more languages.

The mission circle (MC) is responsible for making sure the organization's aim contributes toward the organization's mission.

2.2.2   Domains

Each circle has an aim to carry out. They also need the authority to act. They will need resources, and the right to change and shape their environment in a way that serves the aim.

What is a domain?

A domain defines a circle's area of responsibility for policy making and operational activities. A circle is granted the mandate to work toward their defined aim; in exchange, we entrust them with the authority that is required to perform the tasks that come with those aims.

Defining domains checklist

- [ ] Sets the area of authority over policies and activities necessary to carry out the circle's aim
- [ ] Defined in a way that everyone in the organization understands
- [ ] Set by the parent circle (but could be proposed by child circle)
- [ ] No overlap with another circle's domain
- [ ] No gap between circles' domains

17: Properties of a well-defined domain

We have given circles power, and the power is purposefully distributed outwards to the most specific circles – the most localized level possible. Authority has to go along with that so those circles are free to act. Aims and domains always parallel each other indivisibly. Imagine a Website Circle that has to ask for the password for every change they make. That would slow this circle down. Instead, we want to hand over the authority to manage the password completely (if they are the only ones needing access). The idea is full empowerment: by default, a circle will have the power to act in their domain. The only reason to restrict their authority is because a different group might need some authority as well; not out of a desire to maintain control. The same is true for labor and financial budget: a circle has a budget which is agreed upon by the next-higher circle. Within the limits of their own budget, the circle has full authority over how to spend the money and allocate labor hours. See table 18 and 19 for a examples of (department) circles, aims and domains in food production (bakery) and in a community.

Example: Domains in a bakery

Circle	Aims	Domain
Bakery	Maintaining baking supplies, baking bread and pastry	Workspace 1 (including fridge and pantry), recipes
Front	Selling baked goods and making and serving coffee	Workplace 2 (front desk, fridge in front); design and use of customer area
PR & Marketing	Advertising the bakery, providing and maintaining menus and posters,	All printed materials, website and outgoing material, finances, workplace 3 (office)

18: Circle, aims and domains in a bakery

Example: Aims and domains in an intentional community

Circle	Aims	Domain
Community Connection	Fostering harmonious connections and interactions among residents	Communication system support systems, work system, membership, sales, events
Condo Management	Maintaining and improving community infrastructure	Building systems, building envelope, snow removal, legal and safety issues, condo budget
Outdoor Living	Maintaining and improving commonly owned outdoor space. Fostering harmonious connection and interaction in outdoor space	Outdoor spaces, gardens, lawns, tools, sheds, fences, gates, containers, tree boxes
Extended Home	Maintaining and improving commonly owned indoor space. Fostering harmonious connection and interaction in indoor space	Interior spaces, design and use of facilities, equipment, decoration, furniture

19: Circle, aims and domains in an intentional community

Sub-domains

The overall domain of the organization is the sum of all areas of responsibilities that serve the aim of the organization. We can nest domains by forming sub-domains. Sub-domains live within sub-circles. In that case, the sub-domain is being handed over to the sub-circle and the sub-circle now has full authority in that domain.

> Example: Imagine pastry makers in a Pastry Circle. Pastry Circle is a sub-circle of a circle called Baking Circle. Its sibling circle is Bread Circle. Only decisions that affect both circle's domains are made in the parent circle (see figure 20). We try to make as many decisions as possible in that Pastry Circle. Pastry Circle does not need Baking Circle's approval for decisions in their own domain as long as they are within their own budget.

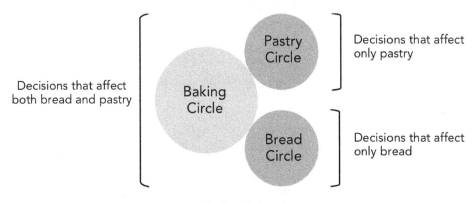

20: Nested domains

A parent circle can pass on distinct subsets of its domain to sub-circles, while some pieces remain in its domain. A circle like that will both be functioning as coordinator between sub-circles but also have "business of their own". This also has the advantage that the parent circle serves as a catch-all for issues and will be able to assign them to sub-circles or take them on itself. For every issue, we try to address it at the most specific level we can find for it.

Each sub-circle has full authority over their sub-domain. Only decisions that involve both other domains (for example shared equipment) are being made in the parent circle. That means we "bump up" an issue into a parent circle only if this is necessary because the topic affects more than the original circle's domain.

What sounds simple here can be quite a change in mindset for groups: a circle is free to act in their domain. As mentioned above, this is also true for decisions that affect people outside of the circle, *as long as these decisions are within the circle's domain.*

> A Membership Circle might have authority over policy that defines membership status for the *entire* organization.
>
> In a community, a Buildings and Grounds Circle might have authority over the roads for *every* house in the community.
>
> In a business, the IT Circle might decide what application is going to be used *organization-wide* for internal communication.

Domains are pivotal for the entire governance system as they guide not only how power is distributed, but also how smoothly the organization will run. This has an implication that sometimes catches new students of sociocracy by surprise. If a domain affects everyone in the organization, a small circle will have authority to make decisions that affect *everyone* in the organization. A circle makes decisions about their domain, and that can be organization-wide, depending on the domain.

Distributed power requires trust. Trust can be earned by gathering feedback from a wide range of people outside of the circle, by transparency and good quality work. The organization runs like an organism with many small self-controlled interdependent system (as opposed to a machine controlled by one big gear in the center). The advantage of small group mandate is focus: not everyone in the organization has to take care of everything. With distributed autonomy and flow of information, more can be accomplished than one person's mind could hold.

When a circle passes on parts of its domain to a sub-circle, anything that is not taken care of by a sub-circle still belongs in the domain of the parent circle. For every issue, we try to address it on the most specific level (i.e. at the "lowest" level we can find for it).

A way to visualize this is figure 21. The domain of the parent circle gets split up "emptied out" as we form sub-domains. The parent circle is responsible for supporting each sub-circle and will be the default circle to deal with the work or decision in case the sub-circle breaks down or if sub-circles need support. The authority follows the principle of what linguists call an "elsewhere condition": something will always be in a circle's domain *unless* it is held in a functioning sub-circle's domain.

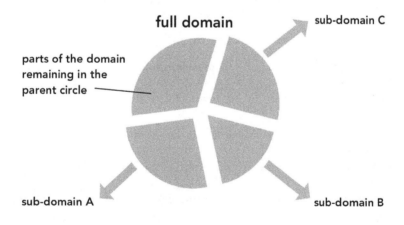

21: A parent circle passes on parts of its domain to three sub-circles

Example: A school divides up a Teacher Circle into 1-6th grade and into 7-12th grade. All coordination work between the two lies in the domain of the next-"higher" circle. Every issue or task that affects curricular work beyond those two groups will remain within the Teacher Circle as business of their own.

Example: A music store that sells string and wind instruments forms a sub-circle for each. The store's focus is not on percussion but they do sell drumsticks as they are high in demand. There is not enough need to form a Percussion Circle, and all percussion-related work can be coordinated by the parent circle.

Clarity of domains

When we define the aims and domains and how they relate to each other, we have to be careful to make sure there is a good fit. Figure 22 shows the cases of gaps and overlap. If there is overlap between the domains of two given circles, the circles might step on each other's toes. How do we notice if they do? Every time there is an argument following one of the patterns below, then we know that there is overlap between domains or lack of education on what the domains are.

- *Why did they do . . . , even though we already did. . . ? Why did they change our. . . ?*
- *Why aren't they taking care of. . . ? Why don't they ever. . . ? Do they not know they should. . .*

The simple answer might be: *"because there was not enough clarity on how the domains are defined."*

In both cases (overlap and gap between domains), there might be feelings stirred up. The most constructive response, however, is curiosity: *"I wonder whether our domains are defined well enough."*

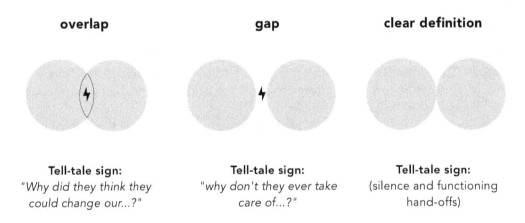

overlap	**gap**	**clear definition**
Tell-tale sign:	**Tell-tale sign:**	**Tell-tale sign:**
"Why did they think they could change our...?"	"why don't they ever take care of...?"	(silence and functioning hand-offs)

22: Overlap, gap and good definition of domains and tell-tale signs

See this in action, on the example of a Community Building Circle:

> Imagine a circle that takes care of the building called Community Building, Community Building Circle. Their domain is everything in the physical sphere of the community building. The circle decides to divide up that domain by forming two sub-circles: one circle takes care of the basement of the Community Building where there is a laundry room, bike storage and a meditation room. Another circle takes care of the first floor of the Community Building.

As easy as this seems, there might be friction. For example, in this example of a First Floor Circle and the Basement Circle – who takes care of the stairs?

- In a situation where we have a *gap* between domains, *no one* is taking care of the stairs. The issue might remain uncovered for a while, and members of the community might complain about the dirty stairway. Eventually, First Floor Circle might get upset with the Basement Circle (*"After all, it's the stairs to the basement, right?"*), and Basement Circle is upset with

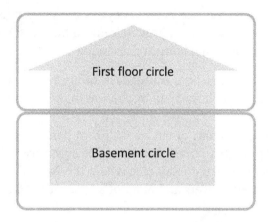

23: Two domains: first floor and basement of a building

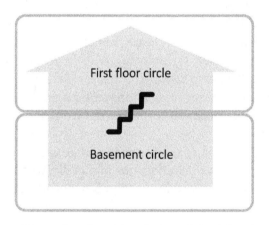

(a) Two domains with stairs in undefined domain

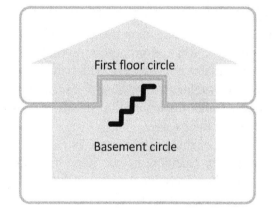

(b) Two domains with stairs in defined domain

24: Creating clarity between two domains

First Floor Circle for being accused (*"After all, when we agreed to take care of the basement, no one was talking about the stairs"*). Feelings point to unmet needs, and the need here is a need for clarity and mutual understanding. There is no right or wrong solution here; all we need is an agreement, a clarification of domains. We might come to the conclusion that Basement Circle should take care of the stairs and we adjust the domains which now include the stairs for Basement Circle. Or we might have reason to assume that First Floor Circle should do it because their clean team cleans more often and the stairs get rather dirty.

- What if they assume *overlap* between the domains of the two circles? Let's assume both circles assume that the stairway is in their domain.

  Basement Circle decides to put an anti-slip carpet on the stairs because there have been reports of people slipping on their way down. Now First Floor Circle is upset because the stairs are visible from the first floor, and the aesthetics are not what First

Floor Circle had in mind for that space. They say the stairs now look like shop floor stairs, but they wanted the community building to have a "living room" look. Both circles assumed they had a say; both circles assumed the stairs were in their domain.

Once we see how the confusion is born out of lack of clarity, solutions are relatively easy to find. The clarification of domains might happen by consent in the parent circle (in this example the Community Building Circle).

Part of a well-defined set of domains of circles is also to define the hand-offs between circles. This is different from overlaps or temporary handovers of authority. With hand-offs, there is no passing on of authority. It is more like a relay race where the baton is passed from one runner to another. See more on domains, handovers and hand-offs in section 2.6.3.

Who sets the aim and domain?

Aims and domains of a sub-circle (child circle) come from the parent circle. If a circle forms a new circle, then that parent circle brings the circle to life by coming up with a way to populate the circle and by defining what the new circle's aim and domain will be. A circle cannot change its aim unilaterally, but it can propose a revised aim to its parent circle for consent. When a circle's aim and/or domains are changed, both parent and child circle must consent.

When switching an existing organization to sociocracy, we recommend that the group consent to a governance document that identifies the circles the organization is starting out with, and their aims and domains.

Over time, there might be adjustments to domains and aims, as we clarify and adjust our organization to changing needs. Keep in mind that the written-down domains and aims are policy like any other decision. They represent the bigger "frame" of how we divide up our work. Aims and domains are your foundational policy. They are not cast in stone; instead, they are in place to support your work.

As we write down aims and domains, go by what makes sense to people in the organization. One does not need a lawyer to define aims and domains. If it is clear enough for everyone who is involved, it will likely be good enough for a start – safe enough to try and good enough for now.

On the question of nomenclature: hierarchy

We have been talking about "sub"-circles and "sub"-aims. Does that mean sociocracy is hierarchical? If so, how does that go together with the idea of governance as equals?

The hierarchy in sociocracy is a hierarchy of specificity of aims and domains, not a hierarchy of oppressive power. A Dishwashing Circle makes very few policies and does a lot of specific, operational work (the dishes!). A Board of Directors does little operational work and spends most of its time on long-term planning and the abstract level of overarching organizational policies that are not made by individual circles. In the original development of sociocracy, the Board of Directors Circle was labeled "Top Circle". People are attracted to sociocracy because of how it embodies egalitarianism. Words like top circle, higher circles, lower circles and even the word leader can trigger discomfort and the assumption of the existence of an oppressive power structure. So we

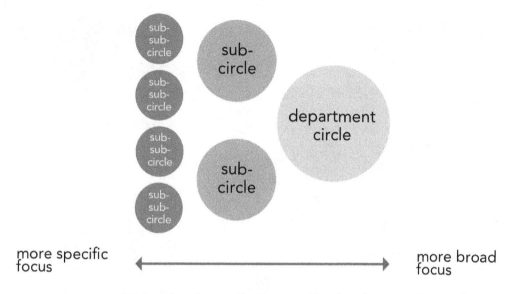

25: From broad to specific. From specific to broad.

look for different ways to describe the continuum of circles from specific to abstract. For example, instead of Top Circle or even Board of Directors, we use the term "Mission Circle".

Organizations can choose the wording they prefer. For sheer simplicity, we often talk of "high" vs. "low" among people who are aware of the lack of oppressive force in sociocracy. To create clarity for those new to sociocracy, we chose to use "sub" as a prefix – the way we also encounter it in power-neutral systems, for example in "submarine" and "subcontinent". It would never occur to us to assume that people in submarines do less valuable work than people in a ship. In the same way, the requirements and the aspects to pay attention to are different for dishwashers than for kitchen planners, although their domains are related.

We often use "broad" vs. "specific" (as in Figure 25) in training contexts where we have more time to explain and can avoid confusion around the terminology. But those terms seem cumbersome and chances are, people might be driven away because it sounds complicated. Our overall aim is to make sociocracy accessible, not to make it sound complicated.

Whatever words an organization uses, here are three ideas to consider. Every organizational structure can be drawn in different ways. The structures in diagram 26 describe the exact same organizational design for an organization, some looking more hierarchical, some less so. We can avoid a perception of linear hierarchy by drawing a more circular structure – but even that comes with connotations (periphery vs. center, peripheral being interpreted as "marginal"). Hierarchy in sociocracy is not a hierarchy of people. Since every circle comes with a piece of the overall aim and domain, and aims and domains are nested, it is not *people* that are in a hierarchical relationship to each other but it is *aims and domains* that stand in hierarchical relationships to each other. Those aims and domains are tied to circles which are filled by circle members and holders of roles.

In a sociocratic organization, it is likely that the same individual can be part of a more specific circle and a broader circle. The same individual may fix bikes and, at the same time, be part of a circle that does long-term planning. The point is that the circle that oversees bike repairs has very

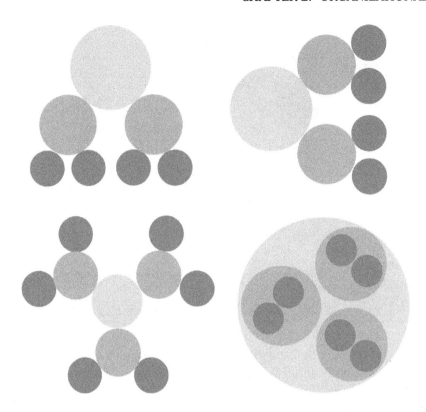

26: Circle structures shown in different ways.

tangible and specific work, while a board deals with abstract long-term planning. Any person might do either job, but the focus is different depending on what we are paying attention to in that circle. (More on power dynamics and how sociocracy challenges the power structures we are used to, see for example 6.10.5 on page 243.)

2.2.3 Membership

A circle is defined by its aim and domain. We also need to know *who* is a member of that circle. Good decisions depend on deliberation among people who have a shared understanding of their work.

A good default group size is a group of 5-7 members. In a group of that size, it is possible to hear each other and to pay attention to each other. Groups can also be smaller or larger. Considerations:

- Policy: How much policy does the circle make? Policy making is easier in a small circle.
- Frequency: If a circle meets often, then a larger circle is doable.
- Duration of meeting: If meetings tend to run long, then a smaller circle is preferable.
- Familiarity and complexity: How much does the circle work together? If workers spend a lot of time working alongside with each other and their operations are alike, they know each other well and meet very often, a larger circle size is possible. If operations are complex and ever-changing, smaller groups and more meetings are recommended.

Defined membership: what and why

Circles make policy decisions by consent. Consent is the default decision-making method in sociocracy that will be described in detail in section 3.2.2, starting on page 83. The definition of consent is that a decision is made if no circle member has an objection.

Consent decision making only works if we know who those circle members are. In a situation where people drop in and out of a group, we will not know who can be counted on and who needs to be asked for consent if we want to make a decision. Protection of any decision-making group is a high priority in sociocracy, so defined membership is an essential feature of sociocratic organizations.

Defined membership does not mean closed membership. A circle can be open to new members while still requiring the clarity of formal membership.

(See more on lack of defined membership in section 6.10.3 on page 242.)

Becoming a member of a circle

In sociocracy, no one can be forced into a circle, and no one can be forced out of a circle.

A circle consents to an individual joining a circle. When an individual expresses interest in joining a circle – no matter whether it is through hiring or a volunteer position – it is a proposal to become a circle member. To accept this proposal, we do a consent process to welcome the new member into the circle (see 3.3.2 on page 109 on the consent process).

The proposal to accept someone as a member is simple, as shown in figure 27: One can do a

---

Example: Proposal for membership in a circle

Facilitator/anyone in the group:

I propose that NN be member of this circle for 1 year because her coding skills would go well with our website project.

27: Accepting a new member into the circle

clarifying questions round, a quick reaction round and a consent round. Questions could be *"I am curious what brought you into this circle"*, or *"what's your experience with. . . "* Quick reactions could be welcoming expressions. This can be a sweet ritual and very affirmative for the incoming member of the circle. *Or* it can be crucial to be honest to protect the functioning of the group – for instance, someone who wants to join a circle for a meeting just because an issue is hot for them. In that case, do *not* consent. We use our right to choose with whom we work. We might also have to work through objections.

> Imagine a Curriculum Circle in a school. A member – Natalie – would like to join the circle and there is a consent round on that person's membership. A current member of the Curriculum Circle objects to Natalie's membership. The concern is that Natalie is

so busy that she might not be able to attend circle meetings on a regular basis which would interfere with the circle working productively. This objection would need to be addressed and resolved for Natalie to join the circle.

If you have ever been part of a group where some people just dropped in from time to time, you know how that can make the circle's work unsteady. In that example, we can see how important it is to have clarity about a circle's members.

Does every member of the organization have to be part of a circle?

There are cases where a member of an organization is not part of a work circle. For some types of organizations, this will be more common (like in platform cooperatives); for others, it will be ruled out (most for-profit businesses). It depends on the requirements for membership in the organization whether or in what way this is possible. Membership in the organization, with its privileges and responsibilities, may be separate from circle membership.

For example, in an intentional community, an individual can be part of the community and do work (dishwash, code, mow the lawn) without being part of any of the corresponding policy-making circles. In a platform coop, not every contributing member will be part of a work circle that makes policy of how the platform is run. If we imagine a sociocratically run town, we would not expect every resident to be part of the administration. (See more thoughts in section 6.7 on page 236.)

The tricky point here is that we have to be aware that sociocracy was not designed for cases of many members that are not connected to the circle system. We have to make sure to hear their voice and consider their needs for all decisions – which is harder if someone is removed from policy making. To give a short answer to a complex topic: no, not every member of the organization has to be part of a circle, but it is easier to run an inclusive organization if as many organizational members are part of at least one circle as makes sense in their context.

How to remove a circle member from a circle

There is also the option of removing a member from a circle. It is crucial to have that option because working together only works if all the circle members are productive in the way that the circle requires. If a member is not able to work well with others (for whatever reason) then making decisions may be challenging for the circle. For example, a member's sarcastic and blaming style of communication may interfere with the well-functioning of the group. If constructive circle members leave a circle because they dislike someone's behavior, an open conversation is overdue. If a circle member's behavior keeps a circle from being functional, that is a clear example of "we cannot work with this", hence an objection to a circle member's circle membership. Sociocracy, while strengthening individual power, also protects groups, and for consent decision making to be possible, groups have to be protected from dysfunction.

Excluding someone from a circle, on the "process level", is easy. It is a proposal *"I propose that XY be removed from the circle"* (with a rationale and term). For example, a member may continually take action outside the aim/domain of the circle or continually push for favorite projects without consideration for the perspective of others.

After presenting the proposal, we can invite clarifying questions and quick reactions. The circle member that is potentially removed from the circle can ask questions and give their quick reaction. In the consent round, that person does not have consent rights. This last aspect makes it slightly more specific from a regular proposal where every circle member has consent rights.

We are aware that removing someone from a circle will be near the end-point of a lot of emotional struggle. We all care about the people we work with and we strive for harmony. It is crucial to know of this option and how to perform it. We highly recommend *defining the steps* that would lead up to this process *before* it happens. Ideas could be:

- Regular, honest performance reviews with concrete, doable requests regarding behavior
- One-on-one conversations between leader and the person who is hard to work with
- Formal mediation/restorative circle

Sometimes groups engage in discussions around ground rules. We have not seen this as effective, especially when those ground rules are made with only one person in mind. Direct feedback is more effective than vague ground rules, especially since, most likely, that particular member, sees themselves as well-intentioned - and they probably are. Hardly anyone would doubt that respect is a basic requirement, but not everyone agrees on what respect looks like, and under what conditions it is appropriate to prioritize, for example, honesty over respect. Make an effort to understand what their self-conception looks like and find good balance on how much time your circle is willing to devote. (See some more comments on "firing" volunteers from only one circle on page 234, and more on how to give feedback in chapter 4.)

2.3 Operations and the internal structure of a circle: Roles

We have described how circles connect to their related circles through linking and how circles have aims and domains that define their work. In addition, circles need some internal structure to function well. Of course, we can define (by consent) what those features might be in a particular organization. What we describe here is what is considered good practice and has been used in many sociocratic organizations. We have not seen any need to deviate from this basic structure, but readers might find their own way.

Why do we define roles? For the same reason that we make policy: for effectiveness, and clarity. For repeating tasks, we do not want to re-invent the wheel every time so we make policy about how it is done. But we also do not want to determine, which circle member is going to take the task every time: that is why we define roles. This is both true for circle roles and for operational roles. It is inefficient to start every meeting having to determine who is facilitator or secretary for that meeting. We want to settle those roles so we can focus on what is relevant. Also, in defining a role, we give the person filling a role the authority to act without having to check back with the circle, and the person a chance to build expertise in that role. Roles in sociocracy are generally about empowerment, building expertise and paying attention.

Some people see a circle as a bundle of operational roles in a domain – the holders of roles are the people who carry out the work of a circle. Another way of looking at it is to see all circle members as people who carry out the circle's operations, while some repeating tasks live in roles. Either way, we are separating roles, like hats, from individuals. One person can wear many hats, but each hat can only be worn by one person. One circle member can hold many roles, depending on resources and skills. Ideally, we would like to see roles distributed among several people as this distributes power. (On rotating facilitation, or roles in general, see section 2.3.4 on page 44.)

There are only two roles that can't be filled by the same person: leader and delegate. Double-linking requires the leader and delegate to be two separate individuals. Readers not familiar with double-linking are referred to section 2.4 on page 45.

2.3.1   Circle roles

- In order to stay in touch with where we want to be heading in the *future*, we need leadership. A circle **leader** (also called *top down link*) is paying attention to the circle's operations in relation to the circle's aim. What needs to be done, who agreed to do it. What is in the future to decide? The leader also serves as a top-down link, bringing information from the parent circle into their circle.
- In order to be *present* with each other, we need a good **facilitator**. Facilitators run meetings according to the format of meetings and decision making adopted by the group. Leader and facilitator are separate roles because facilitation and overseeing operations are different skill sets. They can be held by the same individual.
- In order to manage continuity with the circle's *past*, we need to have written records. The **secretary** manages the notes during the meeting, makes sure the minutes are distributed and accessible. The secretary also manages the records of the circle and is the interpreter of policies. Bigger organizations may choose to have a logbook keeper who keeps the records and the current policies in one central place so they are accessible.
- The **delegate** (also known as the *bottom-up link*, or *representative* or *rep*) is selected from within the circle to represent the circle in the next-"higher" circle. This creates a double-link between two circles. The leader and delegate carry information into the circle and out of the circle, a feature we call *double-linking*. (See section 2.4.)

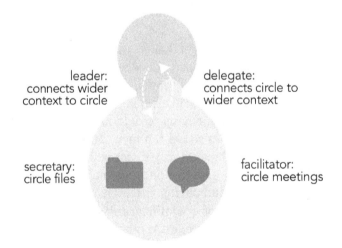

leader:
connects wider
context to circle

delegate:
connects circle to
wider context

secretary:
circle files

facilitator:
circle meetings

28: Circle roles take on a defined set of operations for a longer term

Leader role checklist

☐ Pays attention to the operations of the circle.

☐ Pays attention to the circle members.

☐ Member of circle and its parent circle.

☐ Reports top-down from wider context of the circle.

29: Checklist for the role of the leader

The leader supports forward-motion on the operational level of the circle. Equivalence is embodied in the idea of a double-link of leader and delegate: We increase the chances of more voices being heard when we have a second person forming a link between circles. Facilitator and secretary make sure the circle meetings run smoothly, establishing an effective practice with transparency and equivalence in meetings and between meetings.

Leader

Every circle member is free to act within the frame of policy of the circle. The leader makes sure operations and decisions are moved along so the circle can (continue to) work toward the aim of the circle. The role of the circle leader is both a circle role (supporting circle process) and an operational role (paying attention to operations in the entire circle's domain, see section 2.3.2). The leader operates within the frame of policy to which the circle has consented.

Part of the operational leadership is to pay attention to the whole of the circle. *"What needs doing next? Are circle members doing what they agreed to do? Who needs a check-in, and what might be needed so operations can run more smoothly? What comes from a broader circle that needs to happen here?"*

> Imagine a Membership Circle. Any operation happens within the policy framework given by the Membership Circle. The operational activities of a Membership Circle include outreach, orientations and ongoing education. The circle sets who is responsible for communication with people seeking information about membership. The leader makes sure this actually happens by checking in with people or doing whatever level of management is needed to make sure things happen smoothly. In that way, the leader pays attention to the whole.

Leadership is absolutely essential. Without defined leadership, the circle can easily lack the person who pays attention to the whole and leads the circle forward. Leader-less circles can easily fade away and/or go into "coasting" mode (functioning but not moving forward). Remember that in a system of consent, the leader is not demanding circle members do things they do not want to do.

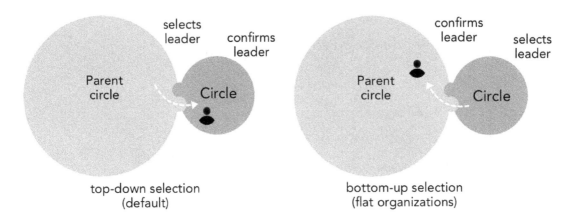

30: The leader can be selected top-down or bottom-up

It is not coercive leadership. Consent or sociocratic leadership is more like a running partner: the person who is paying attention to whether we show up and who checks in if we skip two running days in a row. This running partner does not have power over you; each circle member has given consent to the frame of how work is being done in the circle. The leader is the one who holds the operations and the members together, who is their accountability partner and their cheerleader. Because we have so much experience with the abuses of power, the reactions to leadership will depend on the organizational culture and context.

It is not easy for leaders to find their place if they enter a sociocratic organization for the first time. We often experience leaders as rather cautious around stepping into this role. Despite it being an egalitarian governance system, sociocracy is perfectly compatible with strong leadership. In our view, strong leadership with good listening skills and a good mix of self-reflection and pragmatism is *service* to the circle. It cannot be said often enough: in consent decision making no person can be over-powered. If there is tension around leadership styles, remember three ways to smoothen out the tension: (1) building everyone's communication skills, (2) giving each other feedback and (3) defining the role or related policy better to create more clarity. We encourage an open conversation and reflection on how circle members feel about leadership. It can be an enlightening process to define together in the circle *how* they want to be led!

Who proposes the leader? Which circle proposes the leader depends on the type of organization. In a hierarchical organization, the leader will be proposed top-down, by the circle's parent circle. Traditionally, the leader is the top-down link while the delegate is the bottom-up link (see section 2.4 on double-linking). In a more horizontal organization, the leader can be proposed by the circle. Either way, the *receiving* circle has to give consent to the selection.

The two scenarios are shown in diagram 30. Since roles and membership of a group are always based on consent (an individual consents to being part of a group, and a circle consents to any new member), neither of the two scenarios involves power-over.

Whenever an existing circle creates a new circle, the existing circle will usually select the leader for the new circle to get the new circle up and running well.

Delegate

Each circle selects a delegate to participate in the parent/next-broader circle. The delegate attends the meetings of the next-broader circle and has full consent rights in that circle. Delegates report from their circle to that next-broader circle and make sure their circle's concerns will be heard.

Whose opinions and needs does a delegate represent? Their own or the circle's? Their own. A circle selects a delegate for their capacity to work effectively as a member of the parent circle. The delegate makes sure that policies that the parent circle makes will work well in the child circle. The delegate might not have any operational responsibilities in the parent circle.

Since the leader is also a member of the parent circle, there are now two members from each circle on the parent circle. Hearing more than one voice from a circle in the broader circle supports the flow of information and transparency within an organization. A second voice is particularly useful when there is disagreement within a circle that needs to be represented. More on the psychological effect of double-linking in section 2.4.2 on page 47.

We strongly recommend having a delegate at the very least on your highest-level circles. Whether or not having a delegate is necessary depends on several factors. (See section 2.4.3 on page 48 for a discussion on whether a circle always needs to be double-linked.) Remember: in order to have a double-link, the delegate cannot be the same person as the circle leader.

The delegate is *not* just a reporting voice but a full member in both circles; the delegate has consent rights on *both* circles. This is crucial to establish and sustain equivalence between circles. Having a delegate is an embodiment of providing feedback in both directions.

Delegate role checklist

- ☐ Pays attention to the different voices in the circle.
- ☐ Member of circle and its parent circle.
- ☐ Reports bottom-up to the wider context of the circle.
- ☐ Participates as an equal in the parent circle decision making.

31: Checklist for the delegate role

Who proposes the delegate?   The delegate is selected by its own circle *and* needs to be confirmed by the circle receiving the delegate as a member.

The reason for that is that every circle needs to have full control over its membership. There can be an objection to accepting a member which will make it necessary for the "lower" circle to select a new delegate. As always, the basis for this objection has to be reasoned and in relation to the circle's aim. A dysfunctional general circle can slow down the entire organization – if a delegate is not supporting the work of the general circle, this needs to be taken seriously and addressed. See diagram in 32 and example 33 for a story around this.

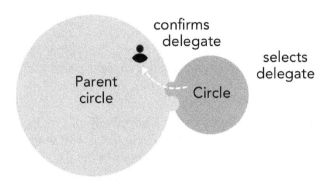

32: A circle selects a delegate; the parent circle confirms that delegate as a circle member

EXAMPLE
Any circle needs control over its circle membership

An organization had been dealing with a dysfunctional General Circle on an international level. When reflecting on this outside of a circle meeting (and with only some members present), there was some complaining about the low level of trust and functioning within that General Circle. *Well, what can we do, that's who they sent us from the department circles!* said one of the General Circle members.
If it's that bad that you don't get any work done in your General Circle and you tell me that this has to do with two of the delegates, and this has been going on for years, then why did you consent to their membership in the General Circle? You can withdraw your consent to their being on General Circle at any time. Tell the circle to send someone else!

33: Make use of your consent rights, including for delegates into the next-"higher" circle.

Secretary

Each circle selects a secretary to take notes and to publish the minutes within the organization. In some organizations, the role of the secretary (also called the circle administrator) might also involve announcing circle meetings, preparing the agenda in consultation with other circle members (see section 5.4 on page 195 on your options of who prepares the meeting agenda), and distributing study materials and proposals. The secretary also tracks what needs to be on meeting agendas, particularly remembering when a policy needs to be reviewed or that it is time for a new selection process for a role whose term of office is ending. As the keeper of the records, the secretary interprets policies when questions arise or if there is disagreement or confusion.

Since decisions in sociocracy are made in small, focused circles, it is vital for the circles and the organization that meeting records are not only written down but also *accessible* to the whole organization – otherwise, no one would hear about new policies that might affect them. In larger organizations, logbook keeping (storing/updating all policies in a central place) can be done by another role, the logbook keeper. In smaller organizations, this will typically be part of the secretary's role. Either way, it is important to define which tasks the secretary is expected to fulfill.

Secretary role checklist

- ☐ Makes sure meeting minutes are taken, approved and stored.
- ☐ Keeps track of all documents of the circle.
- ☐ Interprets the meeting minutes in case of disagreement.
- ☐ Supports planning the agenda from the backlog.

34: Checklist for a secretary

Facilitator

A facilitator is selected by each circle to run circle meetings. Facilitators are responsible for understanding the aim of each item on the agenda so that they are confident they can facilitate each item appropriately and guide the circle through all the steps of decision making. The facilitator may check in with the leader and/or the secretary to plan upcoming meetings. The facilitator supports circle members to be effective participants in the meeting.

Facilitator role checklist

- ☐ Facilitates circle meetings.
- ☐ Pays attention to equivalence during meetings.
- ☐ Supports planning of agenda.
- ☐ Distinguishes facilitator voice from circle member voice.

35: Checklist for a facilitator

Why is the leader not the facilitator? The leader *can* be the facilitator *if* that works well for your circle. In that case the two roles would be filled by the same individual.

Since the skill set of a leader is very different from the skill set of a facilitator, sociocracy separates those two roles so that we are intentional about filling them each on the basis of their own requirements. We might have someone in your circle who is good at *both* leading and facilitation, but there are many examples of great leaders who do not enjoy facilitation and of great facilitators who have a hard time leading operational work. The leader role typically asks for a person who is a doer, who is good at holding people accountable, delegating and paying attention to what needs

Leader	Facilitator
Pays attention to the circle's aim.	Pays attention to equivalence during meetings.
Oversees the circle's operations.	In charge of process during meetings.
Member of their own and of the parent circle.	Understands the aim of each item in a meeting.
	Participating member of their own circle.
Carry the parent circle's information into the circle.	

36: Comparing leader and facilitator

to be done on a broad level while not losing track of details. A facilitator has to be comfortable in front of the group, paying attention to process so equivalence can be ensured during the meetings. A facilitator should be good at listening and synthesizing. Also, it makes sense that the leader has free attention to attend to content during the meeting while the facilitator holds the process level.

Logbook keeper

The logbook keeper manages and maintains the minutes and the set of policies for the entire organization. This role is defined by the general circle if the secretary of the general circle cannot perform those tasks in addition to the regular secretarial tasks.

The objective is to have one person pay attention to the policies, remind circles to update the logbook with new or revised policies, make sure new members have access to the logbook etc. Depending on the size of the organization, this can be a big job. We want to have only policies that are current and want to have them easy to find for maximum transparency. Example 37 shows what a logbook might look like.

Table 38 lists the tasks; more specific arrangements can be made by the general circle.

If desired, any circle that has a lot of policies to maintain can define a role of a logbook keeper just for their own policies and in addition to the secretary role.

Example logbook

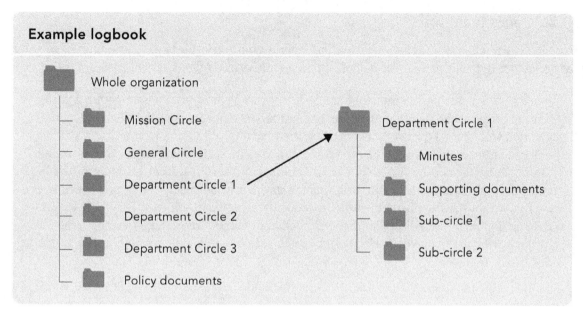

37: An example of a logbook

Logbook keeper tasks

standardization of file and folder names so people know how to find files
(for example: *Minutes 2018.01.13 Buildings and Grounds circle*)

archiving and deleting

safe backup of documents

maintain Policy Manual with policies grouped according to the responsible circle

38: The tasks of a logbook keeper

2.3.2 Operational roles

Most circles will choose to define what we call operational roles: parts of the domain of the circle that are overseen by individual (or paired) circle members in a role as shown in figure 39.

> Imagining a machine maintenance circle in a printing business, a role could hold attention for a special printing machine, its maintenance needs, coordinating repairs, and giving introductions to new workers using the machine. While the printer itself is in the domain of the machine maintenance circle, the operations in relationship to that printer are being performed by the holder of the operational role. Another example might be a membership circle that wants to put some effort into outreach. They might ask one person within the membership circle to coordinate outreach efforts. If this proves successful, and if that is a direction the circle wants to pursue, then the circle might decide to form a separate outreach circle that meets separately, makes its own policy in the domain of outreach.

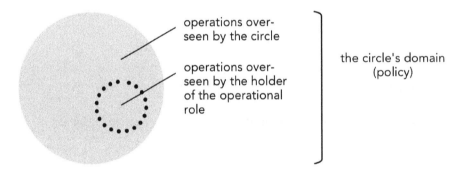

39: Operational roles take on a defined set of operations for a longer term

The advantages of roles for circles are:

- Roles "outsource" the workload in meetings and free the circle's attention so they can address and solve blockages that might be holding back operations in the circle's domains. The maintenance circle should not have to talk about regular service work for each machine unless there is an systemic issue to deal with.
- Separating out particular repeated operations into "packaged" roles supports effective collaboration because we do not need to involve every circle member to do or even talk about repetitive tasks, like scheduling repairs or regular service work.
- Different from job titles, roles allow for a more fine-grained chunking of responsibilities.

Advantages for the holder of roles:

- When the role is well-defined and the holder selected based on qualifications and skills, then the holder of the role has clarity and freedom to act. There is no need for micromanagement.
- The tasks can be performed faster, with more focus and with less need for coordination.
- Holders of roles can build expertise around their role.

Defining operational role checklist

☐ Defines the tasks performed by the holder of the role

☐ Defines and limits the holder's authority for operational decisions

☐ Set by the circle holding the role

40: Checklist for defining an operational role

- Separating work into roles (instead of job titles) allows for flexibility. An area of authority can be passed on, even temporarily, more easily.
- The same individual can hold different roles, with varying degrees of abstractness or concreteness, to create a mix of areas of responsibility that matches the needs and desires of the individual.

Holders of operational roles will typically be circle members – for example if someone is hired to fill the role of the outreach manager, then that person joins the circle that holds that role. Note: holders of roles within a circle domain don't *necessarily* have to be members of the circle that owns the role but it is recommended in order to more easily receive and respond to feedback. The limit here is the circle's attention: we can only distribute authority to the extent we prioritize gathering meaningful feedback. If a circle distributes authority into many roles with half of them not being circle members, it will take a lot of effort to track and support their work and feedback.

In order to create a role, a circle needs a role description. A role description can be generated in the same way other policies are generated – defining a brief needs statement, picture forming and proposal shaping. (See how to write roles in section 3.6.1 on page 130.)

Policy guiding the operations will be made by the circle. The holder of the operational role will operate according to circle policy and has exactly the authority they are given by the circle. They do not have the authority to make policy alone. Most typically, holders of roles will suggest policy to the circle that affects their role.

The circle's job is to create framing for the roles with enough clarity so holders of roles can act without having to check back with the circle and so nothing holds them back. Like any policy, we create the smallest amount of policy – enough to guide, avoiding blockages or clashes with other tasks, without creating unnecessary overhead or bureaucracy. Policy, including role descriptions, is made to free people, not to limit people.

It is a good idea to have some system that creates redundancy (e.g. a second person who knows how to fix the copy machine!) so we do not depend on single individuals and skills, and knowledge can be spread. What is important here is that it has to be clear who is in charge. If two people hold a role, the risk is that they each assume the other one is responsible.

A role description might look like example 41. A circle consents to the role description. Once the role exists, the circle selects someone into that role. The sociocratic selection process serves to

Example for a role description of an operational role

Scheduling system manager

Oversees the online scheduling system. This includes:
- monitoring and responding to alerts from the scheduling software
- offering training and advice about how to use the scheduling system and calendar
- ongoing budget: $2000 a year
- time budget: 3h/week
- writing and maintaining manual on the system's how-to
- educating team members about scheduling system policies

In an effort to support skill-building within the circle, the holder of this role is encouraged to appoint a second person who knows how to use the system.

Term: 1 year

41: Sample description of an operational role.

fill roles based on qualification and skills in a transparent way.

The circle may then create a new sub-circle with its own aim and domain and roles. An operational role might be turned into a sub-circle if this set of tasks grows in complexity, more and more people are involved and the circle wants to move policy-making for this role out of the circle. The important difference between an operational role and a sub-circle (besides, typically, the number of members) is the fact that a sub-circle *owns* the domain of the sub-circle and can make policy in its own domain instead of "just" carrying out operations.

2.3.3 Terms

Every person is selected into operational roles for a set term. The length of that term is completely up to the circle. Often, groups will have a standard term that they modify if there is a reason.

With short terms, we have to do a selection process often, which takes up meeting time. With long terms, we might miss opportunities to spread leadership.

During the selection process, the term will be part of the proposal and can be modified like any other aspect of a proposal.

2.3.4 On rotating or sharing roles

Groups often ask whether they could just "share" the facilitation. In our own circles, we prefer to have the role of the facilitator filled for a year at a time – this applies to all the roles.

Facilitation can be rotated among members under two conditions.

- Only one person is facilitator per meeting (or a section thereof; there might be a good reason to fill in, for example if the facilitator is strongly attached to an outcome or triggered by a situation).

- If facilitation rotates throughout individual meetings, it must be clear who is responsible for the preparation of the agenda – does that rotate as well, or does only the actual facilitation rotate? In our experience, if meeting preparation rotates, it can be hard to keep track of who does what! (It basically means someone will have to remind people that it is their turn to prepare the meeting which creates an extra step.) Preparing the meeting agenda is an important part of effective decision making. While preparing the agenda, the facilitator – ideally with the circle leader and the secretary – thinks about next steps for each agenda items: Are we doing picture forming? Is there a proposal ready? Is everyone present at the meeting who we want there to gather feedback or make a decision? Just putting an item on the agenda is no guarantee of an effective meeting. Being clear about what is realistic and desired as a next step is a crucial ingredient for boosting the circle's productiveness and will be highly appreciated.

We see more disadvantages than advantages in rotating facilitation. Filling a role for at least a few months frees the circle's attention to take care of operations instead of tracking facilitation tasks. Also, building skills takes time and repetition.

The group can still spread the facilitation skills by having short terms for the facilitator, for example 4 months. That way, it is still clear who is responsible for making the agenda and facilitating the meeting. However, this comes at a cost also: the circle will have to do a selection process every four months which takes away from meeting time. We want to be intentional about how long a term we choose for selections. We can choose the terms separately every time we select and they can be different for every role. We can tailor our system to our needs at all times.

2.4 Double-linking

In sociocracy, as much authority as possible is distributed into specific circles. All circles are related but each circle has full authority in their domain. Giving a circle full authority in their domain often leads to an increase in productivity. But how do we avoid silos? How will the circles know about each other's work?

What we need is a way to connect the circles. Let's assume that in image 42 (a), the domains of the two circles are related. Circle 2's domain is a piece of circle 1's domain. Circle 2 will be a sub-circle of circle 1. The connection between circle 1 and circle 2 will be done by double-linking. Double-linking is the sociocratic way of connecting two circles. Two circle members will be *full* members of *both* circles as shown in diagram 42 on the right.

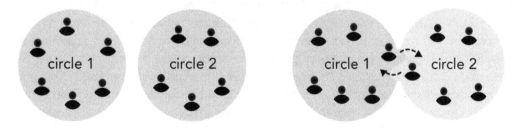

42: Unlinked vs. linked circles

More precisely, we will consider one of the two links the "top-down link" (or the "leader/lead link"), and the other link the "bottom-up link" (or "delegate" or "representative"). The top-down link carries the parent circle's matters into the sub-circle and makes sure all actions serve to carry out the sub-circle's aim. The bottom-up link reports from the sub-circle into the larger organization by reporting to the next 'higher' sub-circle what there is to know from the sub-circle (what decisions have been made, how the sub-circle is doing, the impact on the sub-circle of policies made in the parent circle etc.; see diagram 43).

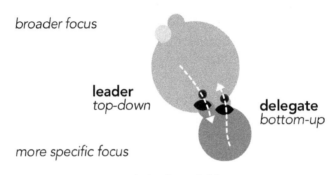

43: Leader and delegate

2.4.1   Circular hierarchy

With both links, we get what is called "circular hierarchy". Linkage is not only top-down and not only bottom-up but *both* at the same time. Information flows in an infinite loop from one circle to the next, in both directions. That also allows the circles to take care of each other if a circle struggles.

We need flow of information to make sure everyone and everything works well together. The two links also serve as a filter – no one in an organization can (and wants to) hold all the information from all the circles. Attention is a scarce resource and we have to protect it. That way, each circle can focus on what's important to them. Only what is relevant is passed on. The top-down link filters information coming from the next-'higher' circle and passes on everything that is relevant for this circle. The bottom-up link only reports what is important to the next-'higher' circle and filters out details that are not relevant to know on that level.

On the other hand, issues can also be amplified. For example, some regional work circles of the same organization might report a problem that does not seem to be huge on their scale – but the circle on the national level starts seeing a pattern that points to a systemic issue. We *want* that kind of information to bubble up. A parent circle does not need to know who is performing what task within the circle. However, a circle might want to report to the parent circle that it is hard to find people to do extra tasks because all members of the circle are overcommitted. This might be a systemic issue that needs attention on a general level. It could also be that the IT solution that the organization is working with is too complicated and create a disconnect between people. This again would be important information. Decentralization and the filtering/amplification of information is a relief. Flow of information will not lead to overload.

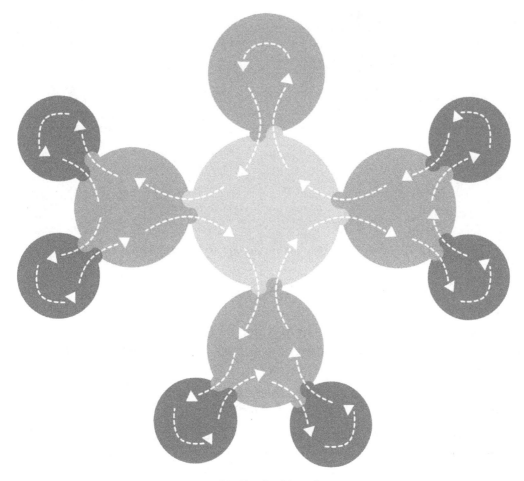

44: Circular hierarchy

See the list below for relevant topics that can be reported on. There might be policy regulating what is reported (like a set of defined measures).

- any formal request of the sub-circle to its parent circle
- policy the sub-circle is working on
- a general sense of the morale of the group (*"Overwhelmed, content, excited, burned out?"*)
- production data; measures of effectiveness
- successes and challenges in progress toward the aim

2.4.2 The psychological effect of double-linking

Delegates report from their circle to the parent circle on a regular basis. Picture this: *both* the leader and the delegate will be present as they are both full members of both circles. Both the leader and the delegate will have been part of any decision or challenge that is being reported. Whenever delegates report from their sub-circle, the other one will be listening too and might add

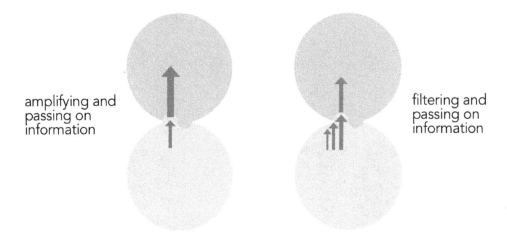

45: Flow of information in the context of circular hierarchy: amplification and filtering

to it to complete the picture. By hearing two voices, we get a more complete picture of what has been going on in the circle.

But there is more to double-linking than that, and that is a psychological effect: since leader and delegate *both* know that the other one is present, their awareness will shift. They will monitor themselves internally more:

- *How can I report in a way that all voices from the circle are represented?*
- *Is what I am saying true, and is it the complete picture?*

Just the other person's presence makes a difference in how the other link self-assesses and speaks.

People might own their unique perspective more and acknowledge uncertainties. If people are aware that they do not have access to the only and absolute truth, they are much more open to listening, and to considering other people's point of view. Perspective-taking is a huge learning in this kind of setting.

In organizations with double-linking, a parent or child circle will not be seen as *other*. Imagine a circle does not agree with a decision a parent circle made: if two people who are part of "my" circle are also part of the parent circle, it will increase understanding instead of creating a sense of separation. Since it is harder to dismiss two voices than one, double-linking supports mutual understanding and a sense of togetherness.

2.4.3   Is double-linking mandatory?

Historically, double-linking is one of the defining principles defining sociocracy (with linked circles, open elections, consent decision making). What we find in practice is that some groups choose to skip double-linking and only implement single links. Practitioners do not always see the need to implement double-linking, or they simply do not have the humanpower to fill all the roles. What we recommend is to strive for double-linking, especially on the highest levels (department circles, to the general circle and to the mission circle). Double-linking is a *strategy* to support equivalence in an organization. Below are some of the considerations around the topic of double-linking:

- If more than one person knows what is going on in a related circle (higher, or lower), then this increases the likelihood that we will have access to information from that circle even if members miss meetings due to travel etc. Double-linking helps keep the organization together: if the leader is not present, the delegate will know what is going on in the other circle. If the delegate is absent, the leader will know.

- In a context where members participate in two or more other circles of the same organization, we might pass on formal double-linking, knowing that we will always have enough information from more than one person in the room. Double-linking is critical for any circles that link to the Mission Circle or General Circle. At these levels, having only a single link may result in too little or distorted information sharing and a decrease in equivalence. At lower levels of the organization, particularly in organizations where volunteers serve on multiple circles, there may be enough information flow.

- At minimum, have a delegate "on call". If the leader can't make the circle meeting of the next-higher circle, or if there is a controversial issue, then we have a delegate in place who will be able to report. It seems like a good idea to select this delegate *before* there is an issue, however, or it might turn into a "political" decision.

2.5 Types of circles

2.5.1 Basic circles of an implementation

One can run a sociocratic organization with one circle. As tasks need to be more differentiated and/or the organization grows, we grow into a more complex structure. We will describe the generic set-up here. There are some comments on tiny organizations in section 6.6.

After having talked about circles and sub-circles, we will now look at circles in the context of a complete organization. We call work circles department circles if they are linked to the circle in the middle, the general circle. They are the equivalent of departments in a traditional organization. Other names for the highest level work circles are "main circles", "division circles", or "core circle". We can, of course, call them by any other suitable name.

In diagram 46, there are three department circles. Any number between 2 and 5 will work, although 3 or 4 seems to be the ideal. Any department circle can have sub-circles. Different department circles in the same organization might have different numbers of sub-circles. There is no need for symmetry. The number of sub-circles is determined by the department circles and their needs. It is not shown in the diagram but any sub-circle can have sub-sub-circles, going down to any level of differentiation that might be needed.

One can see the double-link between every level, which is always a leader as top-down link and a delegate as bottom-up link.

Side note: on a sub-circle level, it is easier to have more than 5 circles *if* there is a lot of overlap between people holding linking roles, so that the intermediary circle does not get too big. The balance we are looking for is to have good flow of information in all directions while avoiding big circles.

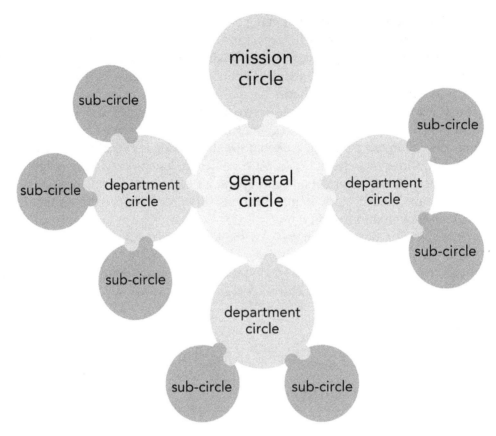

46: A basic implementation

2.5.2 The General Circle

The general circle (GC) connects all the department circles. As such, the GC owns the entire aim and domain of the organization. Note that of course, we strive to "pass on" as much authority as possible to work circles – we do not hold on to that power. The GC has three main tasks:

- The GC holds the department circles accountable and supports their functioning.
- The GC is also the center of the flow of information between circles that carries out the aim. *"What are circles working on? What does Department Circle 1 need to know about Department Circle 3? How can circles support each other?"* Remember that the delegate reports from the department circle *into* the general circle, while the leader – besides their other tasks of leading the circle – take the information *from* the GC into their department circles.
- The GC sets the aims of the circles and supports clarifications of aims. In practice, this means that the GC decides who decides. If a new issue or topic arises, the GC will assign it to one of the department circles. When an issue concerns the aims/domains of more than one department circle, it can be explored and decisions can be made in the GC.

In Diagram 47, the GC would consist of the leaders and delegates of the three department circles, the leader of the GC would be selected by the mission circle.

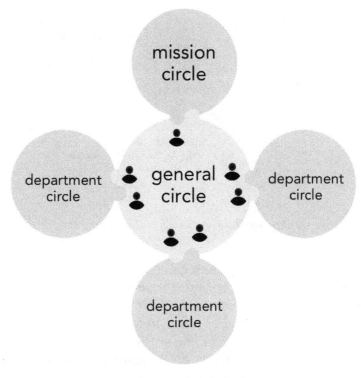

47: The general circle (GC)

2.5.3 The Mission Circle

The mission circle (MC) is a circle that can be compared with the board of directors. A mission circle pays attention to long-term planning and makes sure the organization stays true its mission (and vision) and connected in its organizational and cultural context. As shown in Fig. 48, the MC gives general direction and support, may have legal and financial responsibilities and supports the operational leader. The GC (general circle) supports the aim-related work.

Other names for the Mission Circle

We chose the name "Mission Circle" (MC) because it is the best description of what this circle does: keeping the organization true to its mission. The traditional name for this circle is Top Circle, a term that often raises eyebrows. We understand the cultural baggage the term "top" brings in a hierarchical culture. Other names we have heard:

- vision-keepers circle
- Board of Directors
- Board of Trustees
- strategic planning circle
- root circle
- Council of Elders

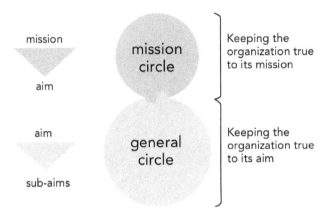

48: Difference between mission circle and general circle

The mission circle offers one of the organization's opportunities for mutual influence between the outside world and the inside of the organization. Thanks to outside members in the MC and to contact with clients, customers, users or members in specific circles, any organization will have mutual influence with the larger community, and as shown in figure 49. There is no *us vs. others* within a sociocratic organization. This is also true for the relationship between the larger community and the MC. The MC is the link with and to the larger community. (Related to this topic, see more on networks in chapter 2.7.)

Who is on the Mission Circle?

The MC consists of:

- the leader of the General Circle
- the delegate from the General Circle
- (if applicable) delegates from stakeholder circles
- experts from inside or outside the organization

Experts from outside the organization may be from areas such as legal, finance, fundraising, communication, sociocratic governance, related content or aim. A few examples:

- A business may bring in legal assistance, an expert from their industry, or a governance expert.
- A producer coop might have someone from the local food cooperative on their board, someone from a cooperative development fund, someone from a different worker-coop in the area and whatever makes sense in relation to the aim.
- An intentional community might have someone from related non-profits in their area on their board, maybe someone from a cohousing association or a community in the area, and a governance or permaculture expert or a trainer for non-violent communication (NVC).

Depending on the aim and the specific implementation, the MC can also include representatives of stakeholder circles, circles that are double-linked to the MC and represent a stakeholder group (see section 2.5.3 on page 56).

The link for coordination between MC and GC is the operational leader, or Executive Director

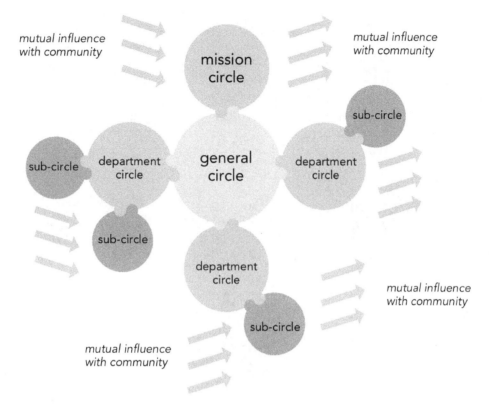

49: Mutual influence between organization and outside world on Mission Circle level and on specific circle level: any organization benefits from this kind of exchange with the outside world; closed systems are not sustainable

or CEO. The bottom-up link is the delegate from the GC. Note that this will likely be a leader or delegate from one of the department circles.

As shown in diagram 51, a worker from the most specific level might be selected delegate into the department circle, and from there become delegate into the general circle and from there become delegate from the general circle into the mission circle.

Representation of work circle delegates on the MC is more than just "being heard" on board level. With consent as the decision-making method, working members cannot be ignored. Sociocracy is more than giving workers a voice in the management. The workers *are* the management. When workers are running the organization, and the decision-making method is consent, workers do not need to be protected because they hold the decision-making power in the first place.

The MC itself will select a facilitator, a secretary and a leader (counterpart of a president of the board) to manage their own circle. The MC typically does not have a delegate because there is no "higher" place to represent this circle inside the organization; this is different for organizations of organizations. An organization may be connected to others in networks and associations. More on these in 2.7.

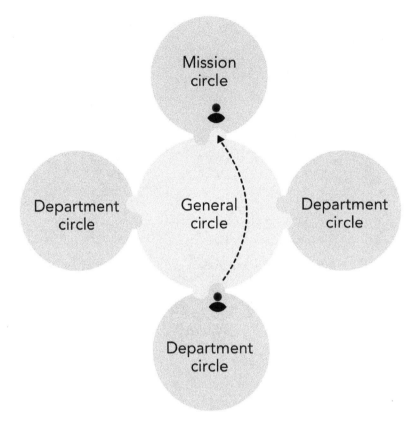

50: One of the leaders/delegates becomes delegate to the mission circle

The difference between traditional boards and mission circles

Below are some important differences between a traditional board and a mission circle. Note that what a "traditional board" is highly dependent on your context.

- Like any other sociocratic circle, an MC operates by consent. There is no factionalism/out-voting/out-numbering in sociocracy. One objection from anyone in the mission circle would require addressing the objection and finding a solution together.
- The double-link. There is flow of information in both directions. Two staff members, namely the leader and delegate of the general circle, are members of the board with consent rights.
- MC members *can* be "working members" if they are *also* members of work circles.

Especially if we come from a domain where it is common to have board-run organizations, there is a noteworthy difference in sociocracy. Separating the operational level (general circle and the circles under the general circle) from the mission-keeping level (mission circle) creates a clean distinction between every-day business and longer-term focus. Both are essential to run a successful organization but they have different angles on what is happening and are therefore best kept separate.

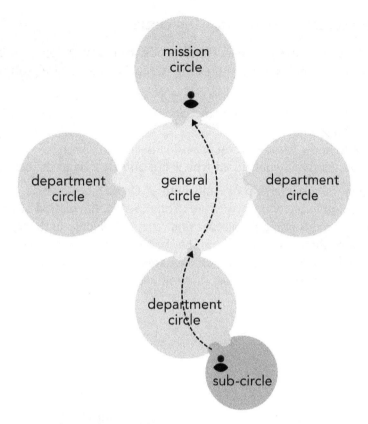

51: A worker can become delegate through all layers of the organization.

Do we need a Mission Circle?

The short answer is: yes. The long answer is: we might start out with only work circles and a general circle, but over time, there will be questions we won't get around to talking about. An organization easily gets tied up in pressing issues. We don't want to give in to "tyranny of the urgent over the important". There will always be something urgent to deal with – but without taking the time to reflect and set a direction, we will lose out in the long run. Not only does the organization need direction but also adjustment and steering because the outside world changes continually. It is false economy to omit time devoted to conscientious steering.

If a group is afraid that having an MC will stretch the organization too thin in a given moment, see section 6.4.3 on page 228 for workarounds and temporary solutions.

> We started without mission circle and had a situation where not everybody had a clear picture of what our mission is and what our aims are. It was hard to align. A mission circle helped us focus and made the implicit explicit.
>
> *(Leif Hanack. Europace, Berlin/Germany)*

Stakeholder representation in the mission circle

A sociocratic MC will usually have members from outside the organization. Those outside members might be individual supporters, experts, or they might represent an entire group of stakeholders.

Questions to ask:

- Who do we want to involve on the mission circle?
- Whose input will be valuable?
- Who would like to know what is going on inside the organization?
- Who needs to be heard and considered who is not directly part of the organization?

It could be the general membership or contributors. Or member-owners, funders or investors. Some groups are reluctant to have "outsiders" serve on the MC: *"But we don't want outsiders controlling our organization!"* On this point, remember that decision making on the mission circle happens by consent. The idea of the outside members, be they investors, funders or anyone else, will be considered but they cannot outvote the other members of the mission circle. Hence sociocratic organizations cannot be subject to takeovers or be moved involuntarily to another location where there are cheaper labor costs etc.

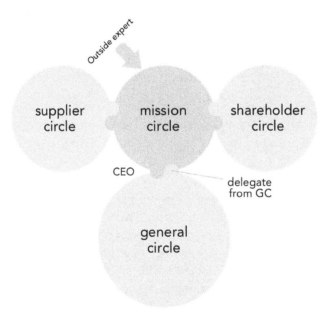

52: An example of the mission circle of a for-profit

Diagram 52 shows what a sociocratic for-profit can look like. Please keep in mind that these are examples – a supplier circle makes sense in some contexts and not in others. The actual organization depends on what constellation works well in the mission circle.

Diagram 53 shows part of the structure of a worker-cooperative. There are two aspects to notice here. First, this cooperative has all workers represented in the work circles, including non-owners like seasonal workers and provisional members. To give a voice to the long-term planning interest of member-owners a voice, the owners form an owner circle that has two delegates in the MC.

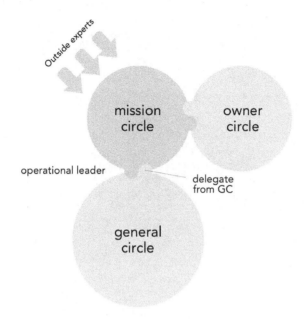

53: A sample structure of a worker cooperative

They also have people from outside the cooperative on their mission circle, for example a co-op developer, or members of other enterprises that are related to their field, like suppliers.

An example of an intentional community is shown in Fig. 54a. There are three outside experts shown. For example, a member of town government could be on the community's mission circle. Someone from a different intentional community, a local farmer, a permaculture design expert, someone with expertise in elder care or in communication skills or in conflict resolution.

For completeness (even though there is not much of a difference), let's explore a non-profit structure as illustrated in Fig. 54b. Depending on the nature of the non-profit, there might be a coherent set of donors. (Coherent enough to select a delegate among them.) They might have an expert from local government or school administration or from another organization with a similar aim. A non-profit may have a membership base which meets occasionally. The membership may select a delegate to serve on the mission circle to represent the interests of the members.

There are many ways to tie stakeholder groups together. The basic ideas are

- to connect within your field
- to seek outside expertise for your organization
- to implement representation of entire stakeholder groups, if that makes sense

Remember that:

- In consent decision making – different from majority vote – number is not a factor. We do not need to have one group outnumber another. Everyone will have to collaborate.
- It is better to keep the numbers manageable. In a large group, people will have difficulties hearing each other and being productive as a group. We can always make policy around rotating stakeholder groups over time if that helps, or ask a stakeholder to visit and report.

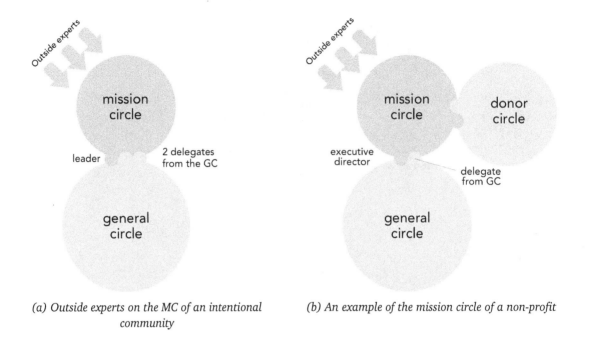

(a) Outside experts on the MC of an intentional community

(b) An example of the mission circle of a non-profit

- Typically, the leader of the general circle (executive director, CEO or other titles) will represent the mission circle on the stakeholder circle to complete double-linking in the usual way. This is another way to ensure flow of information. If we choose to and we value distribution of leadership, we can select another mission circle member (not the leader of the general circle) to link to a stakeholder circle. Whatever works and is decided in the spirit of the principles!
- The MC member who serves on the stakeholder circle is that circle's leader and has consent rights on who that circle's delegate on the MC will be.
- We choose the number of delegates from each group (stakeholder circle or CG) as desired.
- If a group gets anxious at the thought of having all those outside people on the "board", then they can simply have more than one delegate from the GC on the mission circle (see Fig. 54a).

2.5.4   Helping circles

Helping circles are "ad hoc circles" that only exist temporarily for a specific purpose, to accomplish a specific aim within a limited period of time. Usually, helping circles have a limited domain of decision-making. The typical aim of a helping circle is to research, gather feedback, discuss, synthesize, and to come back to the parent circle with a recommendation or proposal.

How to form a helping circle

The parent circle may select the members of the helping circle or select a leader and ask that leader of the helping circle to select the members. All circles must have a clear aim and leadership. The helping circle members can be from inside the parent circle or from outside. It can have two members or many members. A helping circle can exist just for one meeting or for much longer,

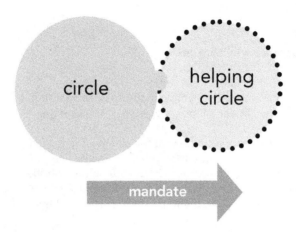

55: Forming a helping circle.

depending on the needs of the parent circle.

Helping circles can also be used to build cross-sectional teams, for example to work out better alignment between two (unrelated) circles or even between two organizations.

Why form a helping circle?

Form a helping circle whenever it would be more efficient to have a few people deal with a question or a task instead of everyone in the circle. Examples:

- The circle needs more information on an issue. A helping circle can gather more information and make a recommendation.
- A written piece requires a re-write. Gather ideas and let a helping circle work out the details.
- A discussion among a subset of the circle comes up and the group has a clear sense that their discussion does not require everyone's presence.

The idea of a fractal circle structure is to reduce the number of items we have to pay attention to in one circle by compartmentalizing tasks into sub-circles. The temporary version of that is the helping circle.

Forming helping circles – common mistakes

The three most common pitfalls are:

- A helping circle without a leader. We can nominate the leader (or all the members of the helping circle) as part of the proposal to create the helping circle or do a selection process after consenting its creation.
- A helping circle without clarity on its aim (e.g. without a clear description of what the outcome or product is intended to be).
- Helping circles without a link to the parent circle; if the helping circle leader is not a member of the parent circle, there needs to be a plan to facilitate flow of information between both circles.

> **Example**
> **An unclear mandate for a helping circle**
>
> An organization runs an annual retreat with about 80 members. The planning of this retreat is within the domain of a circle called *Community Life*. One year, a Retreat Circle was formed by Community Life, with volunteer members outside of the Community Life Circle.
>
> How this played out: the retreat circle went full steam ahead, changed the original ideas and ended up planning most of the retreat before Community Life Circle even met again. Result? Tension, confusion and mixed messages about community priorities. It seemed like the helping circle had overstepped their boundaries. Was the Retreat Circle just a helping circle tasked with getting more information? Or had the Retreat Circle received the authority to plan the retreat?
>
> How much time could have been saved and friction prevented if the helping circle had been given a clear aim specifying the expected outcome of its work?

56: It is crucial to be clear about the mandate given to a helping circle.

Example 56 tells a story from one of our organizations. When setting up a helping circle, use the checklist in 57. If all boxes are checked, it just takes a minute. If not, we'll be glad we noticed!

Helping circle checklist

☐ Aim/expected outcome (report, recommendation, decision)

☐ Authority (domain)

☐ Leadership

☐ Membership

☐ Term/report/complete by

57: Checklist for forming a helping circle

2.5.5 A full-fledged structure

For you reference, Figure 58 is a complete example organizational structure in a generic form. Note that not all circles have to be present in every implementation, and it is intentionally slightly asymmetrical to show the organic nature of circles structures. Notice it also has a helping circle, so one can see all circle types in one structure at a glance. See section 6.4.2 for a step-by-step process on how to approach designing an organizational structure.

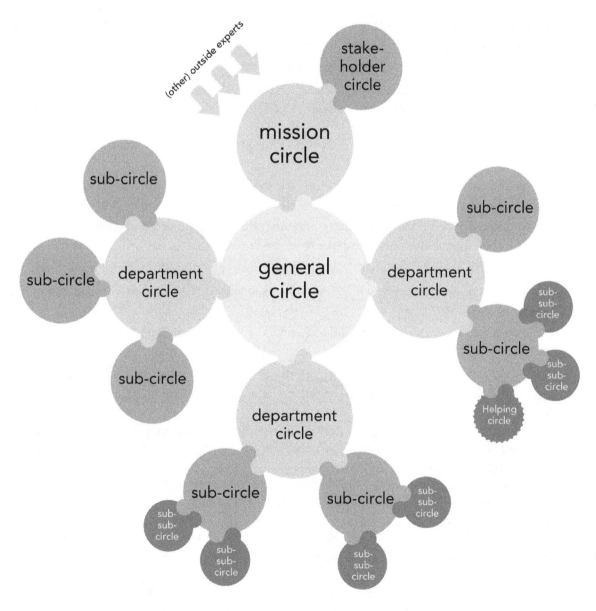

58: A full structure

2.6   Transitions and variations

The structure of an organization is designed to help carry out the organization's aims. No organizational structure is set in stone. The structure has to adapt to the people/mission/needs of the organization, not vice versa.

2.6.1   Growth

How do we know when it is time to grow our organizational structure? Below are some typical signs, including some suggested solutions.

- Symptom: The circle is overwhelmed with detail. Possible solutions:
  - Reassign responsibilities among existing operational roles.
  - Define one or more new operational roles (see section 2.3.2) to take on some of the circle's responsibilities.
  - Form helping circles to review the circle's aims and domain and bring back a recommendation for creating one or more sub-circles.

- Symptom: Many agenda items affecting only a fraction of the circle members. The expectation is that most agenda items are relevant to all circle members. Possible solution:
  - Separate out tasks and/or authority into operational roles, helping circle or sub-circles so that most agenda items are relevant to all circle members.

- Symptom: Many members in a circle say that hearing everyone is hard. Possible solution:
  - Form a sub-circle especially if the circle is responsible for a lot of policy making and has more than 7 members.

To form a sub-circle, define its aim/domain and select the convener or leader. See the checklist in 60 for forming a sub-circle.

- If a sub-circle has a convener but no leader, the sub-circle can select its circle leader in their first meeting. The new sub-circle then needs to review and confirm acceptance of its aim and domain.
- If a sub-circle is formed and the leader of that sub-circle cannot attend the meetings of the parent circle, find a way of gathering the information either through a delegate or by assigning a liaison who checks in with that sub-circle.
- Insist on the sub-circle having a full-fledged internal structure with a facilitator, delegate, secretary and meeting schedule. That helps keep the circle on track. None of these roles can be skipped without good reasons. For example, sub-circles are often tempted to "keep things informal". However, having the roles of a facilitator, secretary, leader and delegate are not implemented for the sake of formality, they are implemented for accountability, full transparency, to save time and to keep good records. (See box in 59.)
- Planning for future growth is fine. However, we don't want to create circles that we can't support in the present moment. Wishful thinking might be informative but acting on it can stretch groups too thin.

> We tried to keep things informal as well. No explicit functional roles, no terms. We learned the hard way that this saved us nothing. Worse, it hindered the learning of and the safety in our sociocratic organization.
>
> *(Leif Hanack. Europace, Berlin/Germany)*

59: What practitioners say

Forming a sub-circle checklist

☐ Aim

☐ Authority (domain)

☐ Leadership

☐ Membership

☐ Term/evaluate new circle by

60: Checklist for forming a sub-circle

2.6.2   De-growth

How would we know that we need to dissolve a circle?

- There might be difficulty populating circles.
- Members do not seem to have the drive it takes to run the circle sustainably.
- The organization cannot afford to pay staff in that circle.

Every parent circle is always responsible for the well-being of its sub-circles. Are the sub-circles getting their work done? Are they making/reviewing policies needed? Are the sub-circle members working well together? We don't want a circle to fall apart without noticing. If a sub-circle decides to fold, the domain and the aim automatically fall back to the parent circle as shown in 61. It is ok if a circle only meets from time to time, as long as this works well for the circle members guiding their work. For example, a circle that prepares the spring and fall fundraising events for a school might meet frequently as the event approaches, once afterwards and then not at all for a while.

What can we do if we need to close down one or more circles? It is easy to do so if we drop the work at the same time. For example, your company decides to drop the line of bathing suits and only to sell goggles. That's fine. Now we do not need the bathing suit circle anymore.

But what if there is still work to do but it is too hard to keep the circle running? We can turn the tasks into an operational role into the next-broader circle. Terminate any "zombie" circles (circles that should be ended because they are not meeting/working but are still kept alive on paper).

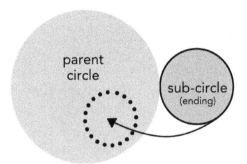

61: Folding a circle into an operational role: aim and domain are re-absorbed into the parent circle

2.6.3   Hand-offs and handovers

What's the relationship between sibling circles? There should not be any overlap between their domains. But we might want to strengthen the connection between sibling circles when domains seem to interdepend. Let's look at an example.

Let's say we have two circles in a land shepherdship context. One circle takes care of the paths, roads and infrastructure – Infrastructure Circle for short. Another circle takes care of the trees and bushes, Tree Circle. It seems that the domains are very well defined. Everything that is a road is

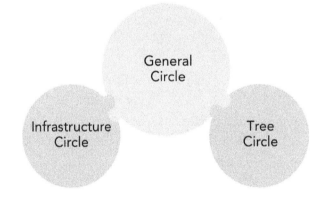

62: The circles with (supposedly) well-defined, non-overlapping domains

in the Infrastructure Circle, for example repairs or cleaning and clearing the paths. Tree circle's domain is also very well defined because we know the piece of land and we have a clear sense of what a tree is. If a tree is damaged, tree circle is going to look into it.

Now, what happens if there is a storm and a branch breaks off the tree and falls onto the path? Who cleans up? There is no right or wrong here, but what we need is clarity between domains. Someone will have to be in charge, make policies around how the clean-up happens and what the budget is for additional machinery that might be necessary etc. This group might decide that the branch is in Tree Circle's domain as long as it is on the tree. Once a branch is not attached to the tree anymore and blocks a path, it falls into Infrastructure Circle. It would be responsible for clean-up because it is in its domain to keep the paths usable. So far, this example is well along the lines of what we have said about clearly defined domains in section 2.2.2.

If this is a big piece of land and tree branches fall often, shouldn't both circles be involved in policy around that? Shouldn't they be *connected* diagonally so that Infrastructure Circle is well-informed which trees are already weak and might fall soon? There are good reasons to create a connection between circles for sharing information, but not shared decision making.

Hand-offs

While domains define the area of responsibility, hand-offs describe how information (or goods or services) flow from one circle to the other. Domains have to do with decision-making authority, while hand-offs have to do with workflow.

> An example of a hand-off would be the transition of a member from active to inactive. The difference in membership status might come with a change in the membership fee (inactive members paying a different amount than active members). The change in status would have to have a clear hand-off from the circle that handles membership to the circle that handles finances so the new membership fees can be tracked correctly.

63: *Handoff between two circles I*

Another membership-related example from a school context could be the transition from prospective student to an actual member.

> Let's imagine a school has a Public Relations (PR) circle that does PR and curates a mailing list of people who are considering sending their child to that school. The school also has an internal mailing list of news for parents of the school. We do not want the prospective parents to keep receiving irrelevant emails, and we do not want school parents to be hit by promotional emails. That means, as a prospective parent turns into a school parent, someone has to take their name off one list and add it to the other. The mailing list for prospective school families might be in the domain of PR circle, and they would have to take the name off and let the curators of the school internal list know that a family has joined the school community.

This is what we call a hand-off. A hand-off is different from a gap between circle domains because it is always clear who can *decide* what.

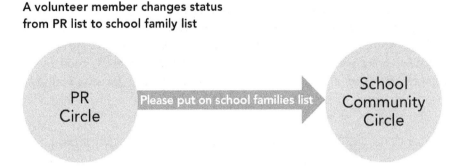

64: Handoff between two circles II

Hand-offs can be defined between any circles, no matter where two circles are in the organizational structure. If necessary, a helping circle with members from both circles can be formed to develop policy and procedures for the hand-offs to be approved by both circles or their parent circle.

Handovers

It is easy to confuse hand-offs with handovers. What's a handover? A handover is when authority is being transferred to a different circle, on a temporary or permanent basis.

For example, let's say fallen branches are in the domain of Infrastructure Circle. A big storm happens and there is a lot of damage to the property. Infrastructure Circle might want to hand over the authority for all the broken branches and fallen trees on the paths to the Tree Circle. Now, on a temporary basis, Tree Circle consents to dealing with the clean-up while Infrastructure is busy doing other things. They are helping out but they have all authority to do so. Obviously, this requires trust and good coordination. If a handover is permanent, it will be manifest in a change of domains. In such a case, the definition of the aims would be changed so that all fallen trees and branches are now in Tree Circle's domain.

hand-off	handover
transfer of information or goods	transfer of authority

65: Hand-off vs. handover

No horizontal linking

The term "linking" usually refers to linking through member(s) being full members with consent rights in both circles. This is not the case in a hand-off. There is no member of Infrastructure Circle that gets selected to be on Tree Circle. Diagonal "linking" is unnecessary since we can use hand-offs. Diagonal linking also waters down the advantages of sociocratic circle structures and creates unnecessary confusion. One of the advantages of small, linked circles is that everyone is part of the circle who matches the domain and the specificity of their work. If we link diagonally (full members of sibling circles), we might end up with a situation where that link does not find the entire meeting of the sibling circle relevant because their work is not in that circle's domain – they are just there to listen in case "their" topic comes up. That is not an efficient use of time. Nothing keeps us from inviting the delegate or leader of another circle to *visit* a circle if necessary, and that way, we can make sure we can keep things relevant for that visitor (for example by putting "their" agenda item first so they can leave after). A visitor does not have consent rights in your circle. If we have a visitor from the same circle often because their presence is important for many meeting agenda items of your circle, then your domains might need some refinement. Another option is to set up a helping circle that supports the interaction between two non-related circles.

We may have some diagonal cross-pollination here and there might be people who are members of more than one circle. They have consent rights in each of their circles, which means nothing prevents double membership. That is different from formal linking. For flow of information, having a few cross-pollinators can be a good idea, and it will often be the reality in contexts where some people have roles in multiple circles.

2.7 Other groups that meet

2.7.1 Gatherings, interest groups and communities of practice

It can be useful, within organizations, to have gatherings that serve for skill building and information sharing. They can meet once or they can be permanent groups. We call any cluster of people within an organization that shares an interest (in addition to/separate from their circle work) an interest group or community of practice. The participants of an interest group may come from multiple departments or external interest groups. They can be formal, like a caucus that is lobbying or raising awareness within the organization, or they can be informal like an annual gathering of all single dads among the parents of a school. They can also be more like communities of practice – a group of people with similar roles that meets on a regular basis. What all gatherings have in common is that they don't have a domain. Confusion can arise from the lack of clarity about the difference between circles and gatherings/communities of practice. Diagram 66 shows the difference between an interest group and a formal circle.

A gathering or interest group/community of practice cannot make decisions that impact the policies in the organization; of course, they can provide information and work out proposals to hand to the circles that hold the relevant domain.

A good example of a community of practice within an organization that is beneficial would be a gathering of all the facilitators. Let's imagine all facilitators of one organization meet to exchange experiences and techniques or guidelines as shown in figure 67. This group cannot make decisions about how any of the circles would be run, even in the domain of facilitation (because that can only be decided by the circles themselves or by the circle that holds this domain in the organization). They can decide for themselves how they meet, but not for others outside their interest group. What they *can* do is work out a recommendation together that might be consented to by each circle. They can train each other or learn together.

	circle	interest group/ community of practice
shared domain/aim/operations	✓	
information-sharing	✓	✓
cross-fertilization	✓	✓
defined cooperations	✓	✓

66: Circle vs. interest group

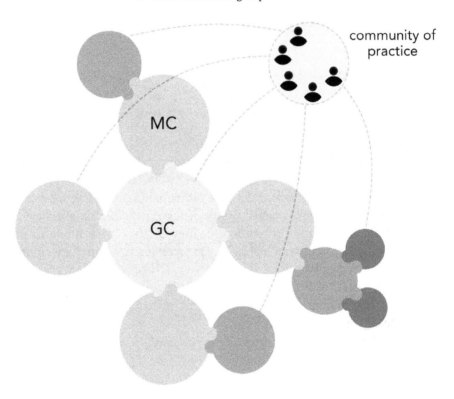

67: A community of practice might give input to the organization

A community of practice might meet and gain momentum. They could visit individual circles and bring up their recommendations or learnings as they relate to that circle's domain, or write proposal drafts to submit to individual circles. However, we do not want to turn our interest groups into "shadow" circles or secret clubs. If we meet half-formally outside of the circle structure (and therefore possibly lose out on strategies supporting transparency like linking, reporting, a

	organization	network
shared domain/aim/operations	✓	
shared mission	✓	
information-sharing	✓	✓
cross-fertilization	✓	✓
defined cooperations	✓	✓

68: Organization vs. network

requirement for meeting minutes, roles etc.), our recommendation is we pay a lot of attention to being transparent and forthcoming. If there is a lot of energy around a topic, groups can consider making it a sub-circle or helping circle with all the usual features so they can benefit from the accountability and transparency that sociocratic design principles bring.

2.7.2 Networks among organizations

When we form networks, we form networks among sovereign organizations. The network cannot make decisions for organizations. The difference between a network and an organization is whether resources and authority have commitment. Networks make recommendations with the overall goal of mutual influence, organizations make decisions and work toward their aim. Note that some groups that call themselves networks really are organizations and vice versa. Organizations are "complete" organizations: they have their aim, domain, mission and members. See the comparison between organizations and networks in table 68.

Interlocking systems of mission circles

There are different ways to design networks. One way is to use the existing organizational structures and connect their mission circles.

Now every organization has information on what is going on in the other organization. (We have already looked when addressing external MC members, see section 2.5.3 on page 56.) Connecting two mission circles is useful when the two organizations are in related fields or for example in a supplier-distributor relationship. Some examples:

- A for-profit organization has a network association with another for-profit organization that distributes their product.
- Two or more intentional communities in the same region want to be connected.
- A private high school networks with elementary schools in its area that are feeder schools to the high school.

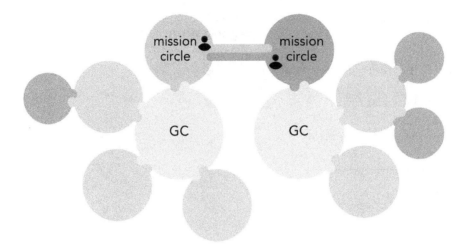

69: Two sovereign organizations with connected mission circles. Connecting two mission circles is useful when the two organizations are in related fields.

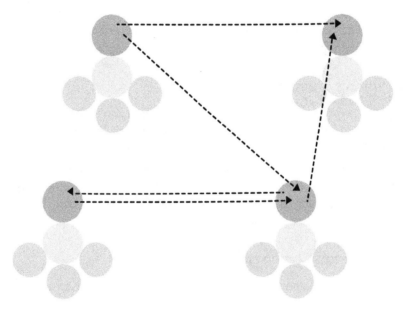

70: Clustering by connecting mission circles

Hubs

We can also form hubs, for example for collective impact efforts (see figure 71). A hub is a gathering (i.e. not a decision-making group) on an inter-organizational level.

The pattern looks like the example of the facilitator circle in the previous section. We can, for example, send the operational leader of the general circle (Executive Director, CEO or whatever the name for that role is in your organization) and/or any other delegate from different organizations

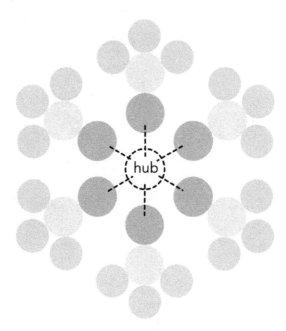

71: Organizations building a network with a hub: no shared decision making but a central place for sharing information

to form a circle. However, the same restrictions apply: this is *not* a decision-making circle to begin with. Since there is no decision making involved, there is no top-down link.

The organizations involved do not all have to be sociocratic to do this. The hub could be running sociocratically (in which case a double representation into the hub would be desirable to hear and speak with two perspectives), and make their own decisions by consent. The organizations connected in the hub would have to commit to making an effort to follow the guidelines developed in the hub. The success of those efforts is highly dependent on the level of commitment in every organization. The decisions they make can be *recommendations* for the connected partner organizations. If those partner organizations are sociocratic (meaning they cannot be controlled by the hub through top-down decision making because even the CEO of a sociocratic organization who might be part of the hub cannot make policy decisions top-down), then those partner organizations are autonomous. If the hub works out a plan that is in line with the partner organization's aim, and the effort seems worthwhile, there will probably be support to adopting recommendations by consent within each partner organization.

International agreements work that way: representatives of nations commit to following climate guidelines, for example, but the actual implementation of these guidelines depends on the decision of the participating governments. Some examples of hubs.

- Non-profits in a state that all work around food justice form a hub for coordination of their efforts.
- Intentional communities in a region form a hub.
- Schools within a school district form a hub around one particular topic.

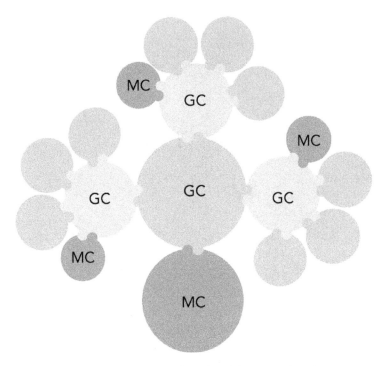

72: *Organizations as work circles with a general circle*

An organization of organizations

While networks are for information-sharing and collective strategizing, things are different with member organizations. Networked organizations do not have to negotiate domains as they are each autonomous. If different organizations decide to become member organizations of a bigger organization, then they will share aim and domain and become semi-autonomous. Organizations now play the role of circles or of members in circles. In this set-up, there *will* be shared decision making. For example, once a set of sovereign countries passes on authority to an umbrella entity – like it was done when the European Union was formed – they are not a HUB but a federation because there are decisions that an EU decision-making body can make that is binding for the member countries.

As another example in the realm of organizations, we could have a global organization of geographically based organizations. Now the general circles of the geographically based organizations act like department circles of a standard organization, and they send a leader and delegate to the general circle of the global organization. Each of those department organizations can have its own mission circle to make sure every organization stays true to its mission. (See diagram in 72.)

Organizations can also serve as sub-circles. Note that, for example, sub-circle 1 in diagram 73 cannot make decisions about organization D. If we have several organizations linked together as member organizations, then we have to be clear about domains so that we know who makes which decisions. Let us imagine that the organization in figure 73 is a global organization. Each department circle has as their domain achieving the same aim in three different parts of the world.

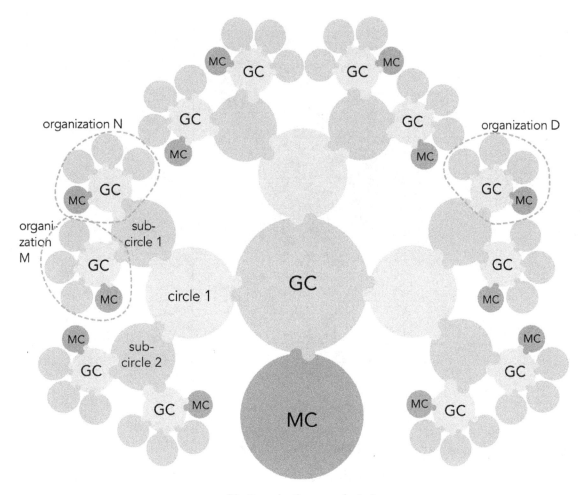

73: Organizations as sub-circles.

Circle 1 might be North- and South America, for example. Sub-circle 1 might be the Spanish-speaking, while sub-circle 2 might be English, Portuguese and French-speaking. Within sub-circle 1, there are two organizations, organization N and organization M, supporting, for example, different Spanish-speaking consulting businesses in the Americas.

Those organizations are all autonomous but they might choose to form bigger organizations. There is no limit to the number of levels we can link together. The structure works like fractals. We can apply the same rules again and again and through recursion, we could, in theory, build a world organization.

This is the power of the fractal nature of sociocratic principles. The rules to build them are uniform. That makes them versatile and adaptive. We can apply them to meet our needs, and we will be able to shift, adapt, and grow. By consent, we can make any changes that make sense in our situation. And we can do all that without ever having to change the basic rule set. No one organization will over-power another organization, and yet, it is possible to form clusters without any restriction in size.

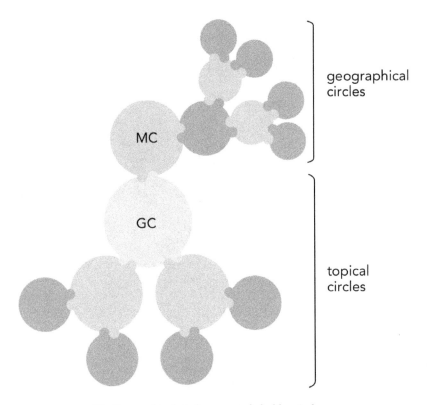

geographical
circles

topical
circles

74: Geographical circles as a stakeholder circle

Geographical circles – topical circles

Global organizations often want a geographical structure mixed with a topical structure. A structure that balances two factors:

- We want to strengthen the bond within and between local, regional, and national groups.
- We want to build expertise on topics, independent of the location of the members interested in those topics.

What we need then is a combination of topical and geographical circles. The geographical circles are either sub-circles under a geographical department circle (in 74), or a stakeholder circle (in 75) depending on how much interaction there is between and momentum in, the topical and the geographical circles. To strengthen cohesion, we can make a requirement that at least leader and delegate from every geographical circle at a certain level be a member of a topical circle as well.

The idea behind these structures is to pay attention both to local peer support and to building expertise. Staying in geographical silos can mean doubling work and re-inventing the wheel (e.g. if every regional organization has to come up with their own mailing list). Topical representation can add experience that can spread into all the circles (e.g. in shared databases supported by the topical circles but open to all member organizations). People with a strong interest on a topical level but without a local group can still join. People with a strong interest on the local level will benefit without being isolated.

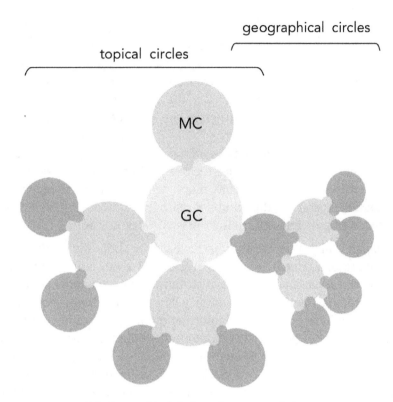

75: Geographical circle as department circle

2.8 Operations – doing the work

Every purpose-driven organization has a mission that translates into organization-wide aims and sub-aims into circles. The aim of any meeting, operational or policy meetings, is to support the clarity and coordination required to do work. The operational work itself does not usually happen during meetings.

The principles for coordinating operations in sociocracy are the same as for all other parts of governance: effectiveness and equivalence. Equivalence is ensured as roles are described and filled by consent, with a clear commitment to feedback and transparency. Effectiveness is supported by putting operations in roles (including the role of a circle member). We strive to give individuals enough authority to do their work well and semi-independently, creating policy to give them freedom within limits.

Sociocracy can be compatible with many ways and tools for coordinating operations and we can pick the tools that are most suitable for our context – the different ways of organizing operations are too different and beyond the scope of this book. By the way, how an organization sets up workflow is a decision about how they do work in general, which makes it policy (see chapter 3 on policy making for creating workflow).

2.8.1   Coordinating operational work

If there are people collaborating on the same task or on interdependent tasks, operational decisions might need coordination. For example, let's imagine a construction business where people need to share tools. We cannot just grab the tool when we want to. It requires coordination. We do not need policy to figure out that member 1 can have the tool at 8.30am and member 2 will pick it up at 11.45am to bring it to the second construction site unless this is a decision we make often (in which case we might want to make policy as a "bulk" decision, see section 3 on page 79).

Any members who are directly affected by a decision in their work will be part of an operational decision. We do not have to involve the entire circle to do this, and we do not have to wait for a circle meeting to coordinate operations. How many people we want to involve and how we want to keep people updated depends on the nature of our organization. The circle leader will be key for coordination. The design principles informing our own workflow are:

- Clarity and balance of power. We want to have clarity about the authority of individual circle members. Define operational roles (see section 2.3.2) so individuals can act freely within circle policies. The circle shapes how to distribute authority among circle members.
- Effectiveness and equivalence. Transparency is a precondition of equivalence and effectiveness. (If we do not have access to full information, then we cannot contribute as well, and it goes along with a loss of power.) Everyone needs to have access to all the relevant information. Technology makes it easier to be transparent.
- We want to keep our eyes open for feedback. If coordination requires too much effort it may be time to give a role more authority. To name a concrete example, if a holder of a role has to come back to the circle for budget requests, maybe it is time to write some defined budget authority into the role description (a policy decision!) so that coordination will be easier in the future. We want to stay on the lookout for places where more clarity and intentionality can make operations smoother.

In Agile, it is common for every team to meet daily in a so-called daily stand-up meeting. This (operational) meeting enables all team members to synchronize. Classically, in a round each team member answers the following three questions:

What did I achieve since we last synchronized (which was yesterday)?
What do I plan to achieve until we meet next (which will be tomorrow)?
And are there any impediments - meaning is there anything that is holding me back?

Sometimes the impediments can be solved quickly, e.g. somebody is lacking the information another one can offer. At other times, more work needs to be provided for resolving the issue.
The original term *daily stand-up* expresses the idea to hold the meeting while standing. The reason is that once people are sitting meetings tend to take more time. Yet, this daily synchronization is supposed to be quick (fifteen minutes at the maximum), and standing up reminds everyone to keep the focus.

(Jutta Eckstein)

76: From agile practice

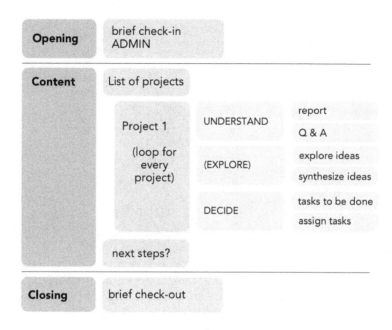

77: Keep your operational meetings short and relevant

2.8.2 Operational meetings

If we meet as a circle (or a subset of a circle) exclusively for coordinating operations, we are holding an operational meeting. *"Is everything happening? Does anyone need help doing their tasks? Is there anything acute keeping them from doing their work?"* These meetings are only for information sharing and case-by-case decisions (if they are not made by the circle leader) to make sure nothing blocks the work of the circle. Depending on the nature of the circle, this can be a daily or weekly meeting, or as-needed. A group of workers in a for-profit will probably meet more often, while a work circle in a community will meet only if there is a workday or a repair to take care of.

Equivalence is core to circle policy meetings so it is important for delegates from child circles to be present at circle meetings. Operational meetings do not depend on equivalence so delegates do not need to attend except in the context of operational roles they may fill in the parent circle.

We can decide to use any process we feel comfortable with, but the diagram in template 77 is a simple and versatile structure to work with. Start every meeting with a brief check-in (shorter than for circle meetings). Then go through your projects and report out so everyone is informed. Make sure to give everyone a chance to ask questions necessary for understanding. After hearing an update on a project, a reflection round can be useful to problem-solve but is not necessarily needed. Depending on the context, the leader of the circle can assign tasks. If there is any need to modify this system, we might make policy on that topic. If a circle notices themselves arguing or getting sidetracked into a discussion, we can make note of the topic in the backlog as a potential policy issue for the agenda of a future circle meeting (as in example 78).

The length of an operational meeting varies considerably. For example, if we plan an event, we might work on coordination of operations for hours; other operational meetings could take minutes.

Example: an brief operational meeting

Anne	Hey all, good morning. Let's do a quick check-in to see how people are doing.
Yagi	I'm good.
Anke	My car broke down so I am glad I even made it here on time. I left my car in a garage on the way here so I have to leave on time today to get it before they close.
Mike	All good here.
Basti	I'm fine.
Anne	Ok, we're all here, that's good. Today is easy, we should be done in 5 minutes. Anything else before we start? *(pause)* Ok, so here is what I have. We're on two construction sites right now. As far as I see, myself and Mike are busy at the Petri's, and everyone else is needed in Sheffield. *(pause)* Let's hear a quick report from each and see whether anything is needed. Mike, would you start?
Mike	Yeah, so we're like three days into doing the drywalls now. We're still working out things with the electrician - what I reported on yesterday - but it seems like all will be smoothened out.
Anne	Great. Any questions? *(pause)* Nothing. Ok, next topic. Yagi?
Yagi	All is well. It's a bit tricky though because starting Thursday, Basti will be out for two days. We had an issue with some parts yesterday and the waiting for the re-order is going to slow us down. We planned to get the roof up before Basti is leaving but it does not look like we can do that. We need another person, so we were wondering whether you, Anne could come over just for Friday morning.
Anne	Hold on. Let me see whether there are any questions. *(pause)* Ok, so you are suggesting for me to help out on Friday. I think that should work. Yagi, what do you think?
Yagi	Works for us.
Anne	Ok, let me write that down for myself. *(writing)* Anything else before we close?
Mike	Yeah, I just want to flag that I want to talk about RH. They sent us the wrong parts again and we're tired of it. I'd like to talk about that at our next circle meeting.
Anne	Thanks, yes. Are you putting that on the backlog? Thank you, Mike. Ok, if there is nothing else, let's close. All thumbs up? *(pause)* See you later!

78: An example of an operational meeting

Chapter 3

Making Policy Decisions

In sociocracy, there are two basic frames of decision making:

- Operational decisions
- Policy decisions

Operations are the tasks we perform to carry out the circle's aim, typically outside of a meeting. We make operational decisions when we perform operations, deciding how to interpret policy that guides our tasks or coordinating operations with each other. Operational decisions are made by anyone with the authority to make that decision.

Policy is made to frame, guide and support operations. It is made by the *circle* for *itself and its domain*. Policy is made by consent. Consent means that no voice inside the circle can be ignored. The circle hears all relevant input and sets a good foundation for working together by equivalence.

Some circles are operations-heavy (more time spent doing work, less time spent in policy meetings), some circles are policy-heavy (more time spent in meetings, less on concrete tasks). The ratio between operations and policy only depends on the nature of the circle.

Operational decisions and policy decisions		
	Operational decision	**Policy decision**
Basis	current policy	previous policy; new needs
Made by	circle members/roles	the circle, by consent
Scope	case-by-case basis	long term

79: Operations vs. policy decisions.

3.1   Why make policy?

There are different reasons to make policy. The most typical reasons are:

- To save time. It might be easier to make one policy decision in the place of many operational decisions.
- To clarify. Policy can be useful if there is a topic that keeps producing tension or friction stemming from lack of clarity.
- To improve. Policy can be made if we observe a mismatch between what we want and what we have. This includes increasing efficiency and effectiveness.
- To create intentionality and equivalence. Different from practices or habits, making policy together means to make a more intentional, informed, and effective choice with more voices heard.

Policy can take different shapes, depending on what kind of decision a circle makes. The different kinds of policy, in the list below, can also be combined into one decision.

- Roles: a statement outlining a set of responsibilities and authorities to be held by one person
- Selections: choosing people to fill roles
- Policy/guidelines: a general statement on what is allowed or not allowed.
- Workflow: a general statement regulating the steps of how to perform operations

The general guidelines, workflow, and role descriptions set the frame in which work is being done. Operational decisions happen within that frame and are made by people who are authorized in a role.

Example: Imagine we hold the role of outreach manager, overseeing communication with prospective members which includes email newsletters. Then our role description – policy – guides us to do it, and it might specify how to do it. In a different context, a policy might frame the conditions of a parental leave for all members of an organization, or the number of outdoor cats allowed in an intentional community.

3.1.1   How much policy should there be?

We only make policy if it is worth doing. Having an aim which is high-level policy might be the only thing necessary to do work well enough to start.

On the one hand, making policy takes time and creates overhead – need for review and adjustments. On the other hand, policy helps create "islands of authority", like roles or other policy, that makes it easy for people to make operational decisions without having to check back with the circle. Policy and the clarity and empowerment it brings supports individuals by giving them freedom to act. Then again, too much policy can feel like being part of a clockwork with no choice or trust. As such, policy is both constraining and freeing: it frees people by creating a clear frame in which they have freedom to act, and it constrains the options of how things can be done.

Each circle has to find its own balance. This might be an enlightening question to ask our circle in an evaluation: are we operating within the sweet spot between limitation, clarity, trust and choice?

3.1.2 Case-by-case and general decisions

A policy typically creates enough structure to be useful but it will leave some room for operational decisions. In the example of the outreach manager, the decision of whether your team sends a newsletter to prospective members at 8.30 am or at 4.45 pm might be a case-by-case decision and might be decided differently every time a newsletter goes out. As such, operational decisions are case-by-case decisions, interpreting the aim and policy ("send out a newsletter") and making choices to complete the task (*"ok, I'll do it this afternoon"*).

The organization might realize that sending the email newsletter in the morning makes it more likely to be opened and read by their addressees. In that case, the circle might review the data and decide that all future newsletters should be sent out before 9 am. This is a policy decision. Without that policy, by operational decisions, the newsletter might have been sent out in the morning one week and in the afternoon the next week. Policy limits choices.

We sometimes call policy decisions "bulk decisions" because instead of making a case-by-case decision, a policy sets a frame for all similar decisions falling under that policy.

An analogy is to consider all the operations (tasks being done in a circle) as water flowing down a river. The water flows within the river bed (the domain) toward a destination (the aim).

- We might take some water out of the river with a bucket here and there and pour that water somewhere else. This is like a case-by-base (operational) decision.
- Policy, on the other hand, is like building a pipe for irrigation. We are making a *general decision* on how we want part of the water to flow. A pipe will have significant impact but it will also require effort to build and maintain.

We would only build a pipe if it seems worth the effort. In the same way, a circle will only make policy where it contributes to getting work done. Do not build pipes where there is no water, or where working with a bucket is enough at the moment.

Note: Operations and policy are not a binary distinction but two ends of a continuum. If we make policy for only a small number of situations, or case-by-case decisions for a set of situations, then the difference between operational decisions and policy decisions can blur. As an example, we might make policy about planning an event before we know how many parties will happen. In that case, making policy (roles, guidelines etc.) might be overdone and simple operational (case-by-case) decisions might be a better choice. If we project that there will be a lot to coordinate or that the party will become a regular event, creating policy might be useful.

3.2   Decision-making methods

3.2.1   Other forms of decision making

Let's look at the most common forms of decision making and their pros and cons.

One person (or a small group) decides. There are two contexts for individual or small group rule. Autocracy means having fairly uncontrolled authority. This seems unacceptable to town or national governance. However, it is still the norm in other areas: in hierarchical corporate structures, public education, families, and in the executive branch of government. We think of autocratic decisions as simple and quick. A downside is that autocratic decisions can lead to a lack of shared information and ideas. And the reaction to autocratic decisions is limited to submission or rebellion.

In the other context in sociocracy, there is a validated form of rule by individuals when a holder of a role has been given authority by a circle to make operational decisions alone within a defined domain.

The majority decides. In majority rule, a group can vote against or in favor of something or someone. The standard is a simple majority rule with 50%+1 of the votes. With plurality voting, the candidate with the most votes is elected to office, even if their vote total is less than 50%. There are also different levels of supermajority vote that refine majority vote.

Preferential voting is a variation of majority vote. Preferential voting is an attempt to include more votes in decisions where there are more than two candidates.

We are used to considering majority vote "fair". Majority vote is fast and can be done easily with very many people and little information. Downsides: majority vote means that up to 49.9% of the group will be ignored – tyranny of the majority. We are likely to miss additional information from the people who vote against (*or* in favor), with an uncertain level of buy-in. Voting rewards divisive behavior because the focus can easily become about winning, not about making a good decision.

Consensus: A decision is made when everyone agrees – a unanimous decision. Consensus seems to be the most inclusive way of making a decision. Buy-in will be high since everyone decides, and the hope is that accountability will also be high. Consensus works well in small, homogenous groups. It is hard to scale to a larger group or organization and can be time-consuming and frustrating in groups where needs and expectations differ. The hidden cost in consensus is that the voices of those who want to move forward may be ignored when decisions are blocked. Consensus tends to give too much power to individuals who can block a decision for an entire group – a tyranny of the minority. (See more on consensus vs. consent in section 3.2.5.)

We often don't operate with intentionality around our choice of a decision-making method. This is noticeable when an argument turns into an argument about the methods of decision making as in example 80. If the decision-making method is unclear, the method itself becomes a contentious issue.

Example
Discussions about decision-making methods

Julius	We still need to decide on the destination for our trip next month.
Anton	Yes! I think we should go for a hike.
Helen	No, go sight-seeing!
Sophie	I think a hike is a great idea.
Helen	Hold on, since when do you get to decide that alone? We're a group here, and we have to decide together.
Anton	It will take us forever to decide together because everyone wants something else. Let's just have one person decide and be done with it. We'll never go anywhere if we try to decide in a group of 6 and that's not even asking the others.
Sophie	No, we are making this decision as a group. After all, we all want to go, so we should all decide. That's just fair.
Jon	Well, then let's vote, that's fair.
Helen	How is that fair if I have to go to a trip that I don't like? You can't just get your way just because you are more people.

80: A discussion in a group with no agreed-upon method of decision making

Sociocracy uses consent decision-making for policy decisions. Operational decisions are made by individuals or by groups coordinating operational decisions. By creating those "islands of authority", operational decisions can be made fast. On the other hand, policy decisions require intentionality and equivalence and are made by consent by the whole circle.

3.2.2   The concept of consent

Consent is a decision-making method that slightly differs from consensus. The definition of consent is: a decision is made when no one objects. To express consent in natural language, we would say *"that's ok"* or *"that works for me"*. Consent is used for:

- policy decisions
- for selections (elections) and
- for decisions about the agenda and the minutes

In order to understand exactly what consent means, one has to understand what an objection is. In its simplest form, an objection is raised when we have a reason to say *"if we approve this proposal, I won't be able to do my work towards accomplishing the circle's aim as well as before"*. On the flip side, one way to express consent in natural language would be *"I can work with this idea for moving forward"* or *"I can still do my work well when we decide this."*

3.2.3 Range of tolerance

A useful concept is the "range of tolerance": everything a person can work with. That does not mean it is their preference. Understanding the difference between range of tolerance and personal preference is vital for sociocracy.

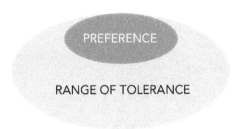

OBJECTION

81: Range of tolerance: what we can live with outside of our personal preferences.

Personal preference: the outcome preferred by an individual.
Range of tolerance: everything that someone can work with, including their preference.
Objections: outside the range of tolerance; everything interfering with carrying out the aim.

For example, a picky vegetarian might not prefer to eat Brussel sprouts – meaning they would not cook them themselves – but they will eat them if served to them. Meat, however, might be outside of their range of tolerance.

Preferences and the ranges of tolerance differ between team members and they also change. Importantly, the deep listening practices and transparency in sociocracy help to build rapport and trust within a group over time, causing the range of tolerance of members to expand over time. As we hear each other, we become willing to accept other people's preferences and to let go of our own.

Conceptually, if we were only able to work in the area of overlap between personal preferences, it would be hard to find common ground to make a decision, in some cases even impossible. Diagram 82 illustrates the overlap between the personal preference of the group members. The sweet spot (darkest) is the intersection where all preferences coincide; The less homogenous a group is, the smaller this area will be because people's experiences and preferences differ. By contrast, the range of tolerance/area of "no objection" amongst group members is quite large. A group will reach consent to proposals more easily when the decision is based on range of tolerance rather than personal preferences.

Consent balances groups and individuals. With consent, individuals will not have as much power as they have in decisions requiring unanimity. On the other hand, with consent, a majority will not have power over a minority.

Consent allows for forward motion. It is easier to find common ground when working with the overlap of our ranges of tolerance. Once we have made a decision, we can carry out our plans and evaluate whether the changes bring improvement. Since we learn with every decision

Shared preferences

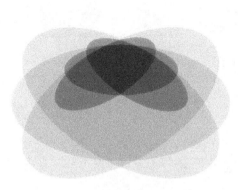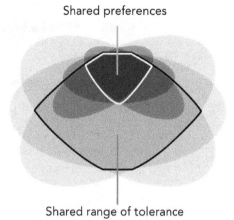

Three people's overlapping
personal preferences
and range of tolerances

Shared range of tolerance

82: The overlap between ranges of tolerances (grey with black outline) is bigger than the overlap between personal preferences (dark with white outline).

made (and we do not learn from decisions not made), every decision made gives us more options to learn and adapt to outside and inside changes. We use the slogan "good enough for now" to encourage groups to innovate and prototype quickly.

Consent is safe. Like a safety net, consent makes sure that no one can be ignored. If someone objects to a proposal, that person will be heard and the objection addressed. Thus, consent secures equivalence. The slogan here is "safe enough to try" which emphasizes that we only move when it seems safe – but then we don't hold back.

3.2.4   What are objections?

Understanding and embracing objections can contribute to more efficient decisions of better quality while making decisions faster and with more focus.

Objections are reasoned

We need to understand the notion of an aim to understand how objections are being defined. As stated in section 2.2 (page 17), aims define what a circle or an organization set out to achieve, for example *"baking and selling healthy bread and pastry in the North Amherst neighborhood."* If there is a new proposal, a circle member objects to that proposal *"if they have reasons to assume that carrying out that proposal would have negative impact on carrying out the circle's aim."* Proposals are intended to contribute to achieving the circle's aim.

In short, an objection to a proposal says: *"if we do this, we won't be able to do our work."*

Imagine a for-profit organization running a co-working space. The overall aim of the organization is *"providing a vibrant co-working space where people network, share resources, form community and are working in a productive way."* The circle that oversees the shared

Definition of objections

Aim
The description of the intention of a circle's work is the *aim*.

▶ **Objection**
The concern that a proposal cannot carry out the circle's *aim* is an **objection**.

▶ **Consent**
A consent decision is made if no circle member has raised an **objection** to a proposal.

83: The definition of consent relies on the definition of objections and aims

resources, like projectors or photo printers, has a sub-aim of *"maintaining and providing shared resources and access to resources for members of the co-working space."* The Shared Resources Circle manages an online system where people check out resources as they pick them up. Someone makes a proposal to allow for equipment to be reserved in advance. Another member objects because they believe people might just book equipment without using it and wants to stay with the first-come-first-serve system.

How is this objection related to the circle's aim? The aim of the circle includes *"providing access to shared resources."* The convenience of online reservations might reduce the availability of resources for everyone because people might book equipment and then not use it. In this way, the new proposal might interfere with the circle's aim. Raising the objection is to say *"I am concerned that we won't be able to do our work of providing access if equipment will be checked out more than it is used."*

Objections are valuable information

We want to create a set of policies that make our operations easier and in alignment with our mission. Since the needs of our aims, people, work, earth and stakeholders create complex interdependencies, it is possible that we could create policy that might work on one end of the system but might create an issue in a different place. If people suspect a potentially adverse "ripple effect", they will object to the proposal.

When a mismatch (or tension) within our current needs and proposed policy is brought to our attention, we have the opportunity to respond and to use the new information. That is why welcoming objections is so important: together with data and feedback, they are precious data we can harvest in a decision-making process.

Objections help us focus

Quite often, differences between people's personal preferences are not worth spending the time we devote to them. We can find ourselves discussing a detail "A or B?" when no one would have objected to either proposal "A or B". In that case, both A and B were within everyone's range of tolerance and the discussion might have spent a lot of time on personal preferences – where we are more likely to disagree.

Objections help us sift through the different concerns so we can filter and focus on what needs attention. The earlier in the decision-making process we do that, the more time and attention we can devote to finding a good solution for an objection.

Objections are a beginning, not an end

Objections in sociocracy are not a roadblock. The proposal is not off the table. Having options of how to move forward by incorporating the objection (see section 3.5) is a core strength of sociocracy. With new information and clearer focus, it will be easier to make realistic and sustainable decisions.

Objections also change culture. Knowing that objections can be integrated encourages members to speak up. We can ease into a place of knowing that our concerns will be taken seriously. If the group can remain in a constant mindset of improvement, there will be more decisions over time, each creating and maintaining a work environment that supports us in making our best contribution possible.

3.2.5 Questions about consent

The difference between consent and consensus

A colleague, Gregory Rouillard, said: *There is no consensus around consensus.* It is hard to compare consensus and consent because consensus is not clearly defined. For some people, consensus is used like consent. That happens when people are willing to agree on a consensus decision even if the proposal is not their personal preference. But that is not something we can guarantee if consensus is not defined as such (and if it were, then consensus would equal consent). Consensus can be *practiced* like consent but does not *have* to be practiced that way.

It is less ambiguous to compare unanimity and consent. If we ask for unanimous decisions, we ask *"do you agree?"*, this question tends to focus people on their personal preferences. In consent, we ask *"do you object?"* and this question includes both the range of tolerance and the personal preference.

We don't see consent as a watered-down version of consensus. In our experience, consent shifts the energy towards doing, instead of convincing others of our own viewpoint. To focus on the range of tolerance instead of personal preferences means to acknowledge that people's experiences and perspectives are different and might remain different. With consent, we can still operate together, guided by a shared aim.

Instead, one can see consent decision-making as an organized, structured form of consensus. It is replicable and supports all voices being heard more effectively.

Can one express a concern? Can one abstain?

Some groups work with "weighted" statements, like numbers to show the level of their support or disagreement to save time, or they introduce "concerns" in addition to objections. To us, the system is binary with exactly two options: either we consent or we object. There is no difference between a concern and an objection, and no difference between an objection and a paramount objection.

Why? All facets of opinions are heard at an earlier point in the process (in the quick reaction round). While our opinions might be multi-faceted with layers and nuances, the *outcome* is binary: either we address the objection or we do not. If we raise a "concern" instead of an objection, we are putting the decision whether or not to integrate our concern on the circle. We prefer for circle members to take responsibility whether or not they would like to integrate their concern.

Neither do we allow for people to pass or abstain in consent decisions. Why not? Let's look at possible reasons that could lead a circle member to abstain:

- The circle member might have a concern without bringing it up. In that case, the group (ideally the facilitator) will try to surface the objection.
- The circle member might not know enough about the proposal to consent. In that case, ideally, the circle member should get access to all relevant information. In a system of distributed power, the people in those decentralized circles *need* to take charge of their domain.
- The circle member might not care. That's ok. What is important to understand is that *not caring* means *not having an objection*. In that case, it is better to say *"I have no objection"*, but we do not abstain. We are actively choosing not to invest more time into the issue – perfectly fine but a choice that comes with responsibility.
- The circle member might not really understand the proposal in depth but might trust the rest of the circle. Since we operate on – to some extent – partial information at all times, not understanding something at depth is not a dealbreaker. If we choose to not object and not to ask for more information, then we are consenting because we don't object.

Issues expressed but unaddressed can create a toxic group culture. Imagine someone consents to a proposal after raising a concern. They skip any attempt to integrate their concern into the proposal but insist on having their concern noted in the minutes. If the action then generated by the proposal is unsuccessful then the person who raised the concern might say "I told you so!". Note that in this example, everyone in the circle heard the concern and everyone (including the member raising the concern) consented. Everyone is equally responsible for the decision made. Consent is not about being right, but about making decisions together that the circle considers safe enough.

Abstaining from a decision will create the same dynamics. Every circle member is 100% responsible for the business of the circle. We *want* the information on the table, and we want to encourage a culture where people are comfortable to object. If there is any reason to object or to ask for more information, any circle member is required to do so. For all other cases, step up and consent – consent decision making also means "no excuses".

Note that by consent, we can decide to use any other method of decision making. For example, we can, by consent to take a vote. By choosing to vote, one would intentionally accept that some voices might be ignored, for example for the sake of saving time. Having more variety in our decision making is useful if we are intentional about our choices and its advantages and disadvantages.

Who decides whether an objection is valid?

Assessing whether an objection is valid can easily turn into a power struggle. It does not make sense to make decisions by consent (defined as "no objections") and to shift the power to someone who then decides what counts as an objection. If there is a judge needed, there cannot be equivalence.

In our experience, when following the process described in this manual, this question does not arise. By default, every objection is valid as soon as it is expressed. As a circle, we can then explore whether we see the proposal interfering with the circle's aim. When people have trust that they will be considered and when they understand the difference between personal preference and range of tolerance, the question of whether an objection is valid or not does not apply. That said, we aim not to engage in "people-pleasing" (fine-tuning a proposal until everyone gets their preference).

Can we make a decision if a circle member is absent?

Consent means that no circle member objects to a proposal. What do we do if a circle member is absent? Can we even make a decision if we do not know whether the absent member has an objection? It is true that we do need every circle member's consent to make a policy decision. This is a reason why defined membership is so crucial (see section 6.10.3 on page 242). However, it is a reality of organizations that people will miss meetings from time to time. In practice, most groups we know assume consent for decisions that do not come as a surprise. Circle members have a history with each other – we often know about where others are at on a topic. Other options:

- Make a policy saying that absent circle members will have to object within 24 hours of receiving the minutes. Otherwise, we would assume consent. (See example 84.) "Lazy consent" works best in a small circle with trust that can track decisions and attendance well.
- All consent decisions are on hold until the absentee consents after the meeting.
- We can get the opinions of people ahead of time if we know that a proposal is going to come to a group. However, it is not uncommon for circle members to change their minds about an issue after hearing everyone. When circle members miss meetings, they not only miss out on being heard, they also miss the transformational process of hearing each other.

The responsibility to catch up when someone missed a meeting lies both in the group and in the circle member. Meeting minutes and a check-in with the circle leader will support this.

> A circle can consent to use an Open space approach for making decisions if a member is absent: One of the Open Space principles states, "Whoever is there are the right people." This means, the circle members present in a circle meeting are the right people for making a decision. There is no waiting for every member being present, no preliminary consenting, no verification, just the trust amongst all peer circle members that they will make the right decision.
>
> *(Jutta Eckstein and John Buck)*

84: What others say

Can people change their mind?

Any circle member can withdraw their consent even if they consented originally. What if circle members change their mind three months after a consent decision was made? Options:

- The policy stays in effect until the circle decides otherwise.
- The circle member may have changed their mind based on new information or a new insight. Share this information with the circle and schedule the topic into next meeting's agenda.
- The circle member may discuss new information with the circle leader.
- At the next meeting, the circle will listen to the concern and come to a (consent) decision on whether to review the policy earlier than the policy's scheduled term end.

We want new information to be considered. But we don't want to waste time un-doing decisions. If situations like these become a source of repeated disruption, we can always make policy on how we handle withdrawal of consent.

Preconditions of consent

Consent decision making can be used in any kind of group, in any non-sociocratic organization. However, there are preconditions of consent, and we strongly encourage organizations that plan to implement (parts of) sociocracy in their organization to be aware of these preconditions.

- The group is able and willing to discuss together long enough to resolve objections. We cannot decide by consent without being willing to work through objections. In taking shortcuts too often, we might create an imbalance in equivalence which can lead to frustration. If all circle members are trained well and know how to deal with objections, the task of "discussing long enough to resolve objections" will be doable and might actually be an enjoyable and connecting experience that strengthens the team.
- The group shares a common aim. Consent decision making requires a shared and defined aim. Objections are defined as interference with aim. If we don't know what our aim is, how will we know what an objection is? (See also page 242.)
- The group can choose its membership. With open or undefined membership, consent will be hard to do. If we do not know who has consent rights, how do we know when we have reached consent? Defined membership is essential for consent because consent means consent by everyone in the circle, not the people present in the room. (See also section 2.2.3.)

Limitations of consent

Not every kind of policy decision can be made by consent, for example decisions made purely by personal preference like design questions. What would be an objection for "blue"? There could be cases where colors have distinct context-specific implication or interpretations that make objections to a color decision reasonable (like if there is existing policy on corporate design). If there is no reasonable basis to object to a color, who gets to choose? We want to avoid power games.

Here is what we *can* do. We can, by consent, make a decision on *how* to decide. For example, we can hear some feedback on color issues and then decide by consent to vote. Or we can delegate to a group or even for one individual to make a decision with or without some limits.

3.3 Making policy – step by step

3.3.1 Measurement-driven process

How often have you walked away from a meeting frustrated about how the meeting time was spent? How can we avoid this?

We want readers to understand all steps so everyone knows the milestones, tools and measures and can make intentional choices. Before discussing decision making, we have to understand some basic sociocratic concepts that measurement-driven process builds on: *lead–do–measure* and *input–transformation–output*. While guiding the process is primarily the facilitator's task, co-creative process depends on good "followers" as much as on good facilitators. The more members of the circle are familiar with measurement-driven process, the smoother processes will be.

Input–transformation–output

Every process consists of three phases: *input, transformation* and *output*. Input is what we know, think, or have when we start. Transformation is whatever we do to that input. Output is what we get out of the transformation process. The kind of output depends on the task at hand:

- If our task is to cook a meal, then the *input* is the ingredients for the meal. The *transformation* is the cooking of the meal. The *output* is the serving of the meal.
- If our task at hand is making stars out of squares using a machine like in figure 85, then squares are our *input*, *transformation* is whatever the magic machine does, and our *output* is stars.
- If our input is agenda items, then meetings transform them into decisions.

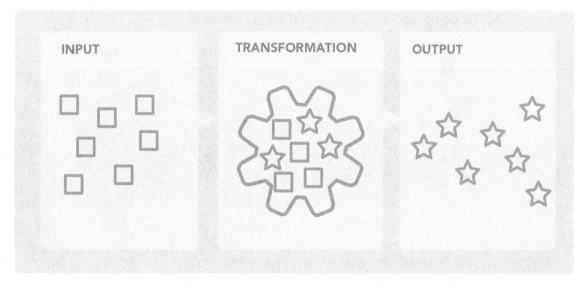

85: Input – transformation – output

86: Lead – do – measure when packing a backpack

Lead–do–measure

Every step along the way, we want to be sure we're being intentional and successful. For example, if we pack a backpack for the day, we might think about what we need to bring first. Then we pack, and finally, we might review to check whether we packed everything we need. Every step in decision making and workflow involves three steps: *lead – do – measure*.

Lead: we make a plan, aware of the outcome we want to have; based on previous experiences.
Do: we perform the action toward the desired outcome.
Measure: we check whether we have actually done what we were intending to do.

The *doing* is where our focus is most of the time; however, both the leading phase and the measuring phase are vitally important. We will not use our time and resources efficiently if we fail to slow down and plan before we act. Equally, if we forget to measure whether what we are doing is reaching the desired results, we do not notice early enough if we get off track.

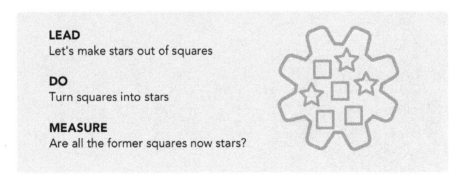

87: Lead – do – measure

Let's assume we want to turn squares into stars using a magic machine like in figure 87. We would make a plan (lead), perform the action (do) and then check whether we reached the desired outcome (measure). As *lead – do – measure* is a standard mindset in sociocracy, it is applied in countless situations, and we will see more examples related to workflow and decision making.

Lead–do–measure *and* input–transformation–output

We can apply *lead – do – measure* cycles to every individual step of *input – transformation – output*. Every smaller step along the way, we plan that step, do it, and then evaluate whether we have completed the step before we move to the next step.

The diagram in 88 shows the steps of *lead – do – measure* in the context of our star-making machine. We make a plan for the input, perform the necessary action (filling the machine), and

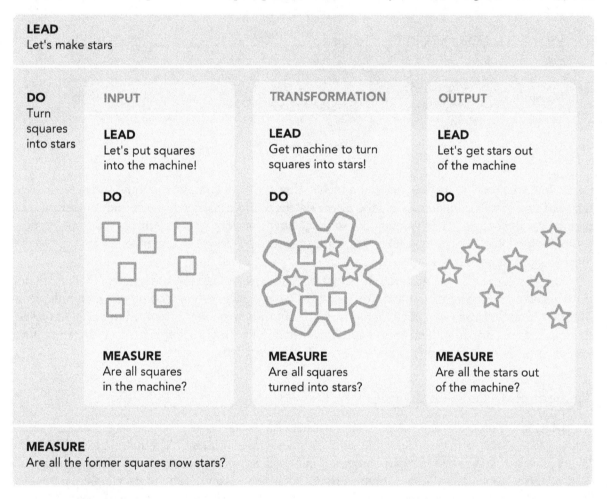

88: Input – transformation – output with lead – do – measure

make sure we completed the input phase. We make a plan for the transformation stage, perform the transformation and measure whether we have completed the phase. We make a plan for the output phase, perform the necessary action and measure whether we have completed the output.

Back to the example of cooking a meal, the same pattern applies. Let's say we are cooking for a large number of people. The day before, we might make a list of ingredients based on a recipe and buy those ingredients. The day of the cooking event, we double-check whether all ingredients are there. Then we look at the recipe again and plan what order to do the steps in and how long it might

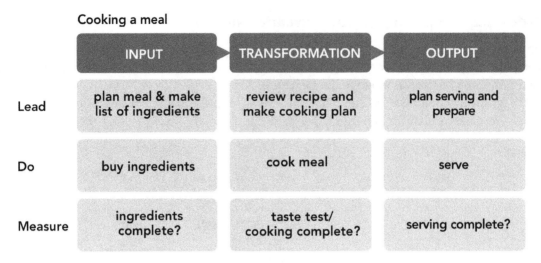

89: *Cooking a meal*

take. Now we cook the ingredients into a meal. After we have completed all the steps, we look at the food and wonder whether it is done now. We check the consistency, taste and temperature to prepare for the output. Then we plan the serving. Bowls or deep plates? Any decoration? We now serve the food and for a second, our eyes wander around, checking whether all is complete as the meal is about to begin.

These are steps that we go through naturally. The need to define the steps explicitly is higher if the process consists of more parts, for example, if the person/group who buys the ingredients is different from the group that cooks and different from the servers, or if we need to order wholesale food in large quantities with an entire workflow instead of a simple shopping trip. We need to have a clean process in place or there will be friction in the workflow.

Application to decision making

For decision making, a group has to think together. All minds have to be connected and synchronized, while allowing for creativity and people's own way of thinking. There are a lot of different layers playing together on top of the content of our decision: process, interpersonal issues, internalized patterns, personal style, performance issues (distractions etc.). The more people participate, the more things happen simultaneously. Shared exploration and decision making is a complicated and complex endeavor. A good and clear system will help.

Chunking We divide the decision-making process into manageable chunks and linearize them so they can be completed together. We want to avoid situations like these:

- One person is still grappling with a detail in wording while the others are ready to explore options. Some get impatient, and the one person feels pressured into letting go their need for clarity.

- Or: half of the group is still wanting to explore options and the other half is ready to decide. Both groups get frustrated.
- Or: a decision is made but soon after, it becomes obvious that not everyone was clear on what the decision was.

We labeled the main chunks of the work-flow process in the star-making machine as *input – transformation – output*. To make this process easier to understand as it applies to decision making, we will label it *understand – explore – decide*. The *decide* step does not have to be a policy decision – it can simply be a conclusion reached at the end of a discussion – the synthesis.

90: We refer to input – transformation – output as understand – explore – synthesize in certain phases of decision making.

- **Understand:** the input step is to understand what needs to be understood. What information do we have and how do we interpret it? What needs are there to consider?
- **Explore:** the explore phase is when we consider wider input, gather ideas etc. This is the generative phase of group processes.
- **Decide:** the decide phase is where we make sure we have a result from our process. A decision does not have to be a final decision – it can just be synthesis that we agree on, for example, a statement describing an issue or a co-created list that serves as input for the next phase.

Figure 91 shows how individuals can move as a group safely through all those steps with a sense of flow: being on the same page and working more or less at the same pace. Everyone might be running in different directions – some might be linear thinkers, some of us have minds that go in little loops, and some of us pay attention to things that tend to go unnoticed. That's ok. The important thing is that for every milestone (1) we start out together and (2) we finish together. We can make good progress following a broad roadmap like in 91.

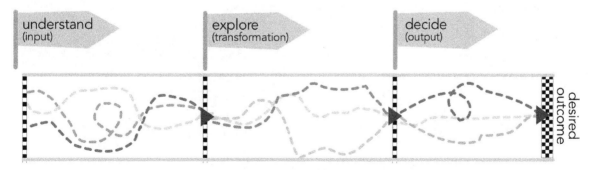

91: Understand – explore – decide in decision making as a team: we have our own ways but we finish together

All the steps in decision making fall into smaller steps, like fractals: as soon as we zoom in with a magnifying glass onto one phase, we find *understand – explore – decide* again. The more in-between steps we consider, the more intentional and effective we can be. The fractal nature is shown in figure 92. Each step now correlates to (a set of) rounds (people in the circle speaking in turn) – which makes facilitation in this format very simple. With many small rounds, each with a well-defined question and scope, every circle member can focus on the content at hand.

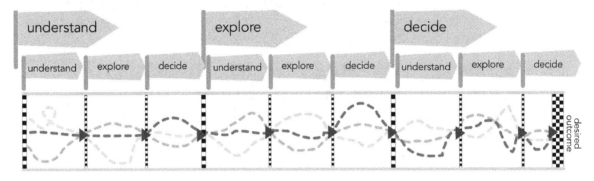

92: The steps fall into more fine-grained steps, like fractals

Choose your tools

- The default tool for an *understand phase* is a combination of report/clarifying questions round.
- The default tool for an *explore phase* is a generative (reaction) round.
- The default tool for a *decide phase* is a consent round.

However, the same milestone can be reached in different ways. Groups can do what is effective in their situation. For example, if the aim is to *understand*, we can do a round where every circle member asks their question *or* ask people to raise their hand in case they have a question. Both approaches will get us there. For any of the milestones, we are free to brainstorm, delegate to one person, survey, dance, sing or act something out; we just want to be aware of our desired outcome.

Measures   As shown in Fig. 93, each phase is wrapped into *lead – do – measure* cycles. Measures like *"Does everyone understand the issue? Have we heard everyone's ideas? Is everyone ready to move to the next step?"* tell us whether we have reached a milestone.

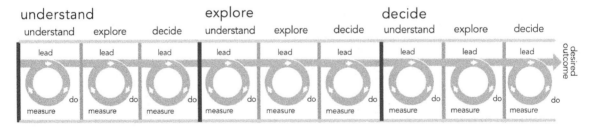

93: Every step has its own lead – do – measure loop

3.3.2   The three phases of policy process

In this book, we will refer to the entire process of making policy decisions as "policy process", while the last phase (consenting to a proposal) is called "consent process". For every step, we are giving the *intention* (lead), the *tools* (do/path) and the measure for telling when a step is complete (*complete when*). In the following sections, we will go through every phase with lots of detail. The detail is intended to support groups in gaining clarity and choice, not to be prescriptive.

Please note that we see the processes described here, based on the classic steps of *input – transformation – output,* are compatible with "classic" sociocracy and with different flavors of sociocracy, for example, Sociocracy 3.0). There are many ways to use and name the process. The contribution in this manual is in listing and explaining the *intention, tools* and *measures* explicitly. If groups deviate in nomenclature or in what tools they prefer, we want to make sure the process integrates equivalence and effectiveness. Especially if groups deviate from what the international community has found to be useful practice over time, we recommend stepping back from time to time and reviewing whether the tweaked process is delivering what is desired.

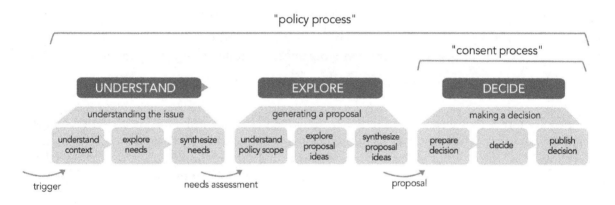

94: Understand – explore – decide

Understanding the need

We start the policy process by understanding the issue that lies under the trigger that brought a topic to our circle. That trigger could be a complaint, or an accident, a drop in sales, or the desire to achieve more. A trigger event points to a deeper need. Before strategizing how to better meet the underlying need effectively, everyone needs to understand it. It can get frustrating when, half-way into the policy generation process, we realize we still do not have clarity about the context, trigger or need. The understanding phase ends with a written or verbally stated "needs statement" that summarizes how the circle understands the issue and needs on the table. The three-step process here is to:

- Understand the trigger and the underlying issue.
- Explore the underlying needs.
- Synthesize the issue and underlying needs.

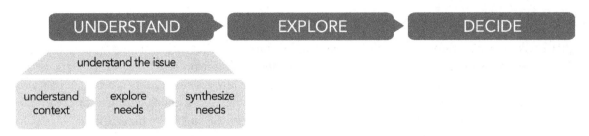

95: The understand phase

Understand the context   An issue comes to the circle. At the very beginning, before we do anything else, we give the circle members some context. How did this topic get on the agenda? Then we describe the trigger that has prompted the topic to come to the awareness of the group.

> **Intention:** Everyone understands the issue.
>
> **Tools:** Make sure all information on context and issue is complete.
>   - Invite reports from all affected or involved (incl. written material).
>   - Ask and answer questions (clarifying questions round or open questions).
>
> **Complete when:** No one has any more questions about the context or trigger.

Example 96 shows what this could sound like. Note that in this example, the facilitator chooses not to call for a full round and just asks whether anyone has questions. This works well in easy cases. Alternatively, we can call for a clarifying questions round (see section 5.5.2). We answer all the questions one by one, or we gather questions first and answer them after – whatever seems easiest.

Explore needs   Shift the attention from the concrete incident to a more general view. Triggers and people's responses are data pointing to underlying needs. In a collective effort to make sense of what we observe, we want to understand the underlying needs so we can find effective strategies.

> **Intention:** Exploring what needs are underlying the issue.
>
> **Tools:** Invite all circle members' interpretations.
>   - A good prompt is *"what do you think this is really about for everyone involved?"*
>   - A round where people offer their interpretation or guess needs (needs list p. 262).
>   - Write down keywords of what is being said in a way that is visible to everyone.
>
> Remember to consider *all* stakeholders. This could be the circle, members, non-members, or the planet. We can have members stand in for others or find other ways to support so everyone's needs can be considered.
>
> **Complete when:** No one has more ideas to add.

Yukio ● Kiara
Imke ● Sanjay

Example: understand context

Imke   The next agenda item was put in the backlog by Kiara. You called it "donor members" when you asked me for time during this meeting and you told me it needed an operational or a policy decision. Tell us more.

Kiara   Ok. In my role as membership coordinator, I was contacted by someone, Mark, who would like to join but says he doesn't have time to work. I told him we have a policy that every member needs to be a working member but he said he'd like to support us and he'd be willing to pay more than the regular fee. Honestly, I did not know what to say so I told him I'd check in with this circle.

Imke   Hm, interesting. Are there any questions? Let's do a quick round. Yukio.

Yukio   I don't think I have a question right now.

Imke   I wonder, Kiara, if you can give us a sense whether there might be more people like that. Who want to be members but not work.

Kiara   That would not surprise me. I think people have asked and I told them about our policy and they backed off. No one has insisted before.

Sanjay   I'd be interested whether he said something about why he is interested.

Kiara   As far as I know it's about the contacts here. Wanting to be connected.

Imke   Ok, any other questions? (Pause) Hearing none.

96: Understand: understand context

Note how in example 97 (page 100), the circle is looking at the issue from different angles, exploring needs of the circle members and the needs of those outside of the circle.

Needs statement   With a clear understanding of the issue and the needs at stake, we formulate a description of the issue and needs (see also "driver statement" in Sociocracy 3.0).

> **Intention:** We synthesize what we know about the needs.
>
> **Tools:** The facilitator or a circle member makes a summary statement (spoken or written).
>
> - Depending on the scope of the issue, a simple statement like *"we need a membership onboarding process that is easier and more transparent"* can be enough.
> - Alternatively, ask a helping circle (an individual or a small group) to write up the pieces collected in the previous step into a coherent document.

Example: explore needs

Yukio ⌒ Kiara
Imke ⌣ Sanjay

Imke	Let's do a reaction round. What do you think are needs at play here? And I mean both for Mark but also for us and others. Kiara, you start, then Yukio.
Kiara	This brings up a whole list of questions for me that I saw coming but that we have not dealt with yet. It's about community, belonging. And in his case, and for our working members of course, it's about contribution.
Yukio	For us, it's about purpose and cooperation. Working members are the ones who make things happen.
Imke	Well, there is the money aspect. More money in the budget supports the working members in making things happen. That's about effectiveness.
Sanjay	Hm.... I don't have anything to add. I guess the way I look at it, it's the balance between contribution through work and contribution through fees. Nothing wrong with either. The question is how we integrate both.
Imke	I think a second round would help. Let's continue. If you want to, you can start thinking whether this is heading towards an operational decision just on Mark's case, or a policy change or whatever else.
Kiara	I agree with Sanjay. We wanted to make sure people have skin in the game and are serious and want to work and not just talk. But we keep running into funding issues. So there is something there. We should re-do our membership policy.
Yukio	There is some hesitation in me but I am ok exploring it.
Imke	I don't have anything to add. Let's make policy to include those cases.
Sanjay	I agree. Let's do it.
Kiara	The current policy just says "every member needs to pay fees and needs to work". So if we made another policy for membership, it would be basically making a new policy. I am happy to do that. It's time.

97: Understand: explore underlying needs

- For a complex issue, we can ask for feedback from people outside the circle who have been affected to ensure that their needs are reflected accurately.
- We ask ourselves whether the appropriate action is to make policy. (See below)

Complete when: There is consent to the needs statement and the next step.

In example 98, the facilitator asks someone in the circle to make a statement as a way to save time. There is typically someone in the circle who is quick at synthesizing. Keep the needs statement as you can use it as rationale when publishing the policy.

Example: needs statement (synthesize needs)

Imke   Ok, so to summarize this, I liked how Sanjay said it. Our current membership practice does not account for members who want to contribute only financially, and we want to make sure everyone can contribute so that the whole organization can be effective and have a sense of belonging. Are there any objections to this summary? (Pause) Sounds like everyone is good with it. I propose that we start looking at membership policy from scratch, going into picture forming. Ok? (Pause) Let's go.

98: Understand: synthesize issue/needs into a needs statement

How to address an issue   Do not take for granted that the most appropriate response to the needs automatically has to be policy. Here are three options to respond to an issue:

- Operational decision. If the issue is covered by existing policy, hold everyone accountable to the existing policy. We might decide to find a way to make the policy better known.
- Give feedback. An often overlooked way to respond is to give feedback, for example to someone who was involved in the trigger event. If they hear about the impact of their actions on other people or the circle, this might already prevent similar events from happening. This is especially true when it is about behavior: much too often, policy is made because we are trying to avoid giving direct feedback. In order to change someone's behavior, a direct and respectful conversation is much more effective than a policy about behavior in general somewhere in the files.
- Adjust policy. Review existing policy to cover the new issue.

Overall, sociocracy practices "lazy" policy-making (like lazy loading in software programming where an item is only loaded once it is requested); we only make policy if the needs cannot be met effectively in any other way. Policy takes time to make, and it requires maintenance over time so do not produce policy if it is not necessary.

If the circle realizes that an issue is not in their domain, they will pass the issue on to the appropriate circle. The original circle may still write up a needs statement to pass it on as input. Keep in mind that the circle that receives the issue has to consent to taking on the issue. (If they do not accept the issue, it automatically lands in the domain of their parent circle.)

Generating a proposal

In the previous phase, we generated clean and clear input so we could work on generating a policy that puts strategies in place that meet our needs. Now we are entering the transformation stage. We are *transforming* the *input* we have (= our understanding of the underlying issue and needs) into a proposal that can be decided in the output phase. Again, this phase falls into three phases:

- Understand the scope of the policy, also called picture forming.
- Explore proposal ideas.
- Synthesize proposal ideas into proposal.

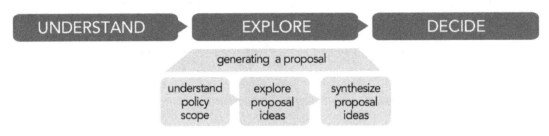

99: The explore phase

Understanding the scope of the policy (picture forming)   Picture forming helps the group prepare for gathering proposal ideas. Before focusing on possible solutions, the circle makes a checklist of items that need consideration that we call dimensions.

If we think about dimensions first, our group will be more likely to cover the entire topic without forgetting central pieces. That way, we can build a good foundation for our policy before emotions get high. It is often astonishing how many good questions come up during picture forming. Starting with opinions can easily distract a group from seeing the issue as a whole. Picture forming offers a phase where we focus on understanding the field before zooming in on solutions.

Intention: Understanding the scope of a proposal by gathering dimensions.

Tools: Ask *"what questions will we have to answer to make good and complete policy?"* Make sure to keep it light with short talking turns.

- Write down all the dimensions and keep the list.
- Gather dimensions in a round or "popcorn style" where everyone speaks as inspired.
- Dimensions will have the format of phrases or of questions, but never of statements.
- If people offer opinions, write them down separately for the next phase (proposal shaping) and help the group get back on track to offer dimensions instead of opinions.

Complete when: There is consent to the completeness of the list of dimensions.

Also, it is helpful for a group to start with something that connects them. For example, if we are debating accountability of dog owners, there might be very different opinions and *strategies* to address it. However, everyone will agree that *something* needs to be said about "leashes/no leashes" in a policy about dogs in a community; everyone will agree that "leashes/no leashes" is a dimension of any complete proposal on this topic (see example 102 on page 106).

Circle members may explain a bit about the background of their dimension. It helps, for example, to name two options (*"do we do A or B?"*). See example 100 for illustration. An experienced group will gather keywords fairly quickly, within a few minutes. Groups get better with experience. The best way to learn picture forming is by example. If the group is new to the process, then someone with experience might model by giving their own dimensions before asking for the group's suggestions. With inexperienced groups, we might have to explain more and perhaps extract dimensions from opinions they share.

Caution: if there are a lot of dimensions, we might be dealing with a question that is too big. We will get way too many proposal ideas and might get overwhelmed. In that case, we can divide up the dimensions into related chunks and deal with them separately or form a helping circle to prepare the next phase.

Yukio   Kiara
Imke   Sanjay

Example: understand policy scope (picture forming)

Imke	Next is picture forming. Let's gather dimensions. In making policy, what are areas of consideration we'll have to cover? What do you want to make sure we don't forget to address? Let's do a round. Kiara.
Kiara	Money, or financial wellbeing of the organization overall.
Sanjay	Ways to contribute outside of work and money.
Imke	Keeping up a sense of community. Structural representation, in our circle structure.
Yukio	Do we make a difference for why someone is not working or not?
Kiara	How do all members know what's going on? Is there a different membership fee for working and non-working members?
Sanjay	Hm....nothing to add right now.
Imke	Membership privileges: do all members have the same rights?
Yukio	Nothing to add.
Imke	Anything else? (Pause) Ok, do we have consent to this list being good enough? (Pause) Alright. Let's put the list up here so everyone can see it.

100: Explore: picture forming (policy scope)

Before moving on, we consent to the list. This is a "good enough for now" decision. It is fine to add new elements coming up later. We ask for consent so we can be sure we are ready to enter the next phase and no one is cut off who still has dimensions to add.

Explore proposal ideas (proposal shaping)   In this phase, we want to hear all the ideas of what could be done to solve the issue, considering the needs of everyone affected (as stated in the needs statement). Have your list of dimensions visible to inform your group on what we want to cover. While dimensions are phrases or questions, proposal pieces are typically statements starting with *"I think we/there should. . . "*, like *"I think we should introduce a membership fee of $50 per month."*

Picture forming and proposal shaping break up the – sometimes daunting – process of formulating a proposal into doable steps. This participatory process draws on group wisdom and can be very creative and productive. At the same time, since no one circle member has to come up with *the* perfect proposal alone and everyone can put their heads together, the task becomes more doable.

Intention: Exploring ideas of how to solve the issue.

Tools: Hear the circle's proposal ideas, preferably in several rounds. Circle members can suggest proposal pieces that cover one or more of the dimensions mentioned.

- It is better to do several rounds of *brief* statements than to only do one round. With short rounds, it will be easier to build on each other's creative ideas.
- This is not the place to lobby and give a long-winded rationale. Ideally, we dictate the proposal ideas and maybe give some context. Avoid any energy that is about *convincing* others as it will inhibit flow.
- Create a safe space. We want every member to speak from their experience. One way to make sure we do this is by only allowing affirmative statements (*"I think we should. . . "*) but no evaluative statements about other people's proposal ideas such as *"I don't think that x is a good idea."*
- The proposal pieces are allowed to flow. They can:
  - contradict each other
  - extend each other
  - make a previous statement more detailed
- It is a good idea to write proposal pieces for all to see, ideally close to the list of dimensions. Appoint a scribe to write down ideas, or let the secretary do it.
- There does not have to be a 1:1 relationship between dimensions and proposal pieces. Some proposal pieces might cover more than one dimension, and a proposal piece can only be a partial answer to a dimension. If we notice a new dimension, we simply add it to the list.
- We can start to group proposal ideas into themes but only if that is easy to do in real time. It is more important to gather proposal pieces than to organize them.
- Proposal shaping can be done asynchronously, for example in a virtual document.

Complete when: No one has another proposal idea to add and every dimension is covered by at least one proposal piece.

While in picture forming, we were trying to understand the issue and its dimensions. In proposal shaping, we want opinions. Example 101 gives us an idea of what this might sound like.

Example: explore policy ideas (proposal shaping)

Yukio   Kiara
Imke   Sanjay

Imke   Proposal shaping. Let me hear your opinions. Remember, everyone says a few pieces and we try to address all dimensions. Sanjay, you start, and send it one way.

Sanjay   I think we should have two membership categories, working members and non-working members. They could have different privileges but I don't know yet. Kiara.

Kiara   I think the membership fee should be the same but I'd encourage non-working members to pay a bit more. Let's see... I don't think it matters *why* someone is not working, so I would just dismiss that dimension.

Yukio   I'd like non-working members to somehow contribute outside of just paying money. I would want them to at least help spread the word but I don't know how.

Imke   All non-working members could be represented on our Mission Circle by a link from a donor circle. And for what Yukio just said, there could be an internal newsletter for donors with things to share on social media so they can help do PR for us.

Sanjay   I am looking at our list for what hasn't been covered yet... the reason why someone isn't working... for me, it does not matter why someone chooses not to work. Could be because they don't have to or because they are caretakers for someone or whatever. Not our business, I think. This policy will actually also create more clarity for people who are out, for example like Jeanette when she had the baby.

Kiara   I'd like to wait before I think about a donor circle. I like the newsletter idea, but it should be for everyone once we have it. And that needs someone doing it...

Yukio   Good point, Kiara. I'd like to track in our bookkeeping how much extra money there is in the bank thanks to non-working members.

Imke   Thank you. Anything else? Are all dimensions covered? There is the piece about sense of community and knowing what's going on. What do we want to say about that?

Kiara   That somehow seems included in the newsletter idea.

Imke   True. So if there is nothing else to add, I think someone should write this up and bring it to our next meeting. Kiara, would you do that? (Kiara nods). Thanks.

101: Explore: explore policy ideas (proposal shaping)

Examples 102 and 103 show how proposal ideas can build or contradict each other. (The lists in 103 are from a real-life process in our family on a chronic source of arguing!)

Example: Dog policy in an intentional community

Needs statement
Dogs and residents of the community want to have a harmonious, healthy relationship.

Dimensions
  areas of the property
  leashes?
  visitor dogs, service dogs
  size of dogs
  dog poop
  safety of children
  how do we measure?

Proposal ideas
  all dogs have to be on leash at all times on the property
  no dogs are allowed in community buildings except for service dogs
  no dogs are allowed in community buildings, including the workshop
  in running field, dogs can be off leash
  same rules apply for member dogs and visitor dogs, dogs of all sizes
  pet officer checks in with dog owners and `dog haters' after 3 months.

102: Needs statement, dimensions and proposal ideas for a dog policy

Synthesize proposal ideas   How do we turn the list of proposal ideas into a proposal?

For this step, we want to keep in mind that we are looking for a solution within a reasonable amount of time that works for everyone (i.e. that lies within everyone's range of tolerance). We are writing down a proposal early because that is what gets the group to the next level instead of continuing a conversation about personal preferences. We put out a proposal so we can surface objections (if there are any) sooner than later.

Intention: Synthesizing ideas into a proposal.

Tools: This step benefits from having only a few people, or even just one individual to write up the proposal. First go through the straightforward parts, the dimensions that only have one proposal piece covering them and that seem uncontroversial. Isolate the proposal pieces that seem contradictory. There are different scenarios:

  • All proposal pieces are compatible and everything is covered. This might be a simple issue – all the proposal pieces seem to go together well and we might

Example from a family: How we decide what show to watch

Needs statement
We keep arguing about what show to watch. We want an inclusive and quick process so we don't waste time arguing and can watch together.

Dimensions
how do we decide?
how do we know this is working?
what if someone does not like the show?
what if a show is too long for time we have before dinner or bedtime?
can one watch longer if one is sick?
do we pause the movie if someone needs to go to the bathroom?
what if someone likes a show but is scared?

Proposal ideas
we take turns deciding what to watch
we make two lists, one for short shows, one for long movies
whoever starts hitting is not allowed to chose
we pause if someone needs to go to the bathroom
success would mean: no more fighting
if someone does not like the show, they can watch something else on mom's phone
if someone does not like the show, they have to wait until it is their time to decide

103: Needs statement, dimensions and proposal ideas for a screen policy (children aged 4-10 contributing)

realize how much we are on the same page. The proposal generating process has guided us through making a proposal draft in a participatory way and we just have to come up with coherent wording.

- Some areas of our proposal pieces seem straightforward, some are highly controversial, incompatible proposal pieces. We now know what is controversial and what will need more attention. Note: we are not trying to solve the controversial issues right now, as that comes later. For now, we just notice the differences in opinion. See below for more guidance on how to navigate controversy.
- We are noticing that we do not have enough information. If there is essential information we need to get before moving ahead, we can do a round on how to gather the information we need, and make an action plan. We do not want to hit the same wall again next time the issue comes up.

We write up a proposal and double-check whether we have addressed all the dimensions so we do not lose information in distilling the proposal pieces. If we leave some proposal ideas out of the final proposal draft, we say so and say why clearly.

Complete when: There is a written proposal that covers all the dimensions.

As in example 104, it works well to either have an individual or two people work on wording the proposal between meetings, or we might take a short break during the meeting to have someone write something up. If there are contradictory proposal ideas, there are at least three options:

- We can do reaction rounds for each controversial proposal idea. That will inform how we can distill the proposal ideas into one proposal.
- We can just make a choice. There is no risk in making a proposal, as anyone can object later.
- We can include the contradictions into the proposal. We can write *"webinars will be held on always the same one day of the week: Tuesdays/Thursdays"* although that is inherently contradictory. That way, we can flag an item for discussion as we integrate objections. Offering contradictory proposals to provoke objections is confusing to some, but it does honor all the ideas that were generated. We only do it with facilitators that feel confident with the process.
- We can break it up. If a subject seems to be sidetracking a discussion, and we are worried about including it in the proposal, we can also break it up into chunks and decide separately.

Example: Synthesize policy ideas

Proposal
All members pay the membership fee of $150 per year. Non-working members are encouraged to pay the $150 plus a donation on top of that.
An internal newsletter is sent out to all members every month with shareable news to spread the word. (Role description to be added to the Membership Coordination role.) The extra income from non-working members is tracked independently from membership fees (request for finance circle). Term: 1 year.

104: Explore: synthesize proposal ideas into proposal

Proposals written by individuals   The more co-creative the proposal-writing is, the more ownership and energy there will be for the proposal, and it will most likely be better quality. There is no requirement, however, that proposals *only* be generated as a group through the process we have described. There are other ways of coming up with a proposal:

- A circle member might write or re-write a proposal and offer it to the circle for approval.
- A circle member might feel inspired to solve a problem or define a workflow and write a proposal down before including the circle.
- The circle might decide to look at an issue together, gather feedback and let one circle member write up a proposal from what they heard, skipping picture forming and proposal shaping altogether. While this is a time-efficient way of working, in our experience the quality of the proposal might be low, which might lead to the circle tweaking the proposal a lot. Sometimes, taking fast tracks like this only makes the process longer.
- The proposal might come from outside the group or even from outside the organization, like from a policy repository or a sample governance document.

Making a decision: the consent process

A group is ready for the consent process when there is (a) an understanding of the need and (b) a concrete proposal on the table.

The three steps for making a decision are *preparing the decision, deciding* and *publishing*. Each of those steps, again, falls into three steps. The structure of this section follows the 3x3 steps:

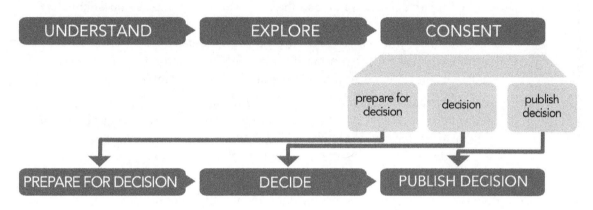

105: The third phase of the policy process falls into three steps itself

Preparing the decision Before we can make a decision, we want to make sure the proposal is ready. Present the proposal and make sure everyone understands it. Then the group gets a chance to react to the proposal. We can make any amendments we want to include in the consent round.

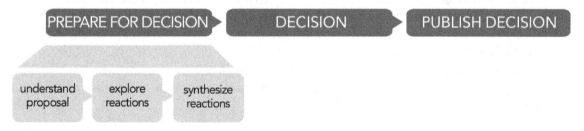

106: The third phase falls into 3 steps

Understanding the proposal Presenting the proposal is important so everyone knows what the proposal *is*. This is especially important when the proposal:

- has had previous versions
- has been generated rather quickly
- has not been generated by the group that is making the decision

Sometimes people only skim a proposal and do not really know what they are consenting to. Make sure everyone knows all the relevant aspects of the proposal. This is the place to gain clarity, *not* the place to question the effectiveness of the proposal – this will come later.

Intention: Everyone in the circle needs to understand the proposal as-is.

Tools: Present the proposal. That means read it out loud, or find another way of ensuring that everyone in the room knows what the proposal says.

- Make the proposal accessible ahead of time, or allow enough time during the meeting for circle members to read the proposal. Allow time for questions.
- Ask questions in a round. A good prompt to start a clarifying questions round is to ask the circle *"what do you need to know so you understand the proposal?"*
- If a group is new to this process, it is helpful for everyone to use a response template so they don't drift into sharing opinions, for example:
  - *"I understand the proposal. I have no questions."*
  - *"I would like to have a better understanding of the proposal. Could you tell me more about the part that says . . . ?"*
  - *"I would like to have a better understanding of the proposal. Could you tell me more about what led you to include the part in the proposal that says . . . ?"*

Complete when: No one has open questions about the proposal

For straightforward questions, we can let the author of the proposal or someone else answer the questions one by one as they are asked in the round. If the questions are more complex or may lead to follow-up questions, then it is often better to collect all the questions in a round first. Doing it this way prevents long digressions that may break the equivalence of doing rounds, and also may prevent drifting into opinions before all the questions for understanding have been asked (see example 107). When all questions are answered, we can ask whether there are more questions that might have come up after hearing the previous questions and answers.

Explore reactions (quick reactions)   In the quick reactions round, everyone gets a chance to give their opinion on a proposal. It is important for every contribution to be brief. Five sentences or less is what a group should be aiming for. If someone has an objection they will have more time to speak later!

Intention: Preparing the group *and* the proposal for decision making

Tools: Do a round where everyone expresses their opinion about the proposal.

- The quick reactions can have different flavors: exploring how circle members feel about it, or whether the proposal is ready for a decision.
- Some groups prefer doing two separate rounds: one for emotional reactions ("reactions"), and one for improving the proposal ("solutions round"; see Fig. 108.)

Never skip the step completely. The minimal version is to ask *"is there anything you'd like to say before we're moving to the consent round?"*

Complete when: Everyone has been able to voice their reaction(s) to the proposal.

Example: Understand proposal

Yukio Kiara
Imke Sanjay

Imke   Kiara, thank you for writing up the proposal. Show us what you've got.

Kiara   Yeah, it boiled down to this simple thing. The fee is the same for everyone, and there are no differences in privileges, everyone gets this new newsletter. Oh, and I noticed that tracking what funds come in extra is something we can't do ourselves but we can ask for it. I can write up a quick role description for producing the newsletter, and I would nominate myself into that role anyway, for the first year. So, that's all! You can read it yourselves. (Circle members are reading silently.)

Imke   Great! Are there any questions? I don't have one. Yukio, and then Sanjay?

Yukio   How did you want to encourage extra donations?

Kiara   Well, I do the new member onboarding interview anyway, and I'd point it out.

Yukio   Ok, thanks.

Sanjay   I don't have a question. Thank you, Kiara!

Imke   No more questions? (Pause) Ok.

107: Understand: understand the proposal

Note: the measure is *not* that everyone agrees with the proposal. We do not attempt to tweak the proposal in an effort to achieve unanimity, as we might lose time over irrelevant details. Instead, we move to consent. If we are not sure whether the group is ready, we just ask, for example by saying *"is there anything else that really needs to be said before we go to the consent round?"* Here are some areas that can be touched on in quick reactions.

- Whether someone likes the proposal or not, as quick as *"I like this proposal because. . . "*
- Members might say that they are planning to object. We can keep it brief in the quick reaction round – the time to explain an objection will come later. For this round, a one-sentence statement like the following is enough: *"I do not support this proposal because I don't believe it effectively supports the organization's (aim to/value of). . . "*
- Appreciation for the author or the process, or other individuals who supported the process
- Improvements in wording
- Small changes that are in alignment with the proposal (in the consensus tradition, those are called "friendly amendments", a term we are adopting – see below)
- We can do a second round if
    - new information has come up near the end of the round, or
    - there is emergence and something is building and we want to explore it. (See box 108.)

> In the original Dutch way of consent forming of a proposal, we learned, after rounds for clarifying questions, to make two rounds for opinion forming, not only one quick reaction round. With only a short summary, the facilitator invites solutions in the second opinion round. Everybody can now bring in their solution ideas after having heard everyone in the first opinion round.
>
> For us in Austria the *second opinion round* is the core of the wisdom of the circle. The solution is emerging in the group process, not in some individuals.
>
> The *second opinion round* shortens the *consent forming* very effectively and minimizes paramount objections.
>
> (Barbara Strauch)

108: What others say

We prefer for people *not* to pass during the reaction round because it is a useful temperature check. We get to hear what others think, where they are with the proposal, what it means to them and what their concerns are, which might not rise to the level of an objection. Especially on controversial topics, it is important to make sure that everyone has been heard sufficiently. However, it is also important to keep statements brief and relevant since it is most effective to devote time to addressing objections. Example 109 shows a quick reaction round and its variant in 110, heading toward an objection.

Example: Explore reactions	Yukio — Kiara Imke — Sanjay

Imke	Let's do a quick reaction round. Sanjay, then me.
Sanjay	Looks good to me. It sounded more complicated than it looks now. I like that.
Imke	Yes, I agree with that. I hope finance circle is going do us the favor of tracking.
Yukio	I'd like to revisit this if they don't want to track. Other than that, it looks good.
Kiara	I am ok with revisiting if finance circle has a reason not to track.

109: Understand: explore quick reactions

Note how in 110, the circle member summarizes the concern in one sentence. The objector-to-be knows he is going to be heard later, so one sentence is enough to give everyone a sense of where this is going. Just saying *"I will object"* without giving any context might be unsettling for a group; but it is also not the right place to say a lot more than a few sentences, so keep it short!

Also notice how the circle just continues with the process – hearing that someone will object does not stop the round. For that reason, it is ok for the facilitator to move to the consent round,

Yukio   Kiara
Imke   Sanjay

Example: Explore reactions

Imke	Let's do a quick reaction round. Sanjay, then myself.
Sanjay	Looks good to me. It sounded more complicated than it looks now. I like that.
Imke	Yes, I agree with that. I hope finance circle is going do us the favor of tracking.
Yukio	I'd like to revisit this if they don't want to track. And looking at it now, I am concerned because I am not convinced the non-workers will have enough connection with us. I'd like to look at that more.
Kiara	I am ok with revisiting if finance circle has a reason not to track. I am curious about Yukio's point.

110: Example of a quick reaction with an objection coming

trusting that the circle member will object and that the group will benefit from the discussion of objections one by one.

Synthesize reactions   We take a moment and reflect on what we learned in the quick reactions. Is the group ready? Is the proposal ready?

Intention: Synthesizing quick reactions

Tools: The facilitator needs to assess whether the proposal is ready.

- The facilitator might choose to take a few moments to think through what might be the best idea. This is a good moment to slow down!
- If there have been several suggested amendments, there are different options.
  - The facilitator can skip, merge, bundle and adjust suggested amendments.
  - The facilitator can decide to move amendments to a later time. For example, the group could consent to the proposal as is and consent to the amendment after.
- The facilitator is always free to ask someone else to state the proposal.

Complete when: The proposal and the circle are ready for the consent round.

If we decide that either the group or the proposal isn't ready, we can arrange for a re-write, schedule the decision for a later date or do whatever we can to facilitate the process towards clarity.

Friendly amendments   Friendly amendments, in the tradition of consensus, are amendments that might come up in the quick reaction round, that seems to be aligned with the spirit of the proposal.

We want to be aware of the pros and cons of friendly amendments so we can understand better what the dynamics are and how to navigate them most effectively and efficiently.

The advantage of a friendly amendment is clear: it can be a fast-track to an improved proposal. But there are disadvantages.

- Friendly amendments can prolong the process. Note that friendly amendments change the proposal, sometimes in unexpected ways. A circle member and the facilitator might assume that an amendment they suggest is uncontradictory. But for a third circle member, an innocent-looking amendment might change how well the proposal works for them and they might end up objecting to the proposal *because* of the amendment. In that case, we have lost time because we will have to process the objection.

- In a similar way, friendly amendments can create frustration. Imagine a group having crafted a proposal very carefully and thoroughly and then pieces of it get changed "on the fly". (Then again, ignoring friendly amendments can create frustration as well.)

- Accepting friendly amendments can create sloppiness and make the process foggy. It can get chaotic and rushed. It is easy to lose track of what version of a friendly amendment made it into the proposal. Slow down.

  - Get clarity by showing the changes visually or by re-reading the proposal.
  - If we make too many changes in the quick reaction round, since you basically have a new proposal, we might have to start at the beginning of the consent process (present proposal, clarifying questions etc.).

We recommend that the facilitator and no one else make the decision of what amendments are accepted in this phase. (Or the facilitator appoints someone to make that decision.) Ultimately, the facilitator is responsible for process during the meeting. Too many cooks will slow down the process with uncertain benefit. The facilitator's task is to avoid confusion and to move the group along without cutting people off. If the facilitator is starting to feel uncomfortable with the process, ask for consent on the original proposal and then ask for new proposals that might build on the just-approved proposal. If someone is making a counter-proposal, we have to be even more alert. (See section 5.5.3 on page 215 on counter-proposals.)

In example 111, things are easy – only a small amendment needs to be considered and the facilitator decides to move to the consent round.

Example: Synthesize reactions

Imke   I'll add this amendment of immediate review if Finance Circle declines. Ok, I think we're ready for the consent round.

111: Synthesize reactions

Decision   Proposal and circle are ready to make a decision. The three steps in this phase are:

- to re-state the proposal
- consent round
- acknowledge consent/objection

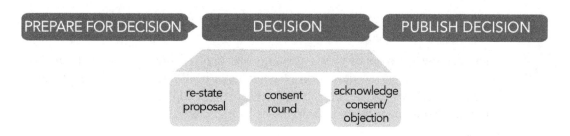

112: The consent phase

Even though all steps might be brief, it helps to be aware of each of them and go through them quickly but in an orderly manner. Rushing through a decision can lead to lack of clarity or frustration.

Re-state proposal   At the beginning of the consent process, we make sure we state the proposal in its most current wording. The intention is to be clear without being repetitive. If the proposal is simple or if it has not changed at all, just acknowledge that and move to the consent round. The more changes there were, the more important it is to read it again in context.

> **Intention:** Make sure everyone has clarity about the (possibly modified) proposal.
>
> **Tools:** Read the proposal, or ask someone else to read it.
>
> **Complete when:** Everyone knows the proposal.

In example 113, the facilitator refers to the written version of the proposal and verbally adds an amendment.

Example: Re-state proposal

Imke   Do you consent to Kiara's proposal as written, with the amendment that we revisit this proposal immediately if Finance Circle is not willing to track the fees and donations from non-working members separately?

113: Explore: re-state proposal

Consent round   It is now time to hear from each circle member whether they have objections. Consent is binary: one either consents or objects. In the consent round, we focus on objections. (See section 3.2.5 on page 87.)

Intention: Hearing objections to the proposal.

Tools: In a round, ask every circle member whether they consent or object. It is important to make sure people notice that this moment is the actual decision phase.

- There are several ways of giving consent, like saying *"consent, I consent"* or *"no objection(s)"*. Given the definition of objections, it all means the same. An answer like "yes" or "no" depends on whether we ask *"do you object?"* or *"do you consent?"* Being too informal often means lack of clarity.

- Consent is an active process. If we sense that someone is giving in, we try to get their hesitation into the open. For some people, it is hard to object (for cultural or personal reasons). Ask *"I heard some hesitation? Anything you want to share?"*

- Consent can be given using hand signs like thumbs up or something comparable if the group has agreed-upon signs.

The best version might be *"Do you have any objection?"* That way, one can affirm in the case of an objection, which is easier to do. Some groups even call the consent round the "objection round" to support members in objecting.

Complete when: Everyone has either consented or objected.

Example 114 shows what a simple consent round without and with an objection sounds like. As in the right-hand example, finish the consent round, hearing from every member.

Example: Consent round (without objection/with objection)			
Kiara	Consent.	**Kiara**	Consent.
Sanjay	No objection.	**Sanjay**	No objection.
Imke	Consent.	**Imke**	Consent.
Yukio	I consent as well.	**Yukio**	I guess I'll object.

114: Explore: consent round without and with an objection

Acknowledge consent/objection After everyone has consented or objected, acknowledge that there is consent or that there are objections. For objections, go through the objection process (see section 3.5).

> **Intention:** Assess and acknowledge consent/objections.
>
> **Tools:** Acknowledge consent or the objection(s) like in 115).
>
> - It helps to say something like *"We have consent, thank you everyone"*, or *"Ok, one objection. Let's hear it."* Not having any acknowledgment can feel awkward.
> - We can do a debriefing round (*"what was this process like? What does this decision mean to you?"*), or celebrate! (This might depend on whether we have worked up to this decision for minutes or months.)
>
> **Complete when:** A consent decision is made.

Example: Acknowledge consent/objection

Imke Terrific, we have consent! Kiara, thank you for taking on the extra role.

Imke Ok, one objection. Yukio, let's hear.

115: Explore: consent given? Acknowledging and celebrating a decision made/an objection.

Publish decision Publishing a decision is a vital step for transparency and effectiveness. Too often, groups fail to publish their decision. The decision has to be known and implemented for it to be effective.

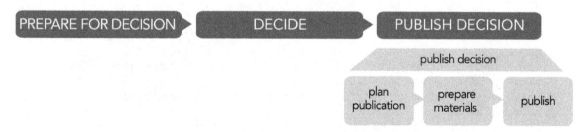

116: The publication phase

Plan publication   A policy is only valuable if people know about it! We make a plan on *how* we are going to get the word out. What needs to happen so people can follow the policy?

> **Intention:** Making a plan of how to publish and implement the policy.
>
> **Tools:** Gather ideas on publication proposals and find consent.
>
> **Complete when:** There is consent to the publication plan.

Prepare materials for publication   We prepare our content (notification, spreadsheet, policy for logbook, tracking sheet) or any other physical object, so the policy can be carried out.

> **Intention:** Creating materials to publish and implement.
>
> **Tools:** What is necessary for this step depends on the nature of your work. Examples: paraphrasing the policy for publication, adding an example to explain, adding the rationale for the logbook, addressing barriers that may keep people from understanding and following your policy.
>
> **Complete when:** Whatever is needed for publication/implementation is prepared.

Example 117 shows a complete policy that is ready to go into a logbook, and 118 provides a checklist.

Example: a proposal

Membership Circle (June 2018)

Background: our previous membership practice did not account for members who wanted to contribute only financially, and the circle wanted to ensure that everyone can contribute so that the organization as a whole can be effective and all members have a sense of belonging.

All members pay the membership fee of $150 per year. Non-working members are encouraged to pay the $150 plus a donation on top of that.
An internal newsletter will be sent out to all members every month with shareable news to spread the word.
The extra income from non-working members is tracked independently from membership fees.

Term: 1 year.

117: Example of a complete policy

Checklist for complete proposals

☐ the policy itself in final wording

☐ the term/evaluation date

☐ optional: measurement (how to measure impact of the policy)

☐ optional: rationale/background (why this policy)

☐ optional: feedback plan (how to give feedback)

☐ optional: action steps for publication stated

☐ optional: action steps for implementation stated

118: Checklist for policy

Publish policy Inform the right people in a suitable way of your new policy. This step is like turning the switch to "on". The policy is now live.

Intention: Making your policy public.

Tools: Publish the minutes according to the publication plan.

- For example, we might have a sign and put it up; we might have a piece of writing. It might be built into the IT system, your email signature...
- The minutes need to be published in an accessible place/logbook.
- We can add a rationale (some text of why the circle assumes the policy will help: a description of the trigger and the needs statement) that informed the policy.
- For writing down policy, especially in a logbook, we want to make sure it is complete. The checklist in 118 on page 119 shows the information we might need.
- We want to make sure to have a reminder for the term end date on a calendar, in whatever system we use to track future items. The term/review practice only works if we follow through!

Complete when: We have carried out our publication (and implementation) plan.

Imagine we make great policy with excellent process. We make a thorough decision and have a great plan for publishing the decision. Then the person who was supposed to write that laminated sign with the new policy on it drops the ball. The sign never gets written. The entire policy process will not have any effect. To prevent falling short, we have to make sure to complete. If all is well, it only takes a few seconds. If adjustment is needed we will be glad we addressed it.

Summary: decision making and measurement-driven process

The table in 119 on page 121 gives an overview of a complete process. Skipping entire phases or steps will often result in stumbling, confusion, and frustration because we forget to listen when we rush through a process. What we call "emotional clean-up" – restoring trust – can be time-consuming, or even worse, never happen and wear on people and turn into social-emotional debt.

If we keep our focus on the intention and measure for every step, we will be able to move through a policy-making process. It might not always graceful or without temporary detours but we *will* arrive at our destination if we know where we want to get, and how we find out whether we're there.

3.4   Improving the policy roll-out

We can improve the quality of policy and make implementation smoother by including measurements and defined feedback channels. These are not separate processes but dimensions of policies that circles can keep in mind for policy making.

3.4.1   Measurement

For every policy, we recommend that circles make it a habit to ask themselves – even before it is put into place – how the effectiveness of policy they are generating can be evaluated. The evaluation will not only come from people but also by gathering data, asking *"for this policy, what would tell us that it is working?"* This could be:

- click rates
- numbers of new members
- donations
- sales
- community members attending meals etc.
- ...

It only makes sense to track the data that the circle is willing to interpret. It's important to make sure to put all the measures in place so the correct data can be tracked. It makes sense to create an operational role so this can happen, especially if there is more than one point in time when data has to be gathered or if a point person is open to feedback on an ongoing basis.

3.4.2   Defined feedback channels

We want to define our feedback channels. New policy means that there might be reactions from others in the organization. The best idea to make sure implementation happens smoothly is to define early on – at the same time as publishing the policy – how the circle wants to receive feedback on that policy. For example, if the circle prefers feedback in a survey, then give access to the survey as soon as the policy is public. If there is a person identified for filling a role of gathering feedback, give their contact information so people can respond with feedback or questions.

Summary: Steps in policy process

STEP/INTENTION	TOOLS	MEASURE OF COMPLETION
1 Understand		
(a) Understand context	Report; clarifying questions (round)	No circle member has unanswered questions
(b) Explore underlying needs	Reaction rounds	No one has another item for the list of needs
(c) Synthesize issue/needs	Write up issue and needs statement	Consent on needs statement
2 Explore		
(a) Understand scope of policy (picture forming)	Round(s) on dimensions	Consent to completeness of list of dimensions
(b) Explore proposal ideas (proposal shaping)	Round(s) on proposal ideas	No more proposal pieces to add, all dimensions covered
(c) Synthesize ideas into proposal	Write up proposal draft	Proposal draft written, all dimensions covered
3 Decide		
(a) Understand proposal	Present, clarifying questions (round)	No circle member has unanswered questions
Explore reactions	(Quick) reaction round	All circle members have spoken
Synthesize reactions	Assert synthesis	Group and (modified) proposal ready for decision
(b) Re-state proposal	Present	Proposal has been presented
Consent round	Consent round	All circle members have spoken
Acknowledge consent/objections	Assert decision/objection	Decision is made (consent)
(c) Plan publication	Rounds on ideas, write up, consent	Consent given
Prepare materials	Write up materials	All materials are prepared
Publish	Publication tools	Policy is published

119: Understand–explore–decide with small steps, tools and measures

The circle can specify:

- How the circle wants to be approached:
  - Who to contact (operational role, leader of the circle, or the entire circle).
  - Through what channel (personal contact, email, a survey, a contact sheet, a physical list or whatever makes sense).
- Whether there is a specific aspect the circle would like feedback on.
- What the circle is tracking (if anything) as a measure of policy effectiveness.
- Whether there is a preferred time frame for feedback.

Inviting and listening carefully to feedback provides learning opportunities for the circle. It also builds trust and reduces the risk of upset among members of the organization.

3.5   Integrating objections: process

Dealing with objections is one of the core skills of sociocratic group process. If we know how to deal with objections in a constructive and time-efficient way, we will turn every concern into a better decision! Listening to and exploring what lies under an objection can take time. Having a way of efficiently dealing with objections will make it doable for an organization to take the time to address objections.

Addressing objections follows the same process of *understand – explore – decide*. The first step is to *understand* the objections thoroughly; then we *explore* what options we have. The amended proposal will be input for the *decide phase*.

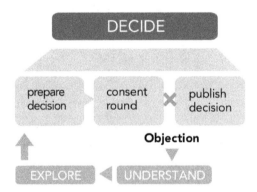

120: Objections send the circle into an extra loop before going back to the process – this time with an even better understanding of the topic and a better proposal on the table.

3.5.1 Understand

121: Understanding an objection

Understand the objection(s)   We start with curiosity in trying to understand the objection.

> **Intention:** Understanding the objection.
>
> **Tools:** The group will try to find out what is underlying the concern.
>
> - We can ask the objector *"what do you fear might happen? How will we know?"*
> - We can synthesize what we hear and reflect back to the objector (and the circle) to find out whether the objection has been fully understood.
> - If there are more objections, we can hear them now. After hearing all objections, the facilitator decides whether to deal with the objections one by one or at once.
>
> **Complete when:** No one has questions about the objection.

Explore needs/relationship to the circle's aim   The circle takes ownership of the objection and identifies how the concerns are related to the circle's aim and needs.

> **Intention:** Exploring how the objection relates to the circle's aim and what needs are underlying the objection.
>
> **Tools:** The easiest way to do this is a reaction round.
>
> - It is not the objector who has to prove that the objection is valid; it is the circle as a whole (including the objector as circle member) that will explore the objection in relationship to the circle's aim.
> - The circle might add to the original objection as they explore the concerns.
>
> **Complete when:** No one has any ideas to add.

A side note: Imagine a situation where someone brings up an objection that is seen by other circle members as a personal preference (no negative impact on the circle achieving its aims).

Consent is not a mechanism that separates objections from preferences in a clear-cut manner. Lack of skill in dealing with objections, like dismissing someone's objection by saying *"your objection is not valid"* and social-emotional backlash can actually *cause* dysfunction and decrease the circle's ability to achieve its aim. It will not help us to have been "right" about the personal preference. If people know they are heard and trust is built, it will be easier to cooperate. To avoid dynamics of people-pleasing, train everyone both on the definition of consent and on communication skills.

Synthesize the objection(s)   After exploration comes synthesizing the information.

> **Intention:** Synthesizing whether there is a need to amend the proposal (see 123).
>
> **Tools:** The facilitator (or an appointed circle member) synthesizes the objection the way it has been understood by the circle.
>
> **Complete when:** There is consent on a synthesized statement.

3.5.2   Explore options

Now that we understand the objection, we explore our options. This phase is similar to generating a proposal. But this time, we are working with improving an existing proposal.

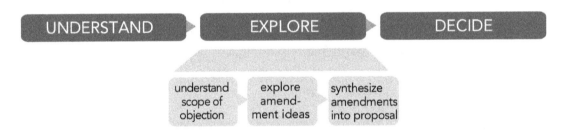

122: Exploring options for improving the policy

Understand scope of amendments   For a thorough process, it is a good idea to spend a minute on understanding which areas of the proposal need changing. Skip this step if the objection clearly only affects a defined area of the proposal and is not likely to have ripple effects. Alternatively, the facilitator may help point the group to the relevant paragraphs that are affected by the objection.

> **Intention:** Understanding what parts of the proposal need changing.
>
> **Tools:** We can either do a round on reviewing what pieces of the proposal are affected and what might remain untouched, or the facilitator offers thoughts and allows for reactions.
>
> **Complete when:** Everyone understands what areas are affected.

Example: Understand objection

Yukio ○ Kiara
Imke ● ● Sanjay

Yukio I thought more about what it would be like with non-working members, and I am concerned that it waters down the sense of community here when they don't really know who is who and what's going on. I am worried that they will walk around saying they are members but can't be good ambassadors for us. Just sending a newsletter does not seem to be enough.

Imke Ok. Does anyone have questions? (Pause)

Kiara Yukio, is this more about you wanting them to feel to connected or you wanting them to be good public advocates for our cause?

Yukio Hmmm. A bit of both I think. I think both concerns are valid.

Imke Ok, I think we can just take them both as they seem related. More questions? (Pause.) Ok, so what comes up for you in hearing this objection? Kiara.

Kiara I see his point. I think I would have been not as concerned because people would only join because they care. But then again, I see that we all know each other from working together in circles, and they would not have that. So, for me it is more about inclusion and community than about desire to control how they represent us.

Sanjay I agree. So instead of focusing on that fear, I'd think about inclusion. Our aim is to create a web of connections between members, so let's do that.

Imke Nice. Thank you for pointing that out. I like how you two think about it. Nothing to add. Yukio, anything to add?

Yukio No, that's good.

Imke So, the objection is about how we can make sure non-working members stay connected and included which entails being informed. Good summary? (Pause.)

123: Seeking understanding for an objection (3 steps)

Explore amendment ideas Now it is time to problem solve! What can we do so that the concern brought up by the objector can be used to improve the proposal?

Intention: Exploring ideas for amendments to the proposal.

Tools: Let everyone give their ideas on what can be changed.

- This is a good place for a reaction round on amendment proposals. Keep going in rounds while ideas keep building.
- Additionally, the facilitator might review the typical strategies for addressing an

objection (see section 3.5.3) to give circle members more ideas and wider view on options.

- Capture amendment ideas in writing.

Complete when: No one else has amendment ideas to add.

Synthesize amendments into proposal   Once everyone has been able to contribute their ideas, the amendment ideas need to be organized so we can go back into the consent process.

Intention: Synthesizing amendment ideas into new proposal.

Tools: The facilitator will either synthesize, or will appoint someone to summarize the amendments and how they fit into the proposal. The aim is to have a coherent proposal to go back to the consent process.

Complete when: There is an amended proposal in writing.

3.5.3   Options for amendments

There are countless options for amendments or modifications, depending on the nature of the proposal and objection. A good solution will come up if everyone has had a chance to express themselves.

There are three go-to strategies that are extremely powerful and can be used in almost any context. It is helpful for the facilitator or others to name the different options:

Modify the proposal   We can change anything in the proposal to integrate the objection. The options for revisions of content are countless and specific to your context. This section cannot possibly cover all the ways one might be changing proposals. Figure 125 on page 128 lists examples of possible modifications.

Shorten the term.   If there is an objection to a policy proposal, one option to move forward is to shorten the term. If a circle member objects to a proposal, they might be willing to consent to trying it out for a shorter time. Oftentimes, this makes it easier for circle members to consent. This strategy works best in combination with the next strategy, *measure the concern*. (See section 4.4.6 on page 166 on term ends for policy.)

Shortening the term of a proposal means the policy will be revisited sooner. We will then see whether the policy brought negative changes and we can then adjust the policy. Therefore, shortening the term of a policy increases a circle's willingness to experiment and innovate. The question changes from *"should we drop this proposal?"* to *"would it feel safe enough to try it for 3 months? 4 months?"*

Yukio   Kiara
Imke   Sanjay

Example: Explore amendments

Imke   Let's see. This is not complicated policy, so we can probably just do a round on amendment ideas. Kiara, then Yukio.

Kiara   I had been thinking about including doing member events, maybe two times a year. We could invite non-working members and see if they show up. And then there is the newsletter. It would be important for people to read it and use it.

Yukio   Yes, the newsletter, since it seems like a lot of work, should be tracked. How many people are opening it, sharing it? How many non-working members are among them? I'd like to track that.

Imke   I like what I heard. Works for me.

Sanjay   The member event sounds sweet - and I like that working members would benefit from that as well. Win-win. More people involved, more money in the bank, more PR happening, no one turned away. Terrific.

Imke   Sounds like we're ready. I'll consider the event a separate topic and propose to put it on the backlog. So as for tracking, Kiara, is it possible to track members and non-members and click rates separately so we can see who really makes use of the resource? (Kiara nods). Terrific. So.... the original proposal is amended with tracking the click rate for opening the newsletter, by member status. I think the term of 1 year is still good, especially considering the events we want to plan. If we consent to this proposal as amended, I will put hosting events as an item on the backlog for planning at a future meeting. I trust Kiara will write a job description for the role of producing the newsletter to approve next time. Any other amendments at this point that we haven't heard yet? (Pause) Ok, I am ready for consent. Are there any objections? (Waits.) Hearing none, that means we have consent! Great job, everyone!

124: Finding amendments for addressing an objection

Measure the concern   An objection is not a reason to drop a proposal. How can we learn?

In sociocracy, we broaden our view using another option: measure the concern. That means that we go ahead and try something (with everyone's consent) but we put a measurement in place so that we don't just hope for the best but actually know what the impact of our policy is.

For example, a non-profit is looking for ways to reduce operational costs. Historically, they have sent out monthly newsletters. The proposal on the table is to reduce the frequency of newsletters to save money. A circle member expresses a concern that the click rate on the website might go down, leading to a decrease in donations. The circle does a quick reaction round where everyone shares a reflection on the concern raised. The circle amends the proposal: by consent, they decide to go ahead with the reduction

---

Examples for amendments modifying the proposal

Proposal: Our organization introduces a membership fee of $20 for all members.

Objection: fee is too high.
Possible amendment: change fee to $15.

Objection: billing every month is too tedious.
Possible amendment: change it to a bi-monthly fee of $40.

Objection: not all members can afford the fee.
Possible amendments: introduce two membership levels, one for students and seniors ($10), one for others ($30). OR introduce a system of work instead of pay OR raise funds to partially cover expenses in a different way.

125: Modifying a proposal

in publications, and at the same time perform a cost-benefit analysis. They want to find out if the savings generated by reducing the operational costs have a negative impact on donor generosity. They craft an additional proposal to measure and monitor the outcome of reducing the frequency of publications. The proposal includes:

- weekly monitoring of the website click rates and donations, for a period of 6 months.
- set measurement parameters, and determine a level at which to abandon the experiment if the rates drop alarmingly.

  - if the click rate drops by 15%, and/or
  - if the donations drop by 10%

- a role is formed to carry out the task and to monitor and report.

At the end of six months, the circle finds that there has been a moderate drop (7%) in clicks and a minor drop (4%) in donations. This feedback provides data for policy review.

The point here is that we don't want to waste time in speculating what *might* happen. We find a way of trying it out. Since we are measuring the concern, we keep the risk as small as possible. In the same way as we might count clicks and donations, we can also count registrations, complaints, count clients or sales. Everything that cannot be counted can still be surveyed: members, staff, workshop participants, hosts, customers. Example 126 is an example of a shorter term and a measurement to see whether concerns are borne out. A habitual nay-sayer may consent if we take their concerns seriously and put good measures in place.

Examples for objections and measuring the concern

Proposal:
To form a new circle under the Membership Circle.

Objection:
We don't have enough people to populate the circle. This might stretch us too thin and we will burn out and lose volunteer members.

Amendment (measure the concern)
We shorten the term of this proposal to 3 months, increase our outreach effort to populate the circle and will reconsider the formation of the new circle, if within 3 months, the circle has under 6 members.

126: Measure the concern and shorten the term to address an objection

An experienced group will combine all the options for amendments. *Always* try to make a step forward. Do not be content with a decision *not* made. Don't kill proposals by being indecisive or by failing to take some action to generate more information. We want to either:

- Make the term shorter.
- Make it safer (measurements).
- Make a plan of how to get more information.
- Make a plan of when/how to talk about the proposal again.
- Even dropping a proposal needs to be a consent decision to ensure intentionality.

3.6   Creating and filling roles (selection process)

All policy is made to support circles in achieving their aims. The three kinds of policy that are typically made are guidelines, workflow policies and the creation of roles. Roles are created to "package" operational tasks within a circle so that the attention and work will lie in the holder of the role instead of the whole circle. In order to move operations into a role, we need to take two steps:

1. Write a role description and consent to it, thereby creating the role.
2. Select an individual into filling that role, also by consent.

In some cases, both steps are taken at once to save time. For example, the proposal might be *"I propose that this task of staying connected to our fiscal sponsor be moved into a role of the fiscal sponsor coordinator for the next two years and that Aliyah fill that role for 6 months."*

   Both decisions will come with a term. To create a role is a decision that needs to be reviewed on a regular basis, including whether it (still) needs to exist, what the tasks, limits and measures might be. At the same time, who fills a role is a decision that needs to be revisited when the term for that person is up. If there is no policy preventing it, any person can be re-elected as many times as the circle sees fit.

3.6.1   Creating roles

Since creating roles is policy, writing role descriptions follows the regular policy process. There is no real difference between regular policy and role descriptions but for convenience and usability, this section fleshes out how to use the policy process to write a role description.

Understand phase

The policy-generating process, as described in section 3.3, encourages circles to make sure the need is fully understood before creating policy. The circle might understand the issue and underlying needs well enough and feel confident that a role might be the strategy that would meet their needs most effectively. Often, creating roles is one part of a larger policy context. This is true when a circle approves a general guideline *and* creates a role to track measures for that guideline. For example if an office is deciding to introduce a new tool for customer relationship management, they might also want to create a role to oversee this process.

Explore phase

The role description can be written by a helping circle, an individual or by the circle. Even for an individual writing the role description alone, it makes sense to go through the regular process.

Explore role scope   For a role description, gathering a list of dimensions to keep in mind and questions that need answers will be vital to explore the policy scope and to create a complete role description – it is really easy to forget crucial parts.

While the dimensions for guidelines will likely be different every time, the dimensions for roles will be based on the very same set every time. The list below shows the most common dimensions for creating a role. Tailor it to your situation.

Dimensions for creating a role

tasks, activities, responsibilities
authority and limits to their authority to make decisions
budget (or budget tiers)
hand-offs with other circles or roles
reporting to the circle and/or circle leader (what/how often)
what measurements/feedback do we ask the role to track?
role held by individual or pair
how to create redundancy/sucession plan/substitutes
minimum/maximum terms?
pay
time budget
term - when will this role description be reviewed?

127: List of most common dimensions for creating a role

Explore role description ideas In the next phase, gather proposal ideas. As usual, a proposal idea might cover one or more of the dimensions, for example

- The holder of Content Resource Management role will work independently.
- Report every 6 weeks.
- The work connected to this role is planned to be performed within 4h per week.
- Time will be tracked in a separate time sheet.

Gather ideas (in a round) and write them down. Stay in rounds until all ideas have been gathered.

Synthesize role description The circle leader, facilitator or any circle member can be delegated to synthesize the ideas into a proposal that will then go to the circle for consent in the usual way (see consent process in section 3.3.2).

3.6.2 Selection process

Everything in sociocracy is designed for both effectiveness and equivalence. Elections are no exception. The sociocratic election process:

- Has the potential to create a wonderful connecting experience for the group.
- Has the potential to spread power and develop new leadership.
- Provides a feedback opportunity where we learn about each other in the circle.

The selection process has three parts that align with the phases of *understand – explore – decide*. (1) First we work on a shared understanding of what we are selecting. (2) Then we explore ideas and give each other feedback so we can form a proposal. (3) Lastly, we decide about the proposal. In cases where there are objections, we deal with the objections until everyone can consent to the proposal. Figure 128 is a summary.

Readers who want to understand the steps of a selection process more deeply are referred to matrix 200 and 201 on pages 264 and 263.

128: All steps of a selection process

We often call elections *selections* to avoid the association between elections and voting. In sociocracy, we do not vote, we nominate. Elections and voting imply majority vote. In our practice, the two terms *elect* and *select* are interchangeable.

Selections in sociocracy are very different from secret ballot majority vote. Society considers the right to secret ballot a foundation of democracy, considering that autocracy was the historical alternative. Open selection processes bring a new depth of participatory democracy.

Understand: what's the role about?

129: Selection process understand phase

Review role   What role are we selecting for? What is the role description? What are the responsibilities and authorities of that role? If the circle is selecting someone for a familiar role, it still helps to review the role description briefly because role descriptions may vary from one circle to another. *"Does the facilitator prepare the agenda with the secretary and the leader, or is there a different agreement? Does the secretary keep the member roster current in case of elections?"*

If we are selecting a delegate, how often does the next-broader circle meet and what day/time? This might inform the selection process.

> **Intention:** Understanding the role.
>
> **Tools:** Paraphrase or read the role description.
> - The facilitator can ask the circle member currently filling that role to give a three-sentence overview of the role.
> - Not everyone in the circle might be aware of who does what and reviewing it increases transparency and learning about your own organization.
> - If there is a reason to change the role definition, then we want to do that before we proceed to select someone. Role descriptions are circle policy, so we have to make sure to be clear and to ask for consent if the role description is updated.
>
> **Complete when:** Everyone understands the role.

Explore term   We can define a default for the term, like one-year terms; however, we set the term intentionally for each selection. *"We're selecting a facilitator for this circle, and I propose the term is our default term of one year. Is there any change from our standard practice that anyone would like to propose?"* What could be reasons to shorten the term or to make it longer?

- Shorter terms if the circle wants to cycle more people through the roles so they gain experience and leadership skills.
- Choose longer terms if the circle does not want to spend much time in selection processes.
- Choose longer terms if the circle wants stability.
- Choose longer terms if the role requires a long learning process for people to become effective in their role.

> **Intention:** Explore considerations on term of role.
>
> **Tools:** State default term, do a round to check if there are considerations affecting the length of term, propose a term and check for consent. This decision might be revisited when a person is chosen to fill the role.
>
> **Complete when:** No objection to the proposed term.

Explore qualifications   On what basis would we select someone for a role? We want to prime our minds so we can nominate based on qualifications and make a good decision. This is even more important for operational roles that require specific expertise.

For example, if the job description says *"types the minutes, especially proposals, into the shared document in real time"* then we need someone who has the capacity to do that. If an operational role requires the capacity to work on weekends or evening, we have to be aware that not everyone might be able to fill that role.

Intention: Exploring what qualifications we would like to see in the holder of a role.

Tools: A round where people name one or two qualifications, continuing until the group runs out of ideas or feels complete.

- Gather the qualifications visible to everyone and keep the list. For established roles, we can just read the list and ask whether there are any modifications to make.
- Just like in other phases of exploration, do not comment (yet) on each other's ideas.
- This step often takes under five minutes.

Complete when: No one has another idea to contribute.

Figure 130 gives a possible list of the 4 process-related roles. Note that these are examples! Any organization/circle might prioritize very differently! Each group needs to compile their own list *and* keep it current and adapt it to whatever is needed.

Sample qualifications for circle roles

Leader

- Good listener
- Good feel for the group
- Experience and knowledge in circle domain
- Capacity (time)
- Trustworthy
- Owning it when making mistakes
- Knows how to delegate tasks
- Accountable
- Reliable

Facilitator

- Good listener
- Good feel for the group
- Facilitation experience
- Skills in non-violent communication
- Knowledge in sociocratic processes
- Confidence in front of people but not ego-driven
- Cheerful
- Excited about process

Secretary

- Computer skills/typing
- Multi-tasking
  (participate in meeting and type)
- Good synthesizer
- Accountable
- Knows how to keep minutes short
  and easy to understand

Delegate

- Good feel for the group
- Capacity to attend additional meeting
- Non-divisive
- Good listener
- Synthesize all the voices in a group
- Long-standing member
- Able to function well at broader level

130: Sample qualifications for leaders, facilitators, secretaries, delegates

Consent to list of qualifications   It is important to end this process with a consent round. If there is an objection, we explore it and see if we can find a set of qualifications everyone can consent to.

For example, in figure 130, the item "long-standing member" for the delegate is not necessarily a qualification everyone will consent to. Someone might have suggested it, it gets written on the list, but we still need to see whether everyone can consent to that. *"Why do you want someone who is a long-standing member as a delegate?"* Accordingly, we might decide that we want a facilitator with only little experience on the job because in that phase of the organization, we might want to put our attention to spreading leadership and we are confident we can work with an inexperienced facilitator. As another example, in training contexts, often someone mentions the qualification *impartial* for a facilitator. We, personally, would not consent to that, so this would give rise to an interesting discussion. (The reasons are that we do not think there is such a thing as an impartial circle member, and the double role – being circle member and facilitator at the same time – is a consequence of *self*-governance. The way we look at it, the facilitator should be willing and able to separate their facilitator role and circle member role.)

> **Intention:** Reaching consent on the list of qualifications
>
> **Tools:** Consent round.
>
> - Note that these are qualifications, not necessarily requirements. No human being will be accountable 100% of the time, or will *always* fulfill the expectation to be a good listener to a maximum extent. We are not, ever, looking for perfect. For operational roles, be sure to define what qualifications are necessary.
> - If we are using an old list, we present it and ask for consent.
>
> **Complete when:** There is consent to the list of qualification.

We now know what role we are selecting, the proposed term and what kind of candidate we are looking for. The only piece missing is *who* we would like to propose to fill that role. It helps to keep the list of qualifications visible to all in the next step so it can inform people's thinking.

Explore: who could fill the role?

In the next phase, the group will share their ideas, allowing ideas to build on each other.

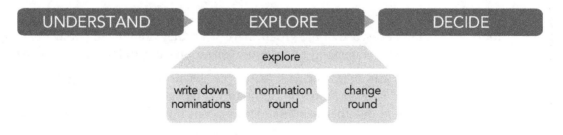

131: Selection process exploration phase

Write down nominations   Everyone in the circle will now nominate someone for the role.

> **Intention:** Circle members reflect on who they would like to see in a role.
>
> **Tools:** Everyone identifies a candidate. Some facilitators prefer nominations to be written down. (See below.)
> **One can nominate oneself** if someone is interested in the role and has reasons to believe they are qualified for the role.
>
> **Complete when:** Everyone has identified a suitable candidate.

Why do we write our nominations down? We want to hear everyone's reasoning without losing information. During the nomination round, it is tempting to just go with the group energy, especially when someone is speaking late in the round. Writing down a nomination *before* the first person speaks will encourage everyone to share their original nomination. Sometimes, the best ideas are the ones that seem peripheral at first!

Some facilitators like to collect the nomination sheets so they can track better who nominated whom. We prefer a grid to get a piture of everyone's nomination(s), as in 132.

	nomination round	change round
Sarah		
Peter		
Victor		
Yuong		

132: Grid for nomination round and change round

Share nominations in round   The circle now enters a shared exploration phase.

> **Intention:** Sharing our nominations and reasons.
>
> **Tools:** In a round, everyone in the group shares who they nominated *and why*. This can be a one-sentence statement, or a slightly longer one, depending on the context.
>
> - The facilitator can fill in the grid as people speak. We will, ideally, hear new information or familiar pieces of information in a new light as people speak.
> - People can *build* on other people's ideas but not invalidate or argue with other people's contributions. The energy is more positive when it is around *"yes, and"*.
>
> **Complete when:** Everyone has shared their nomination and reasons.

	nomination round	change round
Sarah	Yuong	
Peter	Sarah	
Victor	Victor	
Yuong	Victor	

133: Grid after nomination round (and before change round)

Below are some examples of what a nomination will sound like if we are selecting a facilitator:

- *Sarah: "I nominate Yuong because I have seen them facilitate in other circles. They are clear and concise and often explain why we do what, and I enjoy that."*
- *Peter: "I nominate Sarah because she is clear, experienced, quick to understand, and she understands process, and those are the qualifications that most people in the group named for a facilitator."*
- *Victor: "I nominate myself because I am looking for some more practice in facilitation after taking the course on facilitation, and I think I know enough to do a good job."*
- *Yuong: "I nominate Victor because I want to give him a chance to practice."*

Change round   By now, everyone has heard the other people's ideas and reasons and something we have heard might change our nomination. Maybe there was new information, maybe something shifted our thinking or reminded us of something meaningful we knew about somebody. Note that we do not *have* to change our mind, of course.

Intention: Assessing nominations after hearing each other's nominations.

Tools: A round of reactions; people say who they nominate after hearing the others.

- Our standard prompt is *"having heard what you heard, are you moved to change your nomination?"*
- If people change their nomination, we ask what led them to change their mind.
- If they did not change their nomination, we ask them whether they have any new information to share.
- If there is highly relevant information or a compelling argument at the end of the change round, we can ask whether more people speak again, especially the people who spoke early in the change round. Resist the urge to keep going around until everyone nominates the same person, however!

Complete when: Everyone has spoken; relevant information has been shared.

> **EXAMPLE**
> **Original ideas during the nomination round**
>
> We were in the nomination round for a secretary. All but one circle member had shared their nomination and had nominated the most obvious option (the member who always brings his laptop to meetings and gladly writes notes). But then the last person spoke in the nomination round: "*I nominate Katie for secretary because she is hard of hearing.*"
> I remember my initial reaction was "*What?! What kind of reason is that?*" (I am glad it was not my turn so I did not say that out loud!) The circle member continued: "*We often have the issue that we forget that she does not hear well and Katie does not remind us, and I thought that if she is the one writing the notes, we could make sure she asks and we pay attention to whether she can hear everything.*"
> This was so compelling that everyone changed their nomination to Katie in the change round and it was easy to find consent.

134: An example of a compelling reason during a selection process.

Here is how above selection process might continue:

- *Sarah: "I am staying with my nomination for Yuong because of what I said earlier. I think he is a good facilitator."*
- *Peter: "I am changing my nomination to Victor because I had forgotten that he had taken that class, and I appreciate when people learn more, so I want to give him the opportunity to practice."*
- *Victor: "I am staying with my self-nomination for the reasons stated."*
- *Yuong: "I nominated Victor and I am staying with that. I think it is important to give people experience so we all get better at what we do here."*

In this example, maybe not everybody knew or remembered that Victor had taken a facilitation class. Maybe others had not seen Yuong facilitate yet. Thanks to the nomination round and people sharing their reasons, everyone in the group now knows more than before.

The facilitator of the example selection process now sees this grid, preferably written down for all to see. The nominations and the reasons that have been shared will be the foundation for the next step.

Decide: who will fill the role?

This last phase is about synthesizing the selection process into a decision. A candidate is proposed, we do a consent round and acknowledge the decision.

Facilitator proposes a candidate   It is the facilitator's job to make sure a proposal is being made now. That does not mean that the proposal has to come from the facilitator; there can be reasons for the facilitator to ask someone else to make a proposal. In general, it is important to put a proposal out now for reasons of efficiency – we could circle and circle endlessly, weighing all the reasons in search of the ideal candidate. We try to avoid that by making a proposal and focusing on objections.

	nomination round	change round
Sarah	Yuong	Yuong
Peter	Sarah	Victor
Victor	Victor	Victor
Yuong	Victor	Yuong

135: Grid after change round

136: Selection process: decision phase

Intention: Proposing a candidate.

Tools: The facilitator will make sure a proposal is being made.

- Repeat the role and who the candidate is: *"I propose that Victor be facilitator."*
- Share reasons for this choice, referring to the qualifications gathered for this role and to the reasons shared in the nomination round and in the change round.
- Include the term for the proposal, based on the input earlier in the process

For example: *"I propose that Victor be facilitator of this circle, because this would give him experience and he is eager to learn, for a term of one year."*

Complete when: A candidate/term has been proposed.

Consent round/objections   The facilitator now calls for a consent round.

Intention: Hearing from everyone whether they consent or object.

Tools: In a round, let circle members consent or object.

- It is absolutely crucial in this consent round that there are *no negative personal preferences expressed here*, for example in the pattern of *"I consent but I still think that she would be the better choice".* To avoid this, we often review what a possible basis for objections would look like before the consent round begins. *"I ask you to only object if you think your ability to achieve the circle's aim would be harmed if Victor fills this role. Remember that we are not looking for a perfect candidate and that many of us could fill this role. We are only looking for a candidate to fill this role, not the perfect one."*

- If we are only selecting for one role, we always start the consent round so that the nominee goes *last*. By the time the nominee gets to speak, all the other circle members will have given consent or objected. In sociocracy, we want people to step up into power, and sometimes the confidence and faith of a group allow a nominee to consent to taking on the role.
- If there are objections, we aim to integrate them (see section 3.6.3 on page 143 on objections in selections).

Complete when: The circle knows whether there is consent.

Facilitator announces decision The facilitator will assess whether there is consent and will announce the decision.

Intention: Acknowledging and publishing the decision.

Tools: The facilitator will say something like *"Looks like we have consent!"* or *"great, we have made a decision!"*

- Make sure the decision makes it into the minutes, including the term (note when the term is up and set a reminder).
- If you have a central tracking system for roles, update the role there.
- Keep the list of qualifications. We can use that list again next time.

Complete when: The decision is made and is captured in the minutes.

There is a complete example of this selection process in the appendix on page 263.

3.6.3 Frequently asked questions about selections

Can we select for more than one role at a time?

Yes. This makes sense if your choices seem interdependent, for example if we want someone as facilitator but only if he or she is not a delegate. It also simply saves time. We can select all roles at the same time.

How does this work? In the nomination round, people say all their nominations. *"I nominate XZY for. . . because. . . , and . . . for delegate because. . . "* and so on.

The grid in diagram 137 shows how we draw the grid for a multiple simultaneous selection process, in this case for facilitator, secretary and delegate. The change round follows the same pattern. Now the facilitator proposes someone for each of the roles along with the reasons why. If one of the roles is not as easy to fill, it may make sense to consent to the easier choice(s) and to focus afterward on the election that needs more attention.

Selecting more than one role at once

	Facilitator		Secretary		Delegate	
	nomination round	change round	nomination round	change round	nomination round	change round
circle member 1						
circle member 2						
circle member 3						
circle member 4						

137: Grid for nomination round and change round for three roles.

Why do we not ask for willingness first?

Whenever we teach this process, there is someone in the group that asks: *"why don't we ask whether that person wants to do that role? How can we talk about them serving in a role if we don't know whether they are available and willing?"*

The first answer is that having the information reduces the possibilities we have. I (Jerry) was part of a group that had been working together and we were planning to select a facilitator. I had a clear preference for someone and spoke with that person ahead of time, and she shared with me that she was not available. In the formal selection process, everyone but me nominated her in the nomination round, and she ended up being proposed as a candidate and consented to her own selection. Willingness, or lack thereof, may shift.

It makes quite an impression to be told by circle members how qualified oneself is for a role. It is not unheard of that the individual selected says afterward: *"I would have never volunteered for this role, but I was convinced by the positive feedback I heard here. I feel honored to fill this role."* Note that this is not about forcing people into a role. We assume they know that they can say no – and the group needs to allow them that space. They consent to fill the role – which is an active process and very different from being volunteered by not saying *no* loud enough! This process is designed to help people say yes and to create an opportunity of exploring what a *no* means and how it could become a *yes*.

This is why it is best to start the consent round so that the candidate speaks last. To achieve that, just start the round with the person next to the candidate and pass the round in the opposite direction. That way, the nominated person will get to hear everyone else first.

A tricky question is the following: *"I am one of the people that keeps getting nominated, and understand that it is good to give feedback and I understand that people want me in a role. But I am over-committed in this organization. It is just a waste of time to even nominate me as I will object anyway."* Situations and statements like these are tricky, and we'd like to share our thoughts because we assume that what we have to say might be useful. First of all, the people who perceive themselves as overcommitted are often the same people that would like to hear more appreciation of their work. Can we hear this as feedback on how much people appreciate our contribution to our circle? The election process is more than just finding someone as quickly as possible to do the job. It can be a time for reflection too on how we spread the work. If we sit through nominations just seeing them as a waste of time, we are missing the wonderful message in it: *"we appreciate you"*. Also, maybe more importantly, the fact that the same people are nominated again on a regular basis but then object because they are over-committed is very important feedback. What do we as a circle do with that? How do we interpret that? As a circle, do we think we could make better use of that member's contribution? Maybe we could talk about their overall package of tasks in the circle. Maybe we can build more leadership around the easier tasks that person is doing so we can free up time and attention for the more visionary work. Whatever we do with it, we want to be sure to notice the feedback this process gives us.

Why do not we just let people volunteer?

The basis for the decision of who fills the role is qualification. A volunteer might not be the fit person for the job. And the best candidate might not volunteer! Filling roles on a volunteer basis will not get us reliably good results. (Willingness, of course, is *one* factor. If someone *really* does not want to fill a role, chances are they will not perform well in that role.)

Inviting volunteers can get us into a lot of difficulties because it is difficult to object if volunteering is our method of decision making. The ability to object is important for collaboration. An organization is about *doing* something. Whether or not someone is suitable for a role is essential for creating a good work environment.

Self-nomination vs. volunteering

It is important to understand the difference between self-nominations and volunteering for a role. Self-nomination adds *information* since self-nomination includes saying *why* we nominate ourselves. What qualifications do we see in ourselves? What does this role mean to us? There is much more to learn that we would ever hear if someone volunteered saying *"I can do it"*. Self-nominations, like volunteering, express willingness, but being selected into that role does not happen automatically – the other circle members have to consent.

The best way to show the difference is that we have seen it happen many times that people nominated themselves but were not selected. Or they nominated themselves in the nomination round but shifted their nomination to someone else in the change round.

One tricky aspect around self-nominations is that in some cultures, it is not easy to self-nominate, either because those cultures are hierarchical (and some people will traditionally not expect to be allowed to self-nominate), or because they are extremely horizontal in which case self-nomination can look arrogant. We are aware of these patterns and still think that self-nominations are healthy if they are based on qualifications. Even apart from cultural background, self-nomination and changing the nomination from or to oneself require some practice, since those are tied to emotional baggage around how we see ourselves in the group. If it is possible, name those feelings and share them. The more information is on the table, the better the group will be able to hold it with care and respond to it if they choose to.

Can there be objections in a selection process?

There can be objections to any proposal, and selection proposals are no exception.

Let's remind ourselves that objecting means that we have a concern that carrying out the proposal will interfere with our ability to do our work. What does that mean for elections? It means exactly that: *"I have a concern that if XY takes on the role of NN, we will not be able to do our work effectively because. . ."* What reasons could there be to object to someone in a role? It helps to look back at the list of qualifications of the role. Here are a few good reasons, including what the concern is:

- *"I object to . . . being leader because I fear that . . . is too busy to be the leader of this circle. We need someone who has the capacity to pay attention. I am worried that things will slide if there is no strong leadership."*
- *"I object to . . . being delegate because I know our general circle already has a hard time scheduling meetings and . . . as a part-time worker will make it even harder. I am worried that . . . will not be able to attend GC meetings on a regular basis."*
- *"I object to . . . being the facilitator because honestly, in my judgment, . . . does not lead strongly enough and avoids conflict. I am concerned that I'd wind up feeling irritated a lot because my needs for efficiency and effectiveness would not be met."*
- *"I object to . . . being secretary because of the requirement to put minutes up in our online file system and as far as I know, . . . is not comfortable with the system. I guess at least I'd like to understand what NN's thoughts are on that."*

We might find ourselves in a position where we are asked to consent or object to someone who is not our preference. It's good to remind ourselves that in the nomination round, we are being asked about your preference. In the consent round, however, we're asked about our range of tolerance. We only object if we see our participation or the circle's success impacted by that candidate filling that role. Does, for example, selecting Victor as a facilitator potentially harm the circle's work/learning? If so, then we object. If not, then we consent. (On the emotional challenge of objecting to someone, see section 3.6.4.)

Never object based on a personal preference, for instance by saying *"I object to . . . being facilitator because I think that YY would be better in that role."* That is irrelevant information because we are not looking for the perfect candidate. Additionally, comparing people will shift the energy from an affirmative but honest process to a potentially harmful process.

If there are objections, we do not give up right away, for example by nominating a different candidate. First, we check and see if there is a way to turn the *no* into a *yes*. We do so on the basis of the objection. For example, someone might have an objection because the candidate does not have enough experience, and the group has agreed when talking about the qualifications that experience is an essential qualification in the circle's current situation. In general, the three standard ways of integrating an objection apply to selections as well.

- Modify the proposal: what can we modify? For example, if we think someone needs more experience, we make an amendment to get the candidate some extra training.
- Shorten the term: if, for example, one circle member is not convinced that someone is a good candidate to be facilitator, would the objector be willing to try that person for 3 sessions and schedule an evaluation then?
- Measure the concern: what would we need to track so you would feel better about the proposal? For example, if there is an objection on the basis of a circle member not being reliable at preparing agenda items, how would we measure that this is true?
- Combinations thereof: what strategies can we combine? Following the examples mentioned, one might give the person extra training, track how well they are preparing agenda items and fill the role for a short term.

We can follow the template for integrating objections; but at the very least, we would want to go in rounds. We try to tap into group wisdom and be gentle with each other, to find a good solution.

If the nominee themselves objects, for example for lack of experience, we can remind them that the whole group had confidence in them, and ask what they would need to be able to say yes. Their objections are addressed in the same way as other circle members' objections.

Another example: let's assume an employee, Malik, works only part-time because he is taking care of his elderly mother. That does not affect how qualified Malik is as a delegate but it could come up in the form of an objection. Let's imagine this is an international general circle scheduled across different time zones so that meetings can only happen in the afternoon, but this employee needs to leave at 3 pm because that is when the home care person leaves. Let's not forget that if we're even discussing his candidacy, it means that Malik was nominated by his peers for good reasons, for example because he is a well-respected employee with excellent communication skills and this is exactly what the circle saw the need for. If someone objects (could also be Malik himself raising this objection), this is an opportunity to put all the information on the table. An open, transparent process is a better approach than either not considering him in the first place or pretending his time constraints do not exist. Accept the reality so we can work with it, not against it. Once it is in the open in the form of an objection, it is not Malik's *flaw* but instead, it is the shared responsibility and interest of the circle to explore options. In a place of shared power, there is plenty of space to find a creative solution. Could Malik work in his home office and we accept that there might be an occasional interruption? Maybe, the circle might be able to free him up on one morning a month, and he could switch schedules so that the monthly general circle meeting time is free? If there is no good way, don't push too hard. Malik from our example was able to hear how much his skills are appreciated and he will feel the care for him in his situation.

The facilitator can nominate someone else. Since the other nominations are still on people's minds, we don't have to go through the whole process – we can just make another nomination proposal and go into a consent round.

What can we do in a very large group?

Imagine we want to select 4 people among a group of 40 people. If we go around using the usual process of nomination rounds and change round, every round is going to take too long and the contributions people make will likely be repetitive. But we want to hear everyone's input. What can we do? Here is one fairly easy tweak: everyone in the large group nominates a set number of people (for example 4) and writes their nomination on a sheet of paper. Then we ask the first person (let's call them circle member 1) in the round who they nominated. They say the name of their first nomination. We ask everyone else in the room who nominated that person as well to stand up (raise their hand). Then we ask circle member 1 to share why they nominated that person. Circle member 1 shares their reasons, and we ask everyone who feels represented completely in what they heard to sit down/take their hand down. Then ask a circle member who is still standing to share their additional reasons for nominating the same person. Again, everyone who now feels represented completely by what has been shared can sit down. We do that until everyone sits. Then we ask circle member 2 to share who they nominated (can't be the first nominee again but someone else on their list), and the whole process starts again until we have heard all the reasons and nominations, without any repetitions. We can do the same for the change round, encouraging to only speak if there is new information. The rest is the same as the regular process: the facilitator makes a proposal and we can hear objections.

We like getting this visual image of how many people nominated a nominee, and we get to hear all the reasons and at least some sense of how many people agree with those reasons as they sit down but we do not get any repetitions. Maybe not everyone will speak but everyone is represented and can speak if they do not feel completely represented either in *who* they nominated or in *why* they nominated that person. This is time-efficient, without redundant information.

A variation: after the change round, we can put the 5 people with the most nominations in a fishbowl and let them do another change round and the consent round. Other variations are possible as long as the approach and the person filling the role is accepted by consent.

Why not vote?

If we elect an individual into a role by majority vote, then the person with the most votes wins. In general, the issue with majority vote is that in its outcome, up to 49% of the votes are being ignored. In diagram 138 we show how a consent decision could have a different outcome than a majority rule election. Candidate A would win the election by a 4-3 vote (votes are indicated by the letter A or B). But in a consent process, two circle members would object and candidate A would not be selected. On the other hand, there would be no objection to candidate B. This scenario was designed to show the difference between consent and majority rule. Majority rule runs the risk of ignoring valuable information in the form of objections. Sociocracy focuses on effectiveness – enabling the whole circle to make a decision rather than having the decision be made by only some of its members. In contexts where sociocratic decision making is not the accepted practice, there are variations on voting that are more inclusive than majority rule. Describing these is beyond the scope of this book but the reader may want to explore voting alternatives such as preferential voting, approval voting, Borda Counts and others.

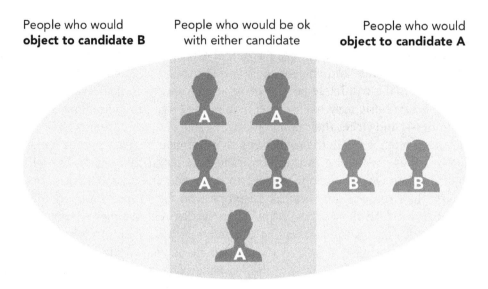

| People who would **object to candidate B** | People who would be ok with either candidate | People who would **object to candidate A** |

138: Majority vote vs. consent

What if there is a tie?

Imagine we have a group of 6 people, and 3 people nominate candidate A, and 3 people nominate candidate B. In majority vote, this would be a tie. If you are the facilitator (and you nominated one of those people) – what do you do?

For consent decision making, we have to know a little more. What is the underlying story? Do we have objections on any side like in scenario 1 below, or do we actually have consent for both candidates like in scenario 2? In scenario 1 in diagram 139, proposing candidate A will get us consent while proposing candidate B will bring objections.

The facilitator's task is to get the group to come to a decision that everyone can work with. If that is true for both candidates, great. We can also say that. *"I am guessing that both candidates could get consent from the group which shows how much skill and trust we have in this group."* Then make a decision, and be specific in your reasoning. We can go back to the qualifications and how we would prioritize them. For example, did we say we wanted to select someone who does not have a lot of experience yet? Then go with the least experienced candidate. Or is there another qualification that makes the difference? Always remember: we are looking to find a candidate that everyone can consent to. The task is *not* to find the best candidate.

We know it can be hard for groups to make a decision if it feels almost arbitrary and both candidates are good and respected. Split decisions are paralysing so any way out of a split decision is better than paralysis. We invite readers to think about it not in terms of fairness. If we try to make it fair, there is hardly a good way out. (Workarounds are typically sharing roles, taking turns etc. which we don't support without hesitation.) Instead of making it fair, look at it from the organization's perspective. It is not a *problem* to have two good members who can fill a role and have the full support from their circle – it's a gift. It's the expectation that things be fair that makes it so hard, not the fact that there is a tie.

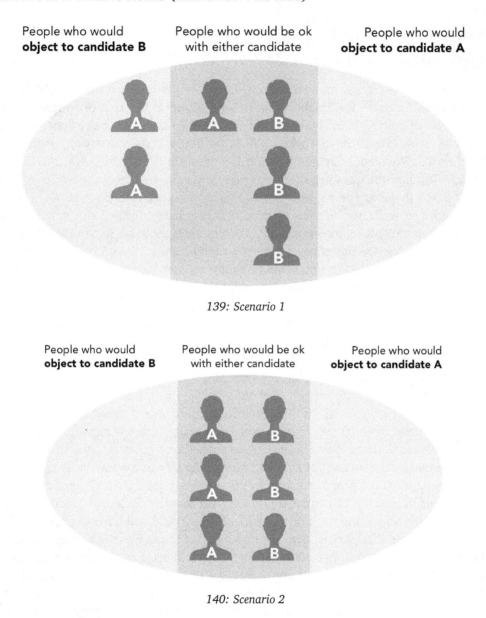

139: Scenario 1

140: Scenario 2

Another aspect of this is that we do the organization – that is, ourselves – a disservice if we don't make a decision or spend too much time on a decision that falls between *good enough* and *safe enough*. Sometimes doing *something* is better.

If it seems worth-while, we can have the two candidates talk to each other, ideally with the circle present. The potential catch here is that internalized patterns around power will be strong in that kind of situation – it will be more likely for a person with less perceived privilege or power to "give up" the role. After the candidates' conversation, the facilitator makes a proposal based on the new information circle members have heard.

3.6.4 Emotional challenges

Triggering someone's feelings

Let's imagine the nominee is not your preference. Or you actually object because XYZ's facilitation style does not work for you. You might feel torn – speak up at the cost of triggering feelings or consent at the cost of holding back relevant information – the fact that you're concerned about the circle's ability to work toward its aim when XYZ is facilitating. As a first step, detach from your personal preference. We want to remember that the question is not *"do I want this circle member to fill the role?"* Instead, the question is: *"If this person fills the role, does that affect you negatively in doing your job?"* If the answer is yes, then we *have* to object. But how do we object when it is someone you know well, maybe even a friend? This is hard, and we can only give you some pointers – doing it might still be uncomfortable. The first thought to keep in mind is that we are not objecting to a person. We are objecting to a person filling a role. We can love a person dearly but their competence in leading, facilitation or writing minutes just does not match the job description. In order to give useful feedback or to object, we will have to be specific. What could that person do differently so it *would* work for us?

Let us tell a personal story here. A friend of mine was nominated for facilitator. I was not happy. I did not want her to be facilitator. I was sitting with the judgment of *"whenever she facilitates, we never get anything done. Her style is too loose, and we'll go round and round the circle without outcome"*. I was judging, not seeing what my own needs are. That lack of clarity kept me from giving constructive feedback. If we are clear about what *we* need, we can make a request and give very clear input that is easy to hear. In this scenario, it could sound like this: *"You all know about me that I value effective meetings. I get impatient when things are not moving, and I realize I get more impatient more easily than most of you. I am concerned that it will be hard for me to sit through meetings. Can we make a deal? I am fine with XYZ facilitating if I can voice when things are moving too slowly for me and be sure I am heard and considered."* I did not object to XYZ, instead our circle just grew in mutual understanding. Of course, if I do not trust that the circle will support me, or if XYZ's facilitation style really affects my work or the work of the circle, I will have to address it differently. The important pointer in this story is: own your own perceptions, feelings and needs first. There is a huge difference between these two statements: *"Your facilitation is muddy and ineffective"* vs. *"I want facilitation to be clear and crisp so I don't lose track of what we're doing, and only that makes it possible for me to be productive in meetings. Therefore I am not confident that XYZ has the capacity to facilitate this circle."* Another way to look at it is that feedback may trigger another person's hurt feeling but the feedback is not the cause. The cause of the pain is the receiver's interpretation. Feedback, when delivered with care, is a gift.

"What about me?"

In the nomination process, it is hard for some if they are not nominated. It might remind them of childhood experiences of being one of the last to be picked for a team. They experience selection process as a trial where the case is *"do my peers know/like me enough to nominate me?"* A selection process is not a popularity contest and neither is it a process that needs to spread appreciation evenly. The circle is trying to fill a role, that's all.

We can take a deep breath and see what we do with the feedback that our skills are not visible to the group. We can nominate ourselves.

(A new group may do a round on what history they bring to the selection process. In a safe group, we strongly encourage being vulnerable. It is possible to say something like *"this selection process was hard for me. I wanted my name to be among the nominations, and I wanted to be needed and considered. I understand that this is not about popularity but I do want to let you know that this was hard."* We could even ask for a quick round of people telling us what we bring to the circle or ask for suggestions about how we could improve your skills so that people would feel confident proposing us for that role in the future. That's a matter of 5-10 minutes of meeting time. Why would it be worth spending those 5 minutes? Because it creates a sense of connection, trust and respect in the circle which is the basis for your collaboration. If we wanted to do a community-building exercise to build trust, we'd be very willing to spend the time on that – so why not go with a real moment? If all circle members learn over time that they can be vulnerable with each other, they can make an immense contribution to the organization.

Facilitator bias

Another challenge comes up if the facilitator is attached to a particular outcome. In that case, the facilitator can acknowledge that bias and can ask someone else to facilitate that part of the meeting. Anyone who owns being biased will earn trust from any group. *"My dear friend/... is being nominated here, I don't feel confident that I can do an unbiased job here. Roxanne, could you facilitate this election?"*

The facilitator can also go through the process and then leave the proposal to someone else. *"Victor, would you be willing to make a selection proposal?"* In the long run, this will have a healing and connecting effect on any group. Often, the tension disappears once it is acknowledged.

If a facilitator repeatedly makes proposals that are uncomfortable for the circle, that feedback should be shared in the meeting evaluation or a separate performance/role improvement review. Any member of the circle can say that they are uncomfortable about an election process because they perceive facilitation bias or they can object to the person the facilitator proposes on the grounds that the proposal was not based on the strongest reasons.

Feelings will come up, no matter what

We can easily forget that volunteering and majority vote come with emotional challenges as well. However, we are so used to considering voting "fair" that we do not acknowledge that. Just imagine what it feels like to get only one vote while there is a head to head race between two candidates who both got more than six votes.

Sociocracy does not magically make everything comfortable and easy, and it cannot make emotional triggers disappear. What the sociocratic process *can* do, however, is give space to talk about one's feelings and interpretations. That requires a lot of maturity, and we are aware of that. To us, this is part of the package and preconditions of doing sociocracy successfully. Selection processes are another example where people are given "air time" to voice their feedback and opinions. Circle members still have to be brave enough to do it. The decision-making process does not do it for them in some magical way. However, what we notice is that groups can grow. Courage and vulnerability, alongside with kindness and honesty, are appreciated. In our training, we *always* teach sociocracy with a compassionate communication (NVC) framework as a backdrop. If the emotional challenges around any governance decision are hard for your group, we strongly recommend educating your group on communication skills. See more on this topic in section 4.

In general, we encourage groups to accept and acknowledge that feelings come up when we make decisions together. Better to be open about it than to pretend they are not there.

3.6.5   Using the selection process for other decisions

The selection process can be used for more than just to fill roles. The selection process is useful whenever we have a discrete number of choices: for example, we can do a selection process where people nominate out of a set of vacation destinations; instead of people, we nominate places.

It also works with numbers. We can do a selection process around the question *"should our membership fee be zero, $10, $20, or $50?"* Then people would nominate an amount and share reasons why they nominated that amount. After hearing everyone, do a change round: *"Having heard what you heard, what amount would you nominate now?"* The facilitator then makes a proposal and the circle is asked to consent or object. Our own community used the selection process to determine by how much the condominium fee would increase for a given year.

With a more complex grid and interdependent choices, the process can be used to assign vegetables to rows in a garden, we can select a new hire or select which construction company will renovate our store.

The first time a group uses the selection process for something that is not selecting people into roles, it may not feel as familiar but it is worth keeping selection processes in mind as another option.

> I use the selection process for complex choices that cause a lot of fear in teams. For example in IT infrastructure teams who have to choose one of several technical solutions implying a change of technology and processes which affects people in their ability to keep their jobs.
>
> (Stephane Brodu)

141: What others say

Chapter 4

Feedback and Learning

4.1 Basic concepts

Many people are afraid of feedback. *"Can I give you some feedback?"* is typically announcing criticism, and humans do not do well with criticism. When we face criticism, the most typical reaction is to shut down, get reactive, defensive or to withdraw. If we want our feedback to be heard, criticism is not going to be effective.

4.1.1 Universal human needs

Our aim as human beings is to survive and thrive. Everything we do we do to meet needs. We all have needs, met and unmet, in every moment of our lives. Not only food and shelter but also the need for connection, belonging, contribution, to be heard and seen, to matter. At the level of needs, we are all connected because all needs are universal. Needs are like the universal language everyone understands.

Although all human beings can relate to all those needs, the priority those needs have for someone will vary from moment to moment. If generally, we would say we are not someone for whom harmony is a priority, a painful disagreement with a family member might bring out our need for harmony to a higher priority.

In diagram 142, we can imagine the same individual in different situations. Cooperation is a need that tends to rise for that person, but it can be trumped by other needs, depending on what is going on. On the other hand, if we imagine the same diagram showing the same situation for different individuals, it shows how the same situation can bring up different needs for different people. The point is that needs are at the same time universal – everyone has them – and highly personal and situational.

Table 143 shows a list of the most common needs.

4.1.2 Personal strategies

What we choose to do to *meet needs* is referred to as *strategy*. Strategies are not good or bad. But some are more effective than others, and that depends on the context. Going to the movies is an

142: Different needs take priority in different moments

Universal needs list

Connection
Acceptance
Affection
Clarity
Communication
Confirmation
Compassion
Intimacy
Understanding
Love

Autonomy
Choice Space
Spontaneity

Peace
Beauty
Ease
Harmony
Order
Wholeness

Interconnection
Belonging
Consideration
Community
Cooperation
Dignity
Mutuality
Support
Trust

Meaning
Contribution
Creativity
Hope
Inspiration
Purpose

Celebration
Joy
Mourning
Play

Competence
Effectiveness
Efficiency
Growth
Learning
Power

Honesty
Authenticity
Integrity

Basic Survival
Shelter
Food & Water
Rest
Safety
Security
Touch

143: A partial list of universal needs. The list is also on the meeting sheet for facilitators in the appendix on page 262 and we are providing a list including feelings in the appendix on page 260.

effective way of meeting the need for connection for some people. For some it is not, and they would choose to do something else to meet their need for connection. When we are not aware of our needs behind our strategies, it is very easy to get side-tracked into astonishingly ineffective strategies. Have you ever steamed out of a room, upset because what you really needed was connection? Leaving the room does not seem to be an effective strategy to get connection. Or when we yell at children because what we need is quiet? This is neither right or wrong in a moral sense, but it certainly is not effective.

Movies or dinner out – we can argue over strategies. But who can argue with the need for connection? *All* humans share this need. And that is true for every universal need, like stimulation, autonomy, cooperation, love, or the need to be seen. Our basic set of universal needs is probably roughly the same between people, we just differ in how important some needs are for us in the moment. On strategy-level, there is a lot more variation. What works for us might not work for someone else. There is no 1:1 relation between needs and strategies. The same need can be met by different strategies. For example my need to be seen can be met by writing a post on social media, or by having a conversation with a neighbor. And a strategy can meet several needs, for example the conversation with a neighbor can meet my need for stimulation, for connection, or for belonging.

4.1.3 Feelings: you can't make me angry

Feelings are pointers to met or unmet needs. We all walk around having needs that bubble up. What happens if a need is not being met, for example our need for connection? We might get sad. Or mad. Unmet needs will trigger feelings. On the flipside, when an important need is met, we might feel happy: when we get an unexpected phone call from a friend in a moment when connection was what we were longing for, we will probably feel happy or excited. There is a list of feelings in the appendix together with the needs list on page 260.

Feelings are caused by met or unmet needs, not by situations. That means that no one and nothing can directly cause your feelings. *"You made me angry"* is not an accurate description of what is going on. Let's look at the figure in 144. Something happens and we react to what we *hear*, not to what has been said or done. We see and hear everything through a layer of interpretation. But for this chapter, it is even more important to see the next step, what happens *after* we receive (and interpret) a message. Consciously, or unconsciously, we evaluate. How does what happened to contribute to my needs being met or not met? It is the evaluation that triggers the feelings.

If our interpretation remains on the level of feelings or strategies, we cannot find out what is really going on. Going to the level of needs enables us to make more informed guesses about what might be an effective strategy. Sometimes people who hear about non-violent communication fear that they will "not be allowed to say what is really going on". The opposite is true for us. Feelings and observable strategies are merely surface phenomena. Since needs are underlying everything we do and feel, talking about needs *is* talking about what is really going on. Some people who start learning about needs and feelings consider this semantics. The fact that feelings are not directly caused by others, however, creates space for choice. Seeing the difference between strategies, needs and feelings creates space for inner freedom, and an opportunity for change.

4.1.4 Requests

Requests are when we ask someone to do something. The more specific and doable a request is, the more likely it will be effective. The other person is *invited* to say *yes*. We naturally want to contribute and because we also want choice, we naturally resist demands.

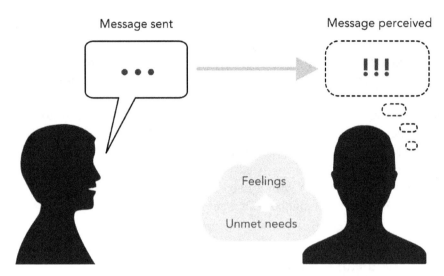

144: Feelings are triggered by messages but not caused by them.

Non-violent communication (NVC) makes a distinction between action requests and connection requests that is very useful to organizational life. Action requests are simply that – *"would you make copies of this form? Would you call that potential donor or customer?"* Sometimes action requests are requests for collaboration: *"Would you help me brainstorm ideas for a new webinar series on sociocracy? Would you be willing to sit with me and talk about how we could improve our relationship?"*

The only reason anyone would ever say no to a request to contribute to our needs is that they are saying yes to meeting their own needs. The *no* becomes the invitation to connection – a mutual understanding of each other's needs. Therefore, there are two kinds of connection requests. To be understood: *"Would you be willing to tell me whatever you heard me say?"* To understand: *"Would you be willing to tell me what comes up for you when you hear what I said?"* Imagine what we could accomplish if (a) we could eliminate misunderstandings and (b) hear each other more empathically!

4.2 Creating change

Change comes from evaluating past actions and experimenting with new approaches we hope will be more effective at meeting needs. This is the *lead* function in the *lead – do – measure* cycle. Feedback useful for the change process emerges much more from curiosity about universal needs underlying behavior than from unexamined right-or-wrong thinking.

4.2.1 Beyond right and wrong lies creativity

When we are friends with someone, we want to hear when their need for connection is not met and they feel lonely (or whatever they might be feeling). It is not anyone's "fault" if they are lonely. Everyone's needs are their own, and the responsibility to meet them is no one's but theirs. They have a need for connection, and there are many strategies to meet that need. One of the strategies would be to call a friend and talk. Another strategy would be for them to look at old pictures. Or to spend time on social media, go out to dance or call their sister. Only they can pick and choose what might work for them in that moment.

> *If you want to live in absolute hell, believe that you are responsible for what other people feel.*

> Marshall Rosenberg

Let's say a coworker calls. I do not like talking on the phone. Talking on the phone for me simply does not work as a strategy in most cases. Maybe it is because my hearing is not good, so listening without visual cues is straining. I am also concerned that talking in my shared office space will interfere with my colleague's focus. I also don't like being interrupted because I enjoy the flow state of focused work. What works well for me is messaging. So I do not answer the phone but I message back. My coworker, however, prefers talking on the phone. For her, not a fast typer, it is more effective to talk on the phone than to message back and forth. She might get annoyed when I don't answer the phone but message back. Did I *make* her upset? No. Her being upset is her reaction to her own needs for connection. My messaging instead of answering her phone call is *my* way of meeting *my* needs for ease, flow and consideration. Now what?

If we have no awareness of needs, both sides might be rolling their eyes and have thoughts like *"why doesn't he just answer the phone instead of making it so complicated by messaging back and forth?"* and *"why is she interrupting me by calling all the time. Does she think she is the only person working here?"* What can we do to meet our needs more effectively? We can give feedback based on our needs. The first step is to share our experience.

> Hey, thanks for messaging back when I called but I prefer talking on the phone because it's faster and helps me get clarity.

> Messaging is easier for me because I was in such a good flow state. And I did not want to interfere with my colleague's focus who I knew was having a tough issue to work on.

145: Sharing your experience with reference to needs.

In example 145, notice how both people are able to share their experience without labeling the other person or even talking about the other person. Once that first step of mutual understanding is complete, the path is open to a shared decision. With everyone's needs on the table, a strategy may be found that works for everyone. Maybe arrange a time to talk on the phone? Leaving the office to talk on the phone while the co-worker needs space? If the issue comes up more often, maybe re-thinking the shared office space?

We are rarely short on strategies once we have clarity about needs. The more information we have, the more we are in choice about what strategy works best in that moment.

4.2.2 Effective feedback

What other people do affects how well our needs can be met. This is important feedback for others. In sharing your observations and interpretations, we are sharing what the impact of someone's actions or words is on us. If we tell other people that they are "wrong" or "mean", they will probably stop listening.

Instead of saying *"you make me upset when you don't answer the phone"*, saying something like *"when I try to call and don't get through, I get upset and anxious when I am not productive when my questions aren't answered"* is more adequate to what happened. In the latter version, the person is talking about their own experience. Constructive feedback is feedback that

- shares information
- can be heard
- fosters connection

No one has access to absolute truth, thus we strive not to present what we say as absolute truth. What we all do have access to is what we can observe, what we interpret or project (both needs to be marked as such) and what the impact is on us. All of those are data that the other person can work with.

Feedback that can be heard is feedback that is free of blame. Any added layer of blame will cover up the data we want to be known. Making sure that the other person is in a good enough place to receive the feedback is part of that as well. An easy way to do that is to ask something like:

- *"I am sitting on some judgment here. Are you open to hearing it? And if yes, now or at another time?"*
- *"I have been observing something. I might be wrong but I thought maybe it might help you to hear what I have been thinking. Do want to hear it?"*

Keep in mind that although what we say matters, just saying the words will not be enough. Only when it is truly felt, will it be genuine and effective. People have a very fine radar and can sense judgment underneath anything we say, no matter how "nice" our words might be.

Effective feedback

1. Check whether the person is open to hearing the feedback.

2. Express your feedback describing
   (a) your observations
   (b) your interpretations
   (c) how your needs are met or unmet
   (d) your request

3. Be curious about the other person's thoughts, feelings and needs that arise in response to your feedback.

146: Effective feedback

If done skillfully (and received with an open heart), feedback between people can be a way to foster connection in two ways.

- Contribution. If it is mutually acknowledged that the more information we have, the more easily and successfully we can collaborate, then giving someone feedback is a way to contribute to their well-being.
- Mattering. If someone shares how my behavior has an impact on *them*, it shows that we are connected and interdependent. What I do *matters* to someone else, and what *they* do matters to me.

Do not use recommendations to act as "NVC police". A statement like *"what you said was not good NVC"* undermines everything NVC stands for. A statement like that serves to judge and criticize, and it shuts people down.

If we feel like we are in a good enough place to receive feedback in person, we have to remember that the other person has to be in a good enough place. Check whether they are able and willing to receive first. Then we say what we want to say.

A feedback form can provide a frame for giving feedback in writing. Then begin the dance of mutual understanding. *"I want to make sure I am communicating clearly. Would you be willing to tell me what you heard me say?"* If the reflection is inaccurate, say *"thank you for letting me know what you heard. What I was trying to say was a little different. Can I try again?"* Then *"thank you, that is what I was trying to say. Now I am curious. Would you be willing to tell me what comes up for you having heard what I said?"* You might then confirm what you heard. *"So, this is what I heard you say. . . Is that right?"* Notice that you are confirming that message sent is message received in both directions. This back and forth communication can continue until both have a sense of being understood.

Once mutual understanding is present, then the space is open for making requests of each other that could improve communication and connection going forward.

Box 147 is an example of a feedback form that was used in an organization (slightly changed for privacy). Every organization can agree on additional ways to give (and receive) feedback. If using a feedback form is already an agreed-upon strategy in an organization, it will be easier to do it when we want to actually do it. In the appendix on page 261 is an example of what a practice sheet and feedback form could look like. Any organization might want to design their own. It is a good idea to put the pointers about what to keep in mind for filling out a feedback form right on the form. Remember that everyone who fills out a feedback form will be in a triggered state in some way, so making it as easy as possible for them to act in an effective, constructive manner is key here.

Even if the person is not ready to receive your feedback, it still makes sense to put something in writing and share it. In that case, the inner peace and clarity may come with exploring and expressing our unmet needs. Our clarity may have a positive effect on your interaction with the other person even though they have never seen our feedback.

Being able to give feedback and to do it skillfully comes with practice. We can practice by starting with only appreciations and expressing how your needs have been met – for example when someone fixes a computer problem for us. What need did that meet? Ease because we were able to access our emails? Integrity because we were able to meet a deadline because of the computer

EXAMPLE
A feedback form

What I heard (observations)
I heard a tone of sarcasm when you spoke in our circle meeting. It was hard for me to translate what I heard as sarcasm into the heartfelt content underneath. I went into a shut-down reaction.

What I was hoping for *(needs)*
I want to hear when important values are at stake for you. For myself, I want to be treated with respect even when you disagree with what I said.

What would help me now *(request)*
Would you be willing to review with me what happened at the meeting and see if we can reach mututal understanding? Then I'd love to explore how we might hear each other more effectively in the future.

147: A feedback form. See page 261 for a template

help? Or consideration because that coworker noticed how urgently we needed help?

Practice giving feedback, in person or in written form. It might be a good idea to use a feedback form for the next small incident so that we can reduce anxiety about using it for bigger issues. Giving feedback is like a muscle that can be trained. Do it!

4.3 Compassionate governance is effective

It is the basic, revolutionary, insight from NVC that in using strategies to meet universal needs, there is no right and wrong, only more or less effective strategies. Since needs are not right or wrong (they just are a part of being human), attempts to meet them cannot be wrong or right, they are just more or less effective. Effectiveness is the measure in governance *and* in non-violent communication. Feelings provide data on how well strategies that we choose meet the needs of the people who are affected.

The key to continuous improvement is feedback. Feedback is the information we need to learn, adapt, improve, change. Whether it's feelings or click rates, good governance will strive for effectiveness by taking in all the accessible data.

4.3.1 Aims and policy

We form organizations in order to meet needs as stated in our vision and mission. The strategies we choose to work towards that mission are our aims.

Proposals, like requests, are proposed strategies to meet needs. When people commit to the requests, they are policies. Examples are *"please put all recycling into this bin. Upload your files to this folder. Go through these steps to approve a new member."*

Only feedback (data) can tell us whether policy achieves what it is intended to do.

Requests (NVC)	Policy (sociocracy)
Requests are strategies to meet needs.	Proposals are strategies in support of accomplishing aims.
There are many possible strategies to meet a need.	There are many possible strategies to carry out an aim.
We do not know whether fulfilling a request will meet a need; it is only a guess. We need feedback to find out how effective our strategy is.	We do not know whether acting on policy will meet the aim; it is only a guess. We need feedback to find out how effective our policy is.

148: Requests and proposals

4.3.2   Personal aims and the organization's aim

It is interesting to think about how the organization's need and people's needs relate to each other. In joining an organization, we respond to a need of ours. Getting paid for our work may help meet our survival needs. But there are other needs at play. It could be wanting to contribute, or the need for connection. The "need" of the organization is to contribute to the organization's mission. Every strategy – every operation and every policy – serves the organization's aims. We often ask people about their personal aims in an organization to explore the relationship between their personal aims and the organization's aims. The more they are in alignment, the easier it will be for the individuals to work at fulfilling the organization's aim.

Organizations are complex organisms. Many sub-aims are at play. For example, two circles might be wanting their budget increased. Although they serve the same overall aim, they disagree on strategy-level. This is similar to a person who might be at the same time experiencing a need for connection and a need for peace and quiet. As such, an organization can be just as innerly torn as a person. All needs can be taken seriously, but not all needs can be met. Personal aims and organizational aims sometimes are in synch and sometimes not. We celebrate needs met and mourn needs unmet. With transparency about both personal and organizational aims, we have the potential to work effectively toward meeting both personal needs and organizational needs.

4.3.3   Objections, and social-emotional debt

If the strategy someone is proposing does not work for everyone, this is the basis for objections. Instead of calmly stating an objection, it may happen that someone gets upset. Imagine a proposal like in example 149.   If we fear we may have to leave the organization because we cannot afford the membership fees, we might get sad, anxious or upset because our need for belonging would not be met. Once we identify the need(s) that are unmet, we will be able to object and put the unmet

> I think we should raise the membership fees drastically so we can hire someone part-time to deal with this.

> Raise the membership fees?! Are you kidding me? You can't do that, that's so unfair!

149: A proposal and a reaction

> I think we should raise the membership fees drastically so we can hire someone part-time to deal with this.

> Wow, the moment you said that, I noticed my blood pressure rise. I think what is at stake for me here is that this group gives me a lot. It's community, almost like family. I am worried that I might not be able to afford a higher membership fee. I am also worried that other people might not be able to afford it, and inclusiveness is very important to me.

150: Upset and still easy to listen to

needs on the table so they can be considered.

What is the difference between example 149 and 150? In the first example, there is no inner distance from the feelings. They are interpreted as absolute truth, not as data to work with. The opportunity to use the feelings as an indicator of a need gets concealed, and we have to restore trust and respect in the group. Since restoring trust and respect takes time, we have lost time and energy in two ways: by losing track of valuable data, and by creating "social-emotional debt" that is likely to negatively impact the quality of connection in the future.

We call social-emotional debt the many micro and macro interactions where people experience their needs not considered. Whether or not that is true is not relevant. Unaddressed, this debt builds up over time and creates more and more interpersonal friction.

Everyone is responsible for the social-emotional debt – the people who chose not to speak up or did not speak up effectively, *and* the people who chose a strategy without considering more people's needs and did not ask for feedback.

It is a reality of humanity that feelings come up. If we ignore them, they will leak. People will be sarcastic, discouraged, disengaged. They will withdraw, lack accountability, work to rule, slow down, or undermine the system. Ignoring needs, ignoring feedback has a high long-term cost.

We may not get input from circle members that is as clear as in example 150. But we can work together to complete the picture. A skillful group will be able to deal with *"something here leaves me anxious but I can't put my finger on it"* and will guess the underlying needs. A more advanced group will be able to deal with the raw feeling, will help the group member to center, identify their needs and formulate their concern. The question is not whether feelings are allowed in organizations but how we make use of them.

- Are group members able to be respectful and responsible even if they are emotionally triggered?
- How effectively can we go from experiencing feelings to naming our underlying concerns?
- Are we able to let our decision making be informed by concerns or objections people bring up, so we can make better decisions?

4.4   Increasing feedback

4.4.1   Short feedback loops

We need to check on our data frequently enough to be able to steer successfully. On a social level, short feedback loops reduce the building of social-emotional debt. For our operations, the same is true to be effective. Once feedback is nothing but data, all ways of gathering and receiving data and personal feedback are the same. We have already talked about the process of *lead – do – measure* and how it forms feedback loops that support the evolution: we make a plan, we carry it out, and we evaluate what we can learn. Steering falls into countless loops of *lead – do – measure*. A few examples are in 151.

	Lead	**Do**	**Measure**
policy	make policy	carry out policy	review policy
meetings	plan meeting	carry out meeting	evaluate meeting
workflow	plan workflow	carry out work flow	evaluate work flow
feedback	feedback considered	feedback given	feedback received?

151: Examples for feedback loops

Sociocracy highlights the importance of feedback and evaluation; to steer, to lead is to continually make new plans based on the data analysis. Out of *lead – do – measure*, we typically do a good job on the *doing*. We can often get ourselves to *lead/plan* – but taking the time to evaluate is done too seldom. The diagram in 153 shows how *lead – do – measure* happens on very different scales but its nature is always the same. Sociocracy creates habits around giving feedback, which we fledge out as milestones in this book – intentional stops to make sure we have shared reality. We showed how in policy-making, a group can move swiftly from one phase to the next if we measure whether a phase or step is completed.

4.4.2   Hearing from as many as possible – while keeping groups small

In sociocracy, we want to learn as much as we can and work with all the data we can access to feed into our decision making. We also try to keep the groups who make decisions to a reasonable group size so that all member voices can be heard. A critical aspect of sociocracy is clarity about membership in policy-making circles: every circle has authority over who its members are. Decisions are made through deliberation among people who have made a commitment to work together toward a shared aim. It is crucial to understand the difference between "hearing everyone's feedback" and "including everyone in the decision making". Sociocracy clearly says *yes* to getting as much feedback as your circle can handle, while keeping decision making within the circle that is responsible for the particular content.

What's the difference between being able to give feedback and being a decision-maker? If a membership circle makes a decision to significantly raise membership fees, they might want to hear from people outside the circle about that. They might even want to survey their entire membership. However, that only means that this circle now has more information. They are not bound to anything but to inviting and taking in the feedback they get.

In an organization that is new to sociocracy, be very clear on the difference between "being heard" and "being involved in the decision making". Sometimes when we ask people for their input, they take it personally if you decide different from their advice, even if you have honestly considered their input. That's where transparency comes in: *why* did we decide the way we decided? It helps to let people know the rationale for our decisions if we think it is relevant and that it could be contributing to people's understanding. The strength of sociocracy comes with the ability to make decisions effectively in small groups while including a lot of data through gathering feedback.

4.4.3   Input and information processing

The path from issue to action does not have to be walked alone by the circle, it can include many people or only a few, varying for each step, depending on what's needed. The process is extremely flexible because at any stage (except the consent decision), any number of people can collaborate. We can get input from hundreds of people, or a proposal can be written up by one single individual.

152: Lead–do–measure-loops continue indefinitely as we work toward the aim

meeting
(evaluation)

circle role
improvement

policy
review

aim
review

153: Lead – do – measure happens on different levels of scale

On a general level, in the *understand–explore–decide* (also know as more generally *input–trans-formation–output*) pattern, it is the easiest to include many people in the input/understanding phase, only a few people in the explore phase and fewer people in the phase of decision or synthesis. A circle moves a policy along the path from assessing the need to making a decision. We can use a wider group for input and to craft a proposal in a small helping circle.

Understand/input phase: In the input phase, we want the input from many perspectives to get a good idea of what is going on. We want to gather data, survey and so on. However, we also want to be focused on our question, otherwise we will get a lot of noise to work through. For example, if we ask a group of 200,000 users *"tell us whether you see issues with our new website"*, we will get a lot of unstructured feedback. If we ask many people, we have to focus on few, specific questions, for example, how long users stay on the new website compared to the old one. If we only ask three test users, we can process much more detailed data but we will only get to hear few perspectives. (See next section for more.)

Transformation/explore phase: In the exploration phase, we want deliberation to happen. Deliberation requires trust in a group of people who know each other well. If we want to deliberate and build on each other's thoughts, we have to be in relationship with each other. That's why the transformation phase works best in a medium-sized group like a circle of 4-7 people. This circle is going to process the input and build on it, based on trust and on hearing each other.

- a change round in a selection
- a consent round and integrating objections
- exploring needs underlying an issue

Synthesize/output phase: Output often requires writing. It is easiest to write along or in a small group. Form a helping circle or delegate to an individual tasks like:

- writing up a proposal
- writing up a needs statement
- synthesizing ideas

The consent round is the only phase where we are firm about who gets to be included and who does not. All circle members are included in the consent round and no one else. If you have non-circle members present for a consent decision and you are willing to spend extra time, you could to ask the visitors *"If you had consent rights on this proposal, would you consent or object and why?"*. Have the visitors speak before the circle members – they may have valuable input for the decision. Sociocracy has an intent to include as many voices as possible for input but it is clear on who the decision-makers are.

4.4.4   Who to ask for input

If a circle would like to get feedback about a decision (before or after the decision), options are:

- Interview key individuals inside or outside the organization; key because of their knowledge, their strong opinion, their role in the organization etc.
- Survey a segment of the membership or people outside the organization that might have relevant input. Use qualitative questions, quantitative questions, or a combination of both.
- Invite non-circle members to add dimensions in picture forming or clarifying questions about proposals. Do this in open organizational meetings, on bulletin boards or on online documents.
- They can ask another circle for input (see diagram in 154).

  - A sibling circle, for example if the topic is close or touches the other circle's. domain
  - A more specific circle, if that circle might have some more expertise on the topic.
  - The parent circle if the circle is looking for a broader perspective on the topic.
  - A helping circle.

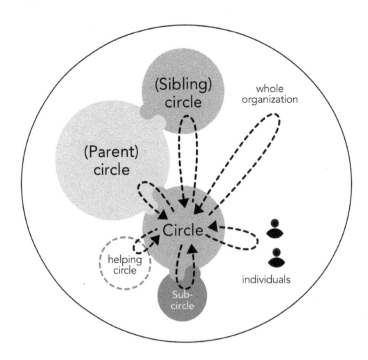

154: The circle-internal support and feedback system – any circle can be asked for help

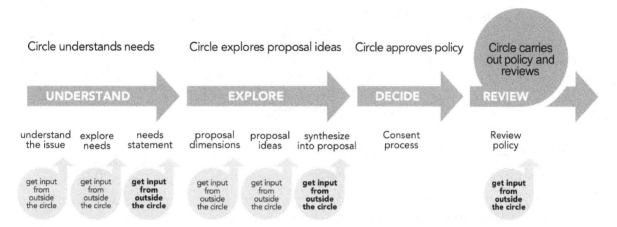

155: *Moments to gather input from outside the circle during the policy process; best moments in bold.*

We encourage every circle to make use of the internal support system but also to reach out outside the organization – we do not have to know everything ourselves.

Surveying the membership is not about involving everyone affected by a decision into *making* that decision. The circle who holds the domain makes the decision. But it *is* about gathering enough input to make a good decision. The small group mandate is based on trust -- an organization trusts a small group of people to make decisions in their domain for everyone. This trust is earned through decisions that take input and feedback from other people in the organization into deep consideration.

4.4.5   When to ask during the policy process

During the policy process, there are good moments to include voices from outside of the circle. Diagram 155 shows the policy process. Theoretically, we can get input all along, every step of the way. A circle will only choose to do so when that is reasonable.

- For a big decision, it might make sense to get input from outside people on the context and the needs statement to make sure the circle is stating the issue in a comprehensive way.
- Gathering dimensions (either in the *understand* phase or during picture forming) is also a good moment to ask for outside help, especially if the circle does not feel confident to have a clear understanding of the scope of the issue and the policy needed.
- The most important time to get feedback is when there is an actual proposal on the table (at the end of the *explore* phase). The more concrete something is, the easier it is to give feedback on it, so the proposal draft is ideal for getting specific input. Of course, in order to ask feedback, there must be a way to ask clarifying questions as well (since that is part of getting feedback).

During the consent process, the circle is best on their own, holding all the input they have heard leading up to this phase in their consideration. After the policy is approved and carried out, the circle will gather feedback on how the policy contributes to the circle's performance.

4.4.6   Metrics in policy evaluation

Any intentional decision on *"how do we do our work"* is policy. How do we evaluate policy? The metrics depend on what kind of policy it is. If the policy is around workflow, we can measure production or lead time, quality, count inputs and outputs. If the policy is more in the realm of "code of conduct", we can count complaints, survey happiness and so on. We have already talked about metrics in section 3.5 on *measure the concern* around objections.

Feedback while the policy is in place

Become intentional about metrics and make a measurement plan. (See also page 120.)

- We think about what metrics we want to measure (and if necessary, we start collecting the data). We collect the data that we think is useful. Examples:
  - If we make a landing page to drive website traffic to our main site, we make sure the flow of website visitors from the landing page to our main page will be tracked right away. That way, we will be able to evaluate the effectiveness very early.
  - If we are trying to reduce the hours you spend scheduling phone calls, we can count the emails sent back and forth for the sake of scheduling to see if buying scheduling software would be a benefit.
- We ask for the feedback we want: we can tell people (1) what the policy is, (2) what we are seeking input on, and (3) how/when to give feedback. The people in our organization are good "sensors" for anything that can be measured qualitatively.
  - For a new membership policy that puts in place a three-month provisional membership, tell people who to send the feedback to, by what day/time feedback would be useful, and what we need to know. (*"We're particularly interested in how this new policy affects our prospective members so please let us know of reactions when you recruit new members: do they still feel welcome?"*)

Term ends

Every policy decision in sociocracy has a term end when the policy will be up for review. It keeps our policies up to date, fresh in our minds and it encourages to strive to improve in every aspect of our organization. It is like a regular check-up of our tools. All in order, all working and doing what we intend them to do?

We can be intentional about term ends and tailor them to our needs. For example, we could make new policy and consent to reviewing it again in 3 months. Or in 10 years. What an appropriate term might be for a piece of policy depends on the nature of the organization. In general, we try to make the cycles long enough to not overload our circle meetings with policy reviews. Sociocracy is about getting work done, not only about *talking* about work!

We want to be sure to keep our policies current. If we only review our policies every 10 years (or never!), we will most likely not keep them current. How many organizations have policies that they are not even aware of? We don't have policies to have them. Policy is made to support us in doing our work. Therefore, every policy has to reflect the current state of how things are being

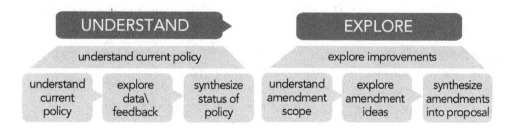

156: Understand - explore applied to policy review

done, otherwise the organization becomes stiff and ineffective. Putting a term end on policy is just a reminder to review policies. If no one sees need for changing a policy, then reviewing a policy can be done in minutes.

Policy is made to *help* people in the organization do their work. If how things are done interferes with the ability of people to fill their roles and do their work, then they need to be changed. This can happen at any time. If there is a reason to change policy, there is no reason to wait until a term is up.

How to review policy

The revision process depends on the feedback gathered on the effectiveness of the policy.

- If it is not a lot and this is just a "standard" revision because the term is up, just start with the beginning of the consent process (present the proposal, clarifying questions etc., see 3.3.2) and work your way toward consenting to a new term, possibly with modifications. If there are many objections and comments and things seem to be getting more complicated with every turn, it's good to back off and either delegate the review process to a helping circle or accept that we need a deeper evaluation.
- If the review process has to be deep because there is a lot of new data, then we treat the proposal and the data as input for a new policy-making process. We can ask a helping circle to analyze the feedback and make a recommendation on the policy. We then enter the consent process with the helping circle's proposal.
- If we have a sense that our policy is not working at all, we can start from scratch. The original proposal and the data collected is now just data for the initial description of the issue. We will now have to look at underlying needs (met/unmet), generate a new needs statement, and go into policy-making. We let the current policy inform our process. We might come up with a completely new approach, given the new information and more experience gained, or we might just make tweaks to the existing policy. A 3x3 chart of this is shown in chart 207 in the appendix.

Reviewing policy follows the familiar steps of understanding current policy, exploring possible amendments and consenting to the modified policy, as shown in diagram 156.

Expressing an objection with reference to a need also gives the circle information on how to address the objection because it points toward a direction: *"How could we amend/change/test the policy to be sure your need can be met?"* Here are a few examples, similar to the ones already mentioned in section 3.5 on objections

- *"I am concerned that if we form another sub-circle, we might be stretched too thin. I am worried that we won't be able to do our work well when our plate is so full."*
- *"I object to this proposal because it lacks information about how we will be able to get prepared on time. I want to make sure I have peace of mind that we'll be able to complete the project on time."*
- *"My objection to this proposal is that if we require bike helmets on scooters and not only on bikes, then no one will take it seriously which will undermine the purpose of this policy. So I have a concern about practicability and ultimately about safety."*
- *"I object because I see no sense in adding a bureaucratic layer. The advantage of this step does not justify the extra work for everyone."*

4.5   Meeting evaluations

How satisfied are we with the product of the meeting? With the process of the meeting? With the interpersonal dynamics?

At the end of every meeting, we evaluate our meeting (preferably in a round). Each person says how the meeting worked for them. If we look at it from a needs/feelings perspective, we all are sharing how well the meeting (a strategy to do work together) met our needs. Did the meeting meet our need for productivity? For connection? Did it give us clarity or maybe companionship? Or maybe we created a policy that contributes to our need for safety or harmony? We can also share feelings that go along with the met needs, for example *"I am happy about how productive the meeting was"*, or *"I was anxious before the meeting, wondering whether the agenda was too full, and now I am relieved that we got through all the agenda items."*

What do we do with "negative" feedback? We share it as well. Better said in the room than as gossip afterwards.

Below are some examples of how to express our meeting evaluation, with a self-awareness of our feelings and needs and without blame, just talking about our own experience with no expectation that we are accessing any absolute truth. Which needs were met:

- *"I enjoyed this meeting because it seemed efficient. I particularly liked how you kept us on topic when we wandered off."*
- *"I am glad about our decision and the sense of integrity it gives me."*
- *"To me, it seems like there was balance in how much each of us contributed, so there was quality and harmony and flow, and I like that."*
- *"I want to appreciate Xiang for giving me space to express myself when I had the objection, everyone made an effort to understand where I was coming from. Thank you."*
- *"This was a fun meeting for me. Stimulating, productive. I felt connected and that really works for me."*
- *"I appreciate that all the agenda items were well prepared. Thank you for that!"*

Which needs were not met:

- *"This meeting was very effective but I would have wished for more connection and time for reflection."*
- *"I noticed some crosstalk in the meeting with people speaking out of turn and that makes it hard for me to be focused. I like the sense of equality and the calmness that comes with rounds. I don't enjoy when I feel like I have to compete to be heard."*
- *"The meeting did not work for me at all. I am curious to hear how other people experienced the meeting but I know that I was sitting with a lot of confusion because I was not really sure what we were doing. I think more structure would help me."*
- *"It was hard for me to be around the vibes of hostility during the meeting. I am not sure whether that is what was going on but that's how it landed on me."*

If we notice patterns around topics that come up during meeting evaluations, we put them on the backlog so they can be tackled. For example, if half of the group is chronically late to meetings, then that might come up in the meeting evaluation the secretary can put topics onto the backlog during the meeting evaluation for a future meeting. The same is true if some people engage in a lot of cross-talk or if meetings are not prepared well. We use the feedback to improve our meetings. Then the leader and facilitator can take it from there when they prepare the next meeting.

4.6 Performance reviews

Performance reviews bring in feedback from the people who know us best in our organization: our coworkers. The person whose performance is reviewed is called the *focus person*. (Note: it can also be an entire circle who is in the focus.) The performance review cycle starts with informing, inviting and scheduling the members of the performance review circle (aka assessment circle). They develop an action plan of how the focus person can improve. It ends with a decision by the focus person's circle to accept the improvement plan.

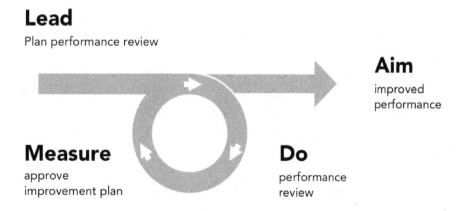

157: Lead–do–measure for performance review

4.6.1   Who is in the performance review circle?

The first step is to have the right people in the room. The aim of a performance review is to give feedback to the focus person in their role(s) in the organization. We can do a performance review in our circle if we are only part of one circle. The performance review can also be done by a group of members who do not usually form a circle. For people in linking roles (leader or delegate), we need the perspective of all circle layers we are a part of. If there is substantial interaction to another circle (for example in a hand-off to a more specific "sub"-circle), then one or two members from that circle can be invited to the performance review. The idea is that every level relating to the focus person is represented. Not everyone in a related circle needs to be invited, keeping the group to a workable group size.

4.6.2   Format

A performance review can take place in a separate meeting, or it can be integrated into a circle meeting. The focus person:

- Determines the members of the performance review.
- Sets a date and time for the performance review.
- Proposes a facilitator.
- Gives the members of the performance review access to relevant documents (previous improvement plans, role descriptions etc).

The feedback circle will come up with an improvement plan. The improvement plan is like any other proposal. Since a performance review works exactly like policy-making, it also follows the same pattern. We can break the process into the usual *understand–explore–decide* (*input–transformation–output* for decision making) as shown in example 158.

We will see that in the meeting sheet for facilitators in the appendix on page 262, there is a more general format that can be done as an agenda item within a meeting.

Understand

Understand: review documents   In the *understand* phase, we review everything that needs to be known

- What *are* the role descriptions for the focus person?
- Is there other data that is relevant here, like reports or evaluations from other sources? (If they take time to read, make sure to distribute them beforehand.)

We'll do two rounds that provide more input: what has the focus person done well, and what could they have done better?

Did well   The focus person speaks first about what they have done well in the areas of production or service, process and interpersonal interaction. Then each person in the performance review circle shares their perspective on what the focus person has done well. The focus person speaks last in the round and summarizes what they heard.

Performance Review

Opening	check-in ADMIN		

Content	Consent to agenda		
		UNDERSTAND	review job description, previous improvement plans
			did well round (focus person starts and ends)
			could do better round (focus person starts and ends)
		EXPLORE	improvement areas
			improvement plan ideas (incl. term/measurements)
			write up improvement plan
		DECIDE	consent to improvement plan
	schedule follow-up		

Closing	meeting evalution		

158: A default format of a performance review if a whole meeting is called just for this purpose

Below are some possible statements that would include effective feedback in that round, both by the focus person and by the other participants of the performance review. Good feedback in a performance review includes general assessments (while making it clear that they are no absolute truth) and specific examples for illustration. We can describe the impact the focus person's actions and way of being has on us.

- *"I enjoy your leadership style. I experience you as reliable, for example when it got forgotten to call the electrician and you noticed that on time and were able to intervene successfully."*
- *"I appreciate your voice in the circle. What you say always seems to add to the discussion. I very much admire how you always pass when you do not have anything new or relevant to say. To me, that just makes your voice more valuable because you seem to choose wisely what needs to be said without taking yourself too seriously."*
- *"I think your energy is great. I feel your attitude as positive and genuine, you seem to give this circle a sense of 'we can do this'. I loved when you pulled out that diagram a few meetings back that showed all the ways of dealing with an objection. What I noticed was how important it was for the circle, and certainly for me, to be aware that we have options. You really moved the circle forward there in my view."*
- *"I like how you seem to be the calm center of the circle. Even when people are stuck or excited and want to do everything at the same time, you keep calm, and in my opinion that contributes so much to the group because you're a needed counter-part to us. That gives me some peace of mind because I know we might drop things but you will notice. That also shows in your writing minutes, they are correct and thorough and organized. That supports us in doing our work."*

Feedback on what a focus person has done well is an implicit request to continue or even do more of what they do well.

Could do better round   Again, the focus person speaks first, then the others take turns and the focus person summarizes what they heard. Both saying and hearing what someone has not done well can be hard to do. It is particularly helpful here that the focus person goes first. This sets up the context where the other speak as allies to the focus person who is welcoming feedback. We encourage kindness, honesty and self-responsibility.

Below are some examples of what is traditionally called "negative" feedback (which, in this case, is not negative feedback but expresses someone's need not getting met sufficiently).

- *"I have a hard time staying engaged during meetings in general, and it helps me when a meeting is structured so I know what's going on. I would love for you as facilitator to support me in that by saying more often, what the frame is for a round and where we are in the process. Maybe we could put a poster up of the different steps, and then you and we could refer to it? That is my request of you because it would help me be more relaxed in meetings."*
- *"I appreciate that you are carrying so much of the load when it comes to our finances. I would like to express some concern because we don't seem to have any redundancy, which also means no one can help you, I would like to have some basic understanding of how our coop is doing financially to give me some peace of mind. I trust you but any role should have some redundancy. I would like for someone to learn from you so it does not always have to be you doing our finances."*

- *"I have something to say that might be a little hard to hear because it is clearly judgmental from my part. It is important to me to feel comfortable in all our meetings, and I am not comfortable when we talk about IT tools. I pick up a sense of impatience on your part, like all the IT is easy to understand for you while I am really struggling. Just taking care of myself for a second, I would like to know that I am seen for my intentions which are to be productive and to be doing my best to learn the new tools. I am curious how my judgment that you get annoyed and brief when it comes to that topic lands on you and how you look at this. My request would be for you to be a bit more gentle with me because I get anxious when I do not feel competent, and I would sense judgment even where there is none. This is hard for me and it is impacting how I participate in our work here."*
- *"There is something that is not working for me. I often come in for my shift after yours and find food on the counter that belongs in the fridge. I am worried about safety and sanitation here. I'd love to hear what comes up for you hearing this."*

Being specific in our feedback makes improvement plans doable. Again, at the close of this round, the focus person summarizes and interprets what they have heard, and circle members can confirm that they have been heard as intended.

Explore

It's time to be creative again. What could be done (by the focus person or elsewhere) so performance could be improved? Before jumping to solutions, we distill from the input we have gathered previously.

Explore: Improvement areas   In the *explore* stage, we now proceed the way we would for policy-making. We now have a complete image of what is relevant to know about the focus person in this context. *Where* do we see areas for improvement? (Not *how* do we want this to be improved?) This is very much like picture-forming in regular policy-making. Examples of dimensions could be:

- communication
- response time to email
- tech support
- public speaking
- flex time

This can also include areas where the improvement would be that we want to see *more* of something the focus person is doing well! This step probably only takes a few minutes or less and is complete when everyone consents to the list of dimensions.

Improvement plan ideas   The next step is to brainstorm action step ideas. *How* would people like to see improvements in those areas? Make it specific and doable. The improvement ideas could be tied back to dimensions. Examples could be:

- *"For communication, I'd like you to get some training in NVC, for example an online class of your choice, by this fall."*

- *"I'd like for you to respond faster to email, like within 24 or 48 hours. I'd love to hear from you whether there is a way to organize that in a way that would work for you."*
- *"You're such an awesome resource for tech help, I'd like to see you bring that in more. I am also concerned about over-loading you. So I'd like for you to reserve 2h per week for that and be intentional about not doing more. I'd like for you to track it. If we find out it takes considerably more time, we should look at that and maybe hire someone for that. We can't just rely on you for tech support. I want to make sure your skills are used well, and that's more than just tech support."*
- *"Since you mentioned public speaking yourself as an area for improvement, I suggest you commit to doing 3 public speaking events by the end of the year and getting more coaching to support that."*

There could also be improvements that affect more than just one person and need to be addressed elsewhere, for instance policies around work time.

- *"We have identified flex time as an issue. Since that seems to be a bigger issue since it does not only affect you, I'd like to send this to work schedule circle to look at."*

Proposal ideas can also be contradictory (as they could be in any proposal shaping process). As usual, we just write them all down.

- *"Yes, you mentioned public speaking as an area of growth but I do not think this needs to be a focus area right now."*
- *"I'd like to modify your role description to include more IT support work."*

If it is easy and straightforward, we can now turn the proposal pieces into a proposal for improvement. The proposal ideas do not only cover actions in the domain of the focus person. They can also be sent somewhere else. As usual, the evaluation can bubble up information that is relevant in a broader context, like a change in the job description or like the flex time policy in this example. This information might not come up anywhere else, so make sure to harvest it here.

Remember, any good policy also has a term. Making a date for a review – and/or the next performance review – is an intentional decision that might depend on the pieces of the proposal (that might each have a timeline, like "3 public speaking events by fall"). The policy will also have measurements and metrics, depending on what we want to measure.

Write up improvement plan   Someone – most likely but not necessarily the focus person – will organize the proposal ideas into a proposal. This might all happen within the meeting or after the meeting. Regardless of when the proposal is being written up, the process continues: the proposal requires the feedback circle's consent. Possibly, it can also also require the consent of all of the circles in which the focus person is a member. (It depends on the focus of the performance review. Find a reasonable balance between a focus that is too wide and a focus that is too narrow. The decision of who is going to have consent rights on the proposal should be made before the performance review begins.)

Decide

The proposal needs to be stated clearly and distributed to everyone with consent rights. Then it needs to be approved, by consent by (at least) the performance review circle – including the focus person – and/or all the circle with whom the focus person works. The improvement plan will be kept in the records in written form (public to the organization) like a policy but not in the policy agreements since it only affects one person.

Once the term gets close, the focus person will start planning another performance review and the cycle begins again. The next performance review acts as a measure for whether the improvement plan has been put into practice, and at the same time as the beginning of a new cycle.

4.7 Self-repairing organizations

If we open our minds and hearts to feedback, we can catch ineffective aspects in our organization sooner. We will be a self-repairing organization. This only works if we are willing to change anything and everything. We might have to change our aim, our circle structure, we might change the way we define roles. Whatever we do, we try to make sure we measure whether change accomplishes what we are hoping for.

4.7.1 There is no right way of doing sociocracy

There is no right or wrong in governance. Groups that are new to sociocracy, from time to time, play the governance police. Sociocracy is *never* rigid. Balance is built into sociocracy, and only a dynamic balance will be resilient. If we catch ourselves being in a "right fight" on how to do sociocracy, we are already on the track toward *right and wrong*. There is no "right way" of doing sociocracy, especially if the discussion around what is right is creating disconnect. What we have been describing here in this book is not "the right way" but rather what we as the authors have found to be effective.

Effectiveness is the measure of governance. Sociocracy is more than how to do a round or how to interpret an objection. It is more than diagrams and meeting formats: it is a *mindset* that there is a way of balancing individual and group needs, in support of equivalence. Anything that does so in an effective way is sociocratic to us.

4.7.2 And there is no wrong way of doing sociocracy

The good news is that there is also no wrong way. We might mess up from time to time. For example, we have facilitated meetings where we assumed that an objection was addressed well in an amended proposal and rushed toward the consent round. When there is upset in the room and all of a sudden everyone wants to speak, that is feedback that we had pushed too hard and continued too fast. We have regretted from time to time erring on the side of effectiveness instead of going for equivalence by slowing down. On the other hand, we have called explorative rounds where everyone passed because there was nothing relevant to say – could we have known that the group was ready for the next step already? Did we just waste minutes on a round that turned out to be unnecessary? That happens. The good thing is: if we have a good system in place, we will still come to a product that is good enough. There is no reason to be afraid to do something wrong. Instead, we pay attention to feedback, because chances are we do things that aren't perfect – the practice is to notice, adjust, and learn.

The measure of effectiveness is about achieving both your aim and the equivalence in your group. Not all measurements have to be around productivity. Pick your measurements based on your aims and objectives. We can measure how happy our members are, how well we protected the planet, how many new members we have been able to give a voice to. Measurement-driven governance and facilitation does not treat people like machines – fill it with what is important to you!

Chapter 5

How To Run A Sociocratic Meeting

Circles hold meetings in order to create clarity for their work. While operational decisions can be made by anyone who is authorized and within the limits set by policy and aims/domains, policy decisions are made by consent by the circle that has this area of responsibility in its domain. Both policy-making and operational coordination may happen during a circle meeting.

Every sociocratic circle meeting follows the same pattern which ensures forward motion while keeping equal voice in all circle decisions. Any meeting falls into three parts: opening, content, and closing. Same as the steps in generating a proposal, each phase in a meeting has *lead – do –measure* loops. It helps to know what the intention is behind every phase of a meeting, what the appropriate tools are and how to measure completion of the phase.

Figure 159 shows a schematic diagram of a typical meeting. It will boost the effectiveness of your meetings significantly if facilitators visually share the diagrams with their circle because it will make it easier to follow for everyone, increasing every circle member's sense of empowerment and trust.

Making the meeting sheet in 199 in the appendix visible to everyone in the circle, is a good way of achieving a shared understanding of the process. (See also downloadable sheets on the book page `www.manyvoicesonesong.com`.)

5.1 Opening

The aim of the opening round is to enter the meeting and be ready for the content of the meeting. The reason there are two parts is because we want to show up as both *human beings* and as *circle members*. Although we are always both humans and holder of our roles, it is easier to focus on them separately.

5.1.1 Check-in

The intention of the check-in is to mentally and emotionally transition into the meeting. Everyone is entering the meeting having left some other activity or mental space. Possible ways to introduce the check-in are:

Meeting template

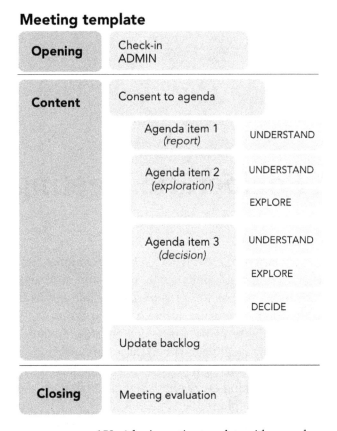

159: A basic meeting template with example agenda items

- (most neutral) *"How are you coming into this meeting?"*
- *"What do you want to say so you can be present with us, and we can be present with you?"*
- (new group) *"What would you like us to know about you?"*

Intention: Transitioning into the meeting and getting ready for the meeting

Tool: An opening round.

- Depending on the group and on how often the members of the group see each other, check-ins can be between two and ten minutes *total*. (For example, a board of directors of a new organization that only meets 6 times a year might want to do a longer check-in so they can give more background in a self-introduction. In a circle that works together in the same space and meets weekly, a long check-in will not be necessary.)
- Even if it seems tempting, do not skip check-ins! Check-ins are essential to transition into the meeting. No matter what your meeting is about, human connection comes first. And connection will ease the flow of the work.

- A formal check-in is an intentional transition marker from chatting to meeting time.
- An alternative to a round is popcorn style; make sure everyone speaks before moving to administrative content.
- We can add a "turn and talk" (everyone talks with a partner for a few minutes) before a meeting, especially if we want people to get to know each other more or if the group is large.
- We do not recommend replacing the check-in of everyone hearing from everyone in a circle of a regular meeting because (a) we want a sense of the whole before continuing and (b) everyone checking in reaffirms equivalence – everyone matters.
- Check-ins can be timed! If we time check-ins, we are putting the minds of those at ease who are only half-way listening because they are anxious about meeting time ticking away.
- A meeting does not need to get hijacked by someone's personal life. If someone shares something heavy, do not go into problem-solving or advice-giving. This is not the place for it.

Complete when: Everyone has spoken and nothing is in the way of starting the meeting.

The context in which circle members find themselves might affect how present and generous they are with their time and energy, and how willing they are to take risks. As we get to know each other more, we are able to see each other in context, be more compassionate and caring.

Themed check-ins (having people check-in responding to a quote or a question/topic) can be done but *always* leave some space for people to share what might be going on for them. For example, someone in the group could be care-taker of an elderly mother, and possibly alarmed by a health scare – confining them to a well-intended prompt might fail to include them where they are in that moment. Someone could be anxious about an agenda item, or upset about something they experienced last meeting. There could be a personal tension between circle members. Someone could be dealing with relationship issues. All these circumstances, and countless more, are meaningful to share *if we choose to*.

If the interpersonal tension or anxiety is circle-related, we might choose to put it on the agenda or on the backlog. Or we might invite a member to share more after the meeting. If someone seems distressed, appoint a person to check with the member after the meeting. We have been to meetings where we lovingly sent someone home after the check-in (with their consent, of course) because given where they were emotionally, that seemed like the only appropriate thing to do to hold them with care.

Remember, all human collaboration starts from connection, and connection can only happen when we are authentic and show up as who we are and how we are.

5.1.2   Administrative: ADMIN

In the administrative section, we talk about everything that concerns the self-administration of the group. Not only *people* but also the *circle* as such has to be ready to enter the meeting.

All the little steps that need doing and are easy to forget form the acronym ADMIN (**a**ttendance, **d**uration, **m**inutes, **i**nformation, **n**ext meeting) so we can memorize them more easily.

> **Intention:** Getting ready for the meeting. Overall, the ADMIN phase makes sure we can focus entirely on content and nothing holds us back or distracts us.
>
> **Tools:** Going through all ADMIN items (see below).
>
> **Complete when:** Nothing keeps us from entering the meeting.

Attendance

Acknowledge the attendance of all circle members. Welcome visitors and the function in which they are present. Make sure the circle is aware of who has what role. Most essential in this moment is to make sure the secretary is present and is taking notes, starting with noting the attendance in the meeting minutes. Make sure to notice who is missing and the implications this has for the meeting.

When all roles are filled or there is a plan for how they can be replaced, the meeting can continue.

> **Intention:** Acknowledging who is present and who is absent.
>
> **Tools:** This depends on the circle's context. The facilitator could introduce visitors and summarize (or ask someone to summarize) who is absent and whether all roles are filled.
>
> **Complete when:** All roles are accounted for.

Example 160 shows a tiny but useful tweak that makes this step much easier in the minutes.

Example: attendance

Membership circle meeting Dec 1st, 2017

Attendance: Anna (leader), Yo (delegate, facilitator), ~~Tim (secretary)~~, Inge, Sebastien (visitor for first agenda item), Simon (leader IT circle)

160: Example of taking attendance in the meeting notes. Make an agenda template that includes a list of all circle members including their roles. Then cross out (but keep visible) who is absent. In this example, the secretary is absent.

Duration

Have you ever been to a meeting where some people thought it was a one-hour meeting, and some expected it to be scheduled for 1.5 hours? Have you ever been to a meeting where the group was unable to make decisions because so many members had to leave early? Talking about the length of the meeting helps circles avoid those situations.

> **Intention:** Acknowledgment of duration of the meeting.
>
> **Tools:** Say how long the meeting is scheduled for. We can ask whether everyone can stay for the entire length of the meeting. People who have to leave early will be reminded to say so. This information will be relevant for planning/adjusting the agenda.
>
> **Complete when:** There is clarity on how long members are able to stay at the current meeting.

Minutes

Make sure the meeting minutes of the previous circle meeting are known and have been consented to. We are only ready to move forward when we have agreement on the status quo.

Consent to minutes can be given between meetings – see section 5.4.6 on page 200. Within ADMIN, we only acknowledge whether or not consent has been given and whether extra action needs to be taken during the meeting.

> **Intention:** Acknowledging consent/lack of consent to the meeting minutes.
>
> **Tools:** The facilitator might have to check with the secretary on the status of last meeting's minutes. If there has been an objection to the minutes or if consent has not been given yet, it belongs on the meeting agenda as an agenda item.
>
> **Complete when:** There is clarity about the status of last meeting's minutes.

Information

Since all circle members are part of the same context of the organization or of several related organizations, there might be announcements from their organization or network. This includes special meetings, decisions, events, celebrations of successes or requests that can be shared in this part of the meeting. While this is an integral part of organizational life, keep this part brief and only report-style.

Any report that lies *within the domain of the circle* should be given as a report during the regular meeting as an agenda item! The clarifying questions and, if applicable, feedback to the report go beyond the scope of the ADMIN phase.

> **Intention:** Hearing announcements relevant to the wider community within the context of the organization.
>
> **Tools:** The facilitator asks whether there are announcements or any other information to share with the circle. Do a round or allow anyone with an announcement to speak.
>
> **Complete when:** No one has more information to share.

Announcements that generate discussions should be ended or moved into the agenda so we can use our meeting time intentionally.

Next meeting

When is this circle meeting next? Many circles and even entire organizations fade away because they miss this step! This agenda item serves to remind groups to pay attention to whether they know when their next meeting time is. Do this now so we don't arrive at the end of the meeting without a next meeting plan – when everyone is too tired or distracted to schedule (and some may leave early).

> **Intention:** Having clarity on the next meeting time
>
> **Tools:** If your circle has a regular meeting schedule, name the next meeting time and encourage everyone to check their calendars. If it turns out that there is a conflict, make either a new date, acknowledge that one member will be absent, or make a plan (appointing someone to take care of scheduling).
>
> - If the next meeting time depends on a decision in the meeting, we might have to push the topic of the meeting time into the meeting in which case we would have to put it on the agenda.
> - If we do not have policy on when your meetings are (i.e. you decide case by case in an operational decision), schedule a time now or make a plan. A circle can consider making policy about their meeting time (*"meetings happen every other week on Wed at 2.30pm"*, for example) to save themselves time in the future.
>
> **Complete when:** There is clarity on the circle's next meeting time.

Going step by step through the ADMIN phase is much more time-efficient than *not* doing it. The confusion and straightening out we have to do if we miss these simple steps will cost us much more time in the long run. That said, this phase does not have to take long. It could just sound like in example 161. The acronym (ADMIN) helps us be consistent, even with no meeting sheet present.

Example: ADMIN phase

Thanks for this check-in, everyone. We're all here except for Eric, but he sent me an email saying he'd be 30 minutes late. We have a guest here tonight, Pablo, in his role of leader of membership circle. Rieke is already taking notes.

The meeting today is scheduled for 90 minutes. Looks we like we have started on time, so we will aim to wrap up the meeting at 11:30. Any time constraints to be aware of? *(pause)*

We already consented to the minutes from last time. Is there anything to say about that? *(pause)*. Does not look like it.

Are there any announcements or events we need to be aware of, besides our annual celebration in 3 weeks? *(pause)* Ok.

Our next meeting as scheduled in exactly in 4 weeks from now, which makes October 15th at the same time. *(everybody double-checking their calendars)* Great! We're ready.

161: Briefly going through all the steps of the ADMIN phase.

5.2   Content

We are ready to jump into the content of our meeting! Now we will hear reports, gather feedback, make operational decisions, policy decisions, run elections and make other decisions that will help us do our work together with as much clarity, efficiency, and forward motion as possible.

The content part of the meeting also falls into 3 phases. First we plan and consent to the agenda – deciding which items from the backlog we intend to talk about. Then we go through each agenda item. The third phase is when we assess briefly what agenda items we have completed, what to-do items remain and what carries over into the next meeting, which we summarize as "updating the backlog".

5.2.1   Consent to agenda

The decision of what we are going to talk about in a meeting is significant. The agenda proposal may have been prepared by someone in the circle, for example the facilitator (see section 5.4), or it might be created in the moment.

Before we start talking about agenda items, we consent to the agenda. This is relevant because there is power in deciding what makes it on the agenda of the day and what does not. Is the circle going to address a challenging topic, or is it going to table that topic again and again? If meeting time is limited, which agenda items have priority over others? How much time is the circle going to give each agenda item? We make those decisions by consent, and in doing so, ownership of the agenda is transferred from the person who prepared the agenda to the circle. Even throughout the meeting, *any significant change in the agenda requires consent!* Everyone in the circle is equally responsible for the agenda.

The *how* of talking, for example, when we do rounds or in what steps a group approaches a topic is in the domain of the facilitator. Suggestions and feedback to the facilitator may be welcome, but the facilitator decides how to run the meeting.

The agenda names all agenda items, gives a sense of the timing for each agenda item and identifies what the desired outcome is (understanding, exploration, decision – see section 5.2.2 below). A checklist for complete agendas is given in figure 162.

> **Intention:** Deciding what will be talked about in the meeting, and how much time will be allotted to each agenda item.
>
> **Tools:** Presenting the agenda proposal, answering questions and consent round.
>
> - Understand: present the agenda and answer questions. (Never consent to an agenda you do not fully understand!)
> - Explore: are there any changes to the proposed agenda?
> - Decide: ask for consent and incorporate objections.
>
> **Complete when:** There is consent to the agenda.

Forming an agenda checklist

☐ Topics and order of topics

☐ Timing for each agenda item

☐ Desired outcome (aim) for each agenda item

162: Checklist for a complete agenda

What would objections to proposed agenda look like? For example, we could decide to table a topic because a circle member whose presence is essential to talking about that topic, is absent. We might decide to postpone an agenda item because we do not have enough information or because we are prioritizing other agenda items. The example in 163 shows that this does not have to be a complicated process and that it benefits from all minds put together.

A side-note on co-created agendas: Some circles meet and make their agenda together, at the beginning of the meeting and without use of a backlog. While this works well enough in some groups, all groups would benefit from a thought-through agenda proposal. It is too easy for agenda items to fall through the cracks and to lack intention and forward motion. In a situation where we start without a prepared agenda proposal, we can make an agenda "on the fly". Steps in co-creating an agenda:

Example
Consenting to the agenda

Baha   These are the agenda items that I am aware of. First we are going to talk about the laundry policy. Then we're going to select a new delegate. After that we're are going to do picture forming about the noise in the cafe area. Any questions? *(pause)*

Hye   What happened to the discussion we had last time about the bike racks in front of the cafe?

Baha   As far as I know, that was passed on to the Maintenance Circle. Any other questions?

Bassim   When is the leader role up?

Baha   Hye, can you look that up?

Hye   In another 2 months.

Baha   Ok, thanks. So if there are no more questions, are there any comments or additions to the agenda?

Karl   Yes, I'd like to give a report from my conversation with Maintenance Circle.

Baha   Ok, thank you. Is it ok to do that at the beginning? Ok. Anything else? (pause) So we're going to do report from Maintenance Circle for 5 minutes, then some more exploration around the laundry policy for 20 minutes, select a delegate -- that probably takes about 15 minutes as well and then do picture forming about the noise which should take about 15 min. Leaves plenty of time. Do you have that written down? Thanks. Are there any objections? *(pause)* Great. Let's begin with the report.

163: Consenting to the agenda

- Understand: Getting an idea of what agenda items need to be talked about (in a round).
- Explore: Any constraints on order, length and priority?
- Synthesize: The facilitator either turns the agenda ideas into an agenda proposal or asks someone to do so. The facilitator presents the agenda and continues as soon as there is consent.

5.2.2   Content block: 3 desired outcomes

For every agenda item, there are exactly three possible outcomes as shown in figure 164 on page 187: *understanding a report, exploring an issue* or *making a decision*. That means that any agenda item will be one of those three, and it's best if a group is able to name which one it is before talking about the agenda item.

As one can see in diagram 164, the desired outcomes build on each other. Every agenda item starts with *understanding,* and for a report that is all we do. If the desired outcome is to ask for feedback, the *understanding* phase is followed by a phase of exploration. If we are aiming to make a decision, we go through *understand* and *explore* and then toward a decision.

Here are examples of how it is helpful to know your desired outcome:

- If an agenda item is to *report* to the group of a decision that has been made elsewhere, then there is no need to go into a discussion. If circle members are aware of that, this agenda item is not going to get out of hand.
- If the desired outcome is to hear feedback and explore, we will have clarity on the scope of this agenda item – no one will expect a decision and we will not waste time trying to come to convergence if that is not what has been asked of us.

The desired outcome might change while we are talking about it. For example, we might notice that we cannot come to a decision during the meeting. In this case, we have to either formally drop this desired outcome (which requires consent since everyone consented to the agenda) or we have to make a plan on when/how the decision can be made. For example, do a round of feedback and then delegate to a helping circle for more research and a recommendation in the next meeting.

Being aware of what kind of agenda item we are dealing with also gives a clearer understanding of what kinds of *tools* might be useful to get to that desired outcome. The most important ones are mentioned in figure 164. These steps align with the different kinds of rounds we use but there is no 1:1 match – there are different ways to hold these agenda items.

Extra clarity can be gained if, for every agenda item, we end by measuring whether we have achieved the desired outcome. Facilitators can make it a habit to pause before moving to a new agenda item by assessing whether the desired outcome has been achieved and by asking the secretary to read out loud what has been written in the notes.

Understanding a report

During reports, the circle is being informed. A report is complete when all clarifying questions have been answered. A report does not require exploration. The reporting member might be a circle member, a written piece of input or a report from an attending visitor. Examples are:

- Reports from operational steps. For example, a circle member was asked to talk with someone outside of the circle to hold that member accountable to policy. After doing so, the circle member reports.
- Reports from decisions made elsewhere. For example, the delegate of the Membership Circle reports that they decided to change the membership fees. In this scenario, there might already have been a lot of feedback given in the process and there is no need for feedback, or feedback can happen outside of the meeting.

Understanding a report

UNDERSTAND

Desired outcome
Receiving and understanding
the input
Tools
Report
Clarifying questions round
Measure
No open clarifying questions

Exploring an issue

UNDERSTAND

Desired outcome
Receiving and understanding
the input
Tools
Report
Clarifying questions round
Measure
No open clarifying questions

EXPLORE

Desired outcome
Enriching and transforming
the input
Tools
Reaction rounds
Measure
All relevant ideas and
reactions shared

Making a decision

UNDERSTAND

Desired outcome
Receiving and understanding
the input
Tools
Report
Clarifying questions round
Measure
No open clarifying questions

EXPLORE

Desired outcome
Enriching and transforming
the input
Tools
Reaction rounds
Measure
All relevant ideas and
reactions shared

DECIDE

Desired outcome
Decision/next step
Tools
Consent round
Measure
No objection to the proposal

164: Three possible outcomes from an agenda item

If the desired outcome for everyone is solely to understand the information given, then this circle does not have to go into a discussion of the subject.

> **Intention:** Everyone hears and understands a piece of information (report).
>
> **Tools:** Present all the information. Allow for clarifying questions and answer them.
>
> **Complete when:** There are no open clarifying questions.

Exploring an issue

If we are asking for shared exploration, we start by giving input (a report, an idea, a request) and making sure that this input is understood. Therefore, the first block in asking for feedback is reporting and answering questions. The second step is inviting feedback. This can take as long as is considered necessary and productive. Examples:

- A child circle is asking for help. The delegate of the child circle reports, makes sure everyone understands what is going on before the parent circle responds to the request. The feedback is being taken back to the child circle and a decision is made there.
- A circle is taking in new information, for example because an outside member wrote an email to the circle complaining about something in the circle's domain. The circle will first try and understand the complaint and then explore their reaction to the complaint.
- A circle hears a report from a meeting of their parent circle. The parent circle is about to make a decision. After the presentation on the matter is understood, the circle does a reaction round to gather some feedback for the parent circle.

> **Intention:** Generating ideas and feedback in relationship to the input
>
> **Tools:** (1) Report. (2) Do one or more reaction/generative rounds where circle members collect their ideas, and reflect on each other's ideas; write them down.
>
> **Complete when:** All relevant ideas and reactions are shared.

Making a decision

To make a decision means to go through the entire cycle of understanding, exploring and deciding. Not all of it has to happen in one meeting. Examples:

- An operational decision (a case-by-case decision) that does not completely follow from policy.

  For example, imagine a meals circle of a community has been asked to make a decision on whether or not there will be a regular meal on New Year's day. The circle decides not to make a policy (i.e. making a general decision on meals on national holidays) but to make a case-by-case decision of skipping that particular meal.

This decision follows the same steps: report what the request was and make sure everyone understands the issue (*understand*), explore what circle members are thinking about it (*feedback*), making an operational decision (*decide*).

- A policy decision. For example, a circle could be making policy on meals on holidays in general and plans to come to a decision in a meeting.
- A selection process. (Following the pattern of understand, explore, decide.)

Intention: Making a decision to create clarity.

Tools: (1) Report (2) Explore (3) Go through the consent process.

Complete when: There are no objections to the proposal.

5.2.3 The flow of agenda items

In some frameworks, operational meetings are strictly distinct from policy meetings. Here, we are assuming they both can happen within the same meeting because the circle decides what to decide in operational, case-by-case decisions and what to make policy on. There can be agreements on doing operational-only meetings, but most policy meetings will contain some talking about operations. (See more on operational meetings in section 2.8.2 on page 77.)

That said, the first agenda item of a meeting might be finalizing policy around topic A and assigning tasks. The second agenda item might be exploring a topic. The third agenda item might be a report from a new issue. The fourth agenda item might be to assign circle members tasks around an upcoming event, and the fifth might be a review of a policy.

An operational agenda item can be very brief (see Example 165). If a discussion about an operational tasks triggers the need for more talking and maybe policy (you can tell by the fact that there is a discussion flaring up, see Ex. 166), remain intentional in your process. Many decisions can be made as a one-time decision. If it seems worthwhile to make a guideline for operations (i.e. policy), decide together (by consent) whether to modify your meeting agenda to fit in a policy decision or whether to put the policy decision on the backlog.

For example, the circle could create a role for a publicity manager that would take all the kinds of action steps discussed. Thereafter, the person filling that role would take off those activities and this topic would not show up on future agendas. New items sometimes arise in the middle of meetings. It is important then not to let the new item take over the agenda without consideration. The facilitator can guide the circle whether or not to change the agenda that was consented to at the beginning of the meeting. If there is no consent to change the agenda, the new item is added to the backlog. The circle may also identify and assign any next steps needed to prepare that item for future discussion.

Remember that a typical policy decision-making process (as described in section 3.3) goes through different phases: (1) understanding the issue, (2) generating a proposal, (3) making a decision. How a group spreads out those phases into meetings is entirely up to the circle. One can go through all the decision-making steps in one meeting, or spread them out over several meetings.

Example: operational agenda item

Pablo	The next agenda item is the upcoming trade show. Let's take a few minutes and talk about that. I'd like to ask Amy as our circle leader to give us an idea of where things are at.
Amy	Yes. The event is 2.5 months away. The status right now is that we're registered and will be assigned a booth pretty soon. I made a list of things that need doing between now and our next meeting. I'd like to put an ad into the local newspaper like we did two years ago for that other fall festival for local businesses, and I'd like to have a new banner printed because our logo has changed since we last used it. One of us should also go through our info material and see whether anything needs restocking.
Pablo	Ok, thanks. Sounds very straight-forward. Are there any questions? Henry?
Henry	Yes, is the new banner in the budget?
Pablo	Amy?
Amy	Yes. They're around $150 and that should be ok. As far as I can see, all of those items were covered last year in a similar way, and the extra banner definitely falls within our publicity line item in the budget.
Henry	Thank you.
Pablo	Any other questions? *(pause)* Seeing none. Is there any feedback that would be relevant to share now?
Charlie	Yes, since I won't be there, I just wanted to let people know that the tent is not quite waterproof anymore. If it rains a lot, it does drip, so maybe bring an extra tarp if the weather forecast is rain. We should have some fairly clean tarps in the tool closet.
Pablo	Thank you, good point. Did you write that down? Good. Any other feedback? *(pause)* Ok, seeing none, Amy, would you read through the list, and Paula, could you write down who does what?
Amy	Take care of the ad—I can do that if no one is wanting to do it. Ok, having the banner printed with the new logo? *(Charlie raises hand)* Charlie, thank you. Charlie, since you know our materials best, would you be willing to see whether anything needs restocking? Ok, great.
Pablo	Anything else? (Pause) I think we're done. If it is written down who is doing what, we're ready to go to the next agenda item. Would you read that back please? (...) Everything ok? Let's continue then.

165: Example of an operational agenda item within a circle meeting

Example: operational agenda item turns into a discussion

Pablo   The next agenda item is the upcoming trade show. Let's take a few minutes and talk about that. I'd like to ask Amy as our leader to give us an idea of where things are at.

Amy   Yes. The event is 2.5 months away. (...) The status right now is that we're registered and will be assigned a booth pretty soon.

Pablo   Ok, thanks. Are there any questions? Henry?

Henry   Yes, I'd like to know whether the people staffing the booth are going to be paid or whether this is volunteer time.

Amy   According to what we have done in previous years, this is paid time.

Henry   *(talking out of turn)* I don't think that's a good idea. It makes quite a difference whether you're working in the shop or whether you're standing around in a booth and might not even do much.

Charlie We've talked about this before. Plus you don't even know how much work it is. Why do you bring this up now? We have already decided that we're doing the fair, and volunteering our time for something that is PR for the coop does not seem fair to me. *(more crosstalk with other people chiming in for 1-2 minutes)*

Pablo   Ok, ok, stop! What I hear is that there are different opinions on whether the time spent at the fair should be fully paid. Correct? *(members nod)* As far as I see it, we only scheduled time here for coordination of tasks, and not to have a whole discussion on general approach. If we went down this rabbit hole now, we will not be able to talk about the other agenda items that are also important and that we agreed to talking about. So what I propose for process now is we either decide to change our agenda, or we postpone this discussion. Let me hear your opinion: talk now or postpone? Let's do a round. Charlie?

Charlie I'm fine either way.

Amy   I'd like to continue with what we agreed to talk about. We really need to get to talking about agenda item number 5 because it affects my schedule next week.

Basti   I want to postpone.

Henry   I'd rather talk now. What I certainly don't want is that this just gets forgotten again!

Pablo   I am ok either way myself, but as a facilitator I am proposing that we continue with this meeting as planned and put the issue around pay at fairs on the agenda next week, and that we make policy then. Our next meeting is still 8 weeks from the fair so that seems enough time. Let me ask for consent here. (Pause. Checks the group visually.) Hearing no objections. Can that go in our backlog please so we don't forget? Let's continue where we left off.

166: How to deal with a discussion coming up in a meeting

Then we see what happens as we implement the policy. Once we review it we make changes if needed, following the same consent process (see figure 167).

All policy decisions in sociocracy have a term end, which forces us to review policy instead of letting it go stale. We might just briefly revisit a policy and decide to leave it as is or do a deeper review.

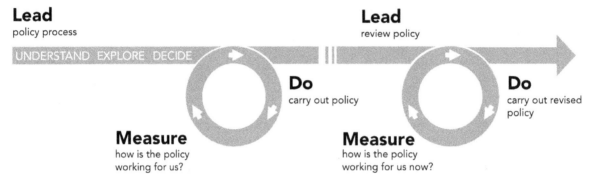

167: Life cycle of policy

5.2.4   Measure: Update backlog

The backlog is a list of topics that require reports, explorations or decisions to gain the clarity needed to do good work. (More information in section 5.4.1.) At the *begining* of the content phase of a meeting, decided what to address. We might generate new backlog items, postponed items or completed topics. Now, at the *end* of the content block, we assess where we are at. What remains to be done? Within a few minutes, we note this down in the backlog while it is fresh on our mind.

> **Intention:** Assess whether all agenda items have been addressed with regard to the desired outcomes.
>
> **Tools:** Depending on the complexity of the situation, we can
>
> - Let the facilitator "think out loud" on where there are gaps (agenda items that got skipped or not covered correctly), and do a reaction round
> - Do a round. "What needs to happen next time?"
> - The secretary either updates the backlog right away or after the meeting:
>   - Agenda items that have not been covered remain on the backlog.
>   - If there is a next step (for example, if a role has been created, we need to schedule a selection process), put it on the backlog.
>   - Delete items that have been dealt with.
>   - Note review dates for decisions made.
>
> Some groups like doing a review of action items generated in the meeting.
>
> **Complete when:** The information to update the backlog is collected

The backlog is vital data to use for the planning of the next agenda. Think of your updated backlog as the hand-off from one meeting to the other. (See section 5.4.1.)

Example: Complete? Next steps? (measure of the content block)

Baha So, that was our last agenda item. Let's see. We did decide to postpone the email policy decision to next time, so that should go on the backlog. I think next time we should also continue to do picture forming on the membership policy change. Anything else? *(pause)* Ok. Mike, is that written down?

Mike Yes.

Baha Great. So let's do our closing round then.

168: Measuring the content phase of the meeting

5.3   Closing: meeting evaluation

Make sure to wrap up the content part of your meeting about 10 minutes before circle members have to leave. Meeting evaluations are an integral part of every meeting. We end the meeting with one or two rounds on:

- *"What worked well in the meeting?"*
- *"What could be improved in future meetings?"*
- *"Is there anything you are carrying out of the meeting that you'd like to get off your chest now?"*

Meeting evaluations are an opportunity to learn from our meetings. We can either talk about content, process, or interpersonal dynamics.

The diagram in 169 illustrates what people can touch on during the evaluation round. The intention is not to cover *all* those areas but to show the variety of topics to evaluate.

If we want to address something interpersonal, remember that effective feedback is feedback that is easy to receive, specific, and blame-free. Of course, a meeting evaluation is not a magic fix. A governance method cannot fix what people have to do: speak up and take action. If there is a circle member that behaves in a way that makes it hard for us to participate, we share the responsibility to speak up. There are many ways to address behavior, but the meeting evaluation can be the first and easiest one. More examples of things to say during meeting evaluations can be found in section 4.5 on page 168.

If something needs attention, the circle will set some time aside in a *future* meeting to address it; for example if the circle meetings go significantly over time on a regular basis, we need to make time at a future meeting to talk about it. In that case, put the evaluation (*"observation: meetings go over time a lot"*) in your backlog right away during the meeting evaluation so that facilitator and leader can decide whether and how to address it before or in a future meeting. Other strategies for improvement might also go into the meeting's notes for later consideration. This could be the need for more training on process, a mediation, or a policy around circle admin matters. Overall, inhabit a mindset of growth: how can these meetings be better next time? Or, even better, what will make our circle meetings awesome? Remember to be specific. Meetings would work better for you if they started on time? Say that! Groups sometimes seem to accept that meetings would be lengthy or irritating. Sociocratic meetings, if well-run, are refreshing, connecting and energizing. That is the benchmark we are aiming for.

Meeting evaluation
General feedback; what worked well, what could be improved?

Process
- Flow of the meeting, facilitation
- Meeting preparation
- Time keeping
- Equivalence of voices
- Is more clarity on certain processes/training needed?

Content
- How do you feel about progress and decisions at this meeting
- How do you feel about upcoming event/activities/meetings?
- Are there agenda items that you'd like to put on the agenda?

Interpersonal
- How do you feel about your membership in the circle?
- Do you have feedback for anyone in the circle, including yourself?
- Are you leaving this meeting with any interpersonal tension?
- Was the tone during the meeting respectful?

169: Ideas on what to evaluate in the meeting evaluation/check-out

Intention: Learning from the meeting around how the circle deals with and learns about content, process and interpersonal relationships.

Tools: A round where everyone speaks.

- We can divide up content, process and interpersonal evaluations into separate rounds.
- The secretary puts items that might translate into an agenda item on the backlog.
- If we get a sense that someone is not sharing relevant data, we can choose to share the impact on us. For example, if there was a lot of tension between two circle members during the meeting and they do not acknowledge that in their evaluation, nothing keeps us from sharing what the impact was on us.

> • Something is brought up in the closing round that triggers strong reactions. In that case it is best to do a reaction round to that and consider if any next steps need to happen operationally or if items need to be added to the circle backlog.
>
> **Complete when:** Everyone has spoken. Evaluations that require an action step are written in the minutes or in the backlog.

5.4 Supporting documents: backlog, agenda, minutes

Backlog, agenda and minutes are documents that support the circle's work. The three documents do not have to be in three different files. The same document can have different sections that serve different purposes. In a digital document, create a space for the backlog, type directly into the agenda and keep adding your minutes within the same file. That way, everything will remain in the same place. Of course, we may have good reasons to keep backlog, agenda and minutes in different files.

5.4.1 Backlog

The backlog is a list of topics that the circle needs to talk about. The backlog is like a rolling to-do list of a circle. It is best to create a backlog in a place that is visible to everyone. Some circles gather their agenda items at the end of the running minutes file, or on a whiteboard or on a digital or physical board.

Between meetings, new ideas for agenda items can be put on the backlog so they can be remembered and tracked. 170 is an example of a backlog. Use whatever sorting supports the group in addressing topics effectively without creating a lot of need for maintenance.

The backlog will ideally be updated during the last content phase of each meeting when new topics, active or resting items, are added to the backlog or items that have been dealt with during a meeting are taken off the backlog. The overall goal of circle meetings is to check topics off your backlog!

5.4.2 Agenda

The agenda is the list of topics that a circle talks about at a circle meeting. Having an agenda set before the meeting is the first step toward an effective and time-efficient meeting. Time is precious for everyone in the room. It can be frustrating to have all the right people in the room but no prepared agenda to make good use of everyone's time!

Who sets the agenda for a meeting? There are two answers to that: one around power and one around logistics. As for power, what is important to keep in mind is that regardless of who prepares the agenda proposal, what we choose to *accept* as the agenda is a consent decision by all circle members. The circle members hold equal responsibility for the agenda once consented to.

Logistics: There is variety in how sociocratic organizations set the agenda for their circle meetings. One practice is to have the leader, facilitator and secretary prepare the agenda proposal. The initiative comes from the facilitator who will contact the leader and secretary. Facilitators will

Example: sample backlog

Agenda items (active, time critical in bold)
  policy around CRM
  talk about budget for coming fiscal
  switch to 1-hour meetings?
  form helping circle for getting circle budget ready
  talk about IPC request (see email June 12, 2018)
  change fiscal year to calendar year?

Agenda items (resting)
  11-2018 review improvement plan for YM
  12-2018 about summer schedule policy
  03-2019 fiscal sponsorship for TG?

Term ends
  8-2019 review calendar policy (start survey process in June according to policy!)
  Delegate: Sept 2019
  Leader: Sept 2019
  Secretary: April 2020
  Facilitator: May 2020

170: An example of a backlog to be carried at the end of the meeting minutes.

have to have an agenda proposal ready at the meeting, so facilitators are relying on there being an agenda more than everyone else. Ideally, the agenda is made by secretary, facilitator and leader, bringing together past, present and future as shown in figure 171.

- The leader will weigh in on what needs to be done in a larger picture. Have circle members identified any new topics? Are there topics from the parent circle or sub-circle that should come to the circle? From the leader's perspective, do some items have priority?

- The secretary will track whether elections are due or whether a policy is due for review. Sociocracy does not prescribe what tool to use for tracking due dates, and there are plenty of options. A tracking tool or simply your calendar will help the secretary remember when those items need to go onto the agenda. Please note that just going back to last meeting's agenda does not provide the long-term planning. For example, when the circle agreed to re-evaluate a decision after 6 months, the secretary (or logbook keeper) needs to remember to put this on the agenda. We might also decide to go for an error-proof option and put all our review dates into our backlog and keep them there (see figure 170 on page 170). Some circles select all their roles on the same day each year. Some organizations ask all their circles to review the policies in their domain at the same time, for example from September to October of odd number years. These are easy ways to support continuity and the additional accountability.

- All the agenda items, new and from the backlog, will be gathered and will be put in order in the agenda proposal or draft agenda by the facilitator. Any complete agenda includes: agenda

171: The agenda unites past, future and present needs

topics, timing and order of topics, desired outcomes for each item (see below).

- The facilitator or leader will make sure the right people are in the room; for example, inviting guests whose input would be helpful to the discussion in the circle.
- The facilitator also makes sure that the agenda proposal with supporting documents goes out to the circle members ahead of time so they can prepare for the meeting.

172: Forming an agenda

Topic, timing, desired outcome

This agenda format is an enriched format that allows for better agendas. Instead of just a list of topics, we add all relevant information.

- Topic: items that need to be talked about.
- Timing: time we plan for each agenda item.
- Desired outcome: understanding, exploration, or decision (see section 5.2.2).
- Further: supporting documents, presenter names.

Agenda items (Topic)   All topics, those from the backlog and new agenda items, will be gathered into a list, prioritized and sequenced. The backlog will likely have more items than can be talked about in one meeting. Prioritize and make a realistic agenda.

Timing   It is essential to put time information into an agenda, at least more or less. The reason to do this is to have *feedback* during the meeting. Timing information does not have to be followed by the book. If we notice in the middle of agenda item 1 that we are already 25 minutes behind our own schedule, we will know that we need to make adjustments. We cannot always predict in advance how long an item will take but we can make a good guess. During the meeting, we compare the plan to reality and consider the implications. What changes do we want to make to the rest of the agenda for this meeting?

Be realistic! If a group does over time chronically, it might work to address it and be intentional about how meetings are planned and run. Maybe we need to increase the meeting time, frequency, outsource reporting out of meeting time, or make more use of helping circles. There are many ways to address timing but the first step is to have a way of assessing how we intend to use our time.

Define your desired outcome   For a more general look at content during meeting agendas it helps to think back to the three possible content items or desired outcomes as described earlier in section 5.2.2 on page 186: reports/understanding, exploration and making decisions (synthesis or output). Each agenda item needs to be assigned one of these desired outcomes. The desired outcomes are measurements for each agenda item.

Don't aim too high. Sometimes just getting to a shared understanding of the status quo is a success! Whatever we do, this is our starting point, as all three desired outcomes have *shared understanding* as a first step. Confirm that people are on the same page and have a shared understanding of what there is to know (to the level of detail that makes sense in your context).

Make sure to share with the circle what the desired outcome is for each item and put it on the agenda.

Be proactive and intentional, instead of just dealing with whatever falls into the circle's lap. Agenda planning should have a longer-term view. This is why the leader's input is important. What is your circle's one-year plan (informed by the aim)? What needs to happen so we can get there?

EXAMPLE
An example agenda

Time	Topic	Desired outcome
0:00-0:10	Check-in + ADMIN	
0:10-0:15	Consent to agenda	
0:15-0:20	Agenda item 1	decide
0:20-0:30	Agenda item 2	understand
0:30-0:50	Agenda item 3	explore
0:50-1:15	Agenda item 4	decide
1:15-1:20	Wrap-up	
1:20-1:30	Meeting evaluation	

173: Example of an agenda. Each agenda item can also name the person responsible for the item and reference any supporting documents

5.4.3 Meeting minutes

In a decentralized governance system like sociocracy, meeting minutes are a significant source of transparency. With so much authority distributed into circles, we need to be able to rely on minutes to hear what is going on in circles, in addition to reporting through linking.

5.4.4 Taking notes

Notes are written, ideally, in real time as the meeting progresses. In our organizations, we type directly into the agenda, which is a document on the secretary's computer or in the cloud. We do not write detailed minutes (no *"who said what"*) but write down only decisions and any content we generate together, as shown in example 174. This includes policy decisions (in their exact wording), selections, action items for operational decisions.

Although sociocracy does not come with special requirements for minutes, we recommend only recording relevant information and keeping the minutes brief so the larger organization can manage the amount of information. If we write wonderful notes but they are very long, people will stop reading them, which will lead to lack of transparency. Transparency and practicability need to be in balance.

5.4.5 Making use of notes during the meeting

It is helpful to write down every decision (policy and operational) that is relevant beyond the meeting. If minutes are available in real time, we can make use of this resource by asking the secretary to read a proposal out loud that is being formed in the meeting before consenting to it.

Additionally, the notes of a particular *agenda item* can be read back to the circle before moving to the next agenda item. This serves as a measure of whether the agenda item has been covered and captured well and can often surface whether the circle is on the same page about what happened.

What goes into the minutes

- circle name
- attendance
- meeting date
- topics
- next meeting date/time

- decisions
  - elections
  - new policies
  - operational decisions

- content that is worth keeping (lists, drafts)

- backlog (future topics)

174: Keep your minutes short and relevant

5.4.6   Approving minutes

Meeting minutes need to be approved so the circle as a whole can take ownership of what has been written down during the meeting. Consenting means to not have any objections to the proposed minutes. A person who missed the meeting cannot object to the minutes since they were not there to witness what has been decided, unless they object to how a report got recorded. (They might object to decisions made but that is different and it is covered in section 3.2.5 on page 89.)

The earlier we can approve the minutes, the better. Minutes need to be approved before the content phase of the next meeting begins. Some options:

- Consent to the minutes as the last content item of the meeting (if the minutes are taken in real time during the meeting and cleaned up on the spot).
- Send the draft minutes out to the circle after the meeting and give circle members 48 hours to object (lazy consent); otherwise assume consent, as described in the example in 177.
- Send draft minutes to circle members and approve them at the beginning of the following meeting.

5.4.7   Publishing minutes

Minutes are filed in the circle's logbook, in an online folder or a binder.

Minutes need to be published within the organization, not only in the circle. At least a brief summary is made available to the whole organization.

Example of meeting minutes published to the organization

Membership circle
Date: Sept 15, 2017
Attendance: Yagi (leader), Anne (facilitator), Anke (secretary, delegate), Basti, Mike

Decisions:
consented to prospective member policy (see full notes)
Anke (re)-elected delegate until Sept 2018

Topics
- prospective member policy
- selection
- exploration of outreach strategy
- report from General Circle

Future topics:
- membership circle is going to focus more on outreach and potentially forming a subcircle for outreach. Talk to Yagi if you have any relevant input.

Next meeting: Oct 14, 2017

Full notes are here (link).

175: Example minutes to go public.

In Agile, we visualize the notes, e.g. on a flip chart during the meeting and take a picture of it as a report. The picture goes on the (internal) wiki.
(Jutta Eckstein)

176: What others do

Minutes in a sociocratic organization are even more important than in other organizations because of the way power is distributed. Transparency and easy access to information is crucial when decisions are made in small groups.

If we consent to a policy in a meeting, the new policy needs to be added to the appropriate document (policy manual, organizational agreements, rules and regulations) of the organization's logbook. Policies are only useful if people know about them. Make sure to implement a logbook system that works for the organization. In sociocracy, in large organizations, there is the additional role of a logbook keeper (see section 2.3.1) so the logbook remains up to date and accessible to everyone in the organization (or even to the public). Note: It is useful to do ongoing education about existing policies to your organization.

Example: Minutes policy

1. Secretary has 48 hours from a meeting to send draft minutes to Circle members.

2. Circle members then have 24 hours to send feedback to the Secretary.

3. Secretary then has 48 hours to publish the minutes to their Circle's Minutes folder in Google Drive and a summary to the community, having used his/her judgment about what to incorporate or not from the feedback received.

Rationale: Balancing aims of transparency and efficiency.

177: An example policy implementing lazy consent for approval of minutes

In a circle meeting there's often the problem that people don't know what wording actually went into the minutes. This requires checking back with the secretary and re-reading the various statements. A more transparent way is to capture the minutes transparently on a flipchart (or prominently on big stickies). This way everyone sees the minutes all the time (if you need more than one sheet of paper, hang them all on the wall). At the end of the meeting the secretary takes pictures of all easels and stores them in the electronic file system.

(Jutta Eckstein and John Buck)

178: What others say

Meeting minutes are a natural place to invite feedback. However, keep in mind that not everyone will read every set of meeting minutes that are published. If we want feedback on something, it helps to be explicit and make a clear request. Just sending out minutes and saying later *"well, you could have given us feedback when we said we were working on this"* is not enough! What channel we use to put out our minutes depends on the nature and the patterns we find in our organization and in our culture. Sociocracy balances out the relationship between individuals and circles. Circles have to make an effort to be transparent, while individuals have to make an effort to respond to the information. There is no right and wrong here – *everyone* is responsible.

5.5 Facilitation formats

Since this book is only about sociocratic methods, we are not covering all other approaches to facilitating conversational processes like Dragon Dreaming, Art of Hosting and Dynamic Facilitation. They are compatible with sociocracy but describing them is outside the scope of this book. We encourage all readers to get familiar with those approaches to build a broad skill set. In this book, we focus on the strength of sociocracy – small groups whose focus it is to make decisions.

5.5.1 Rounds

Although sociocracy did not invent rounds, they are the signature tool. Like all tools in sociocracy, rounds support equal voice and effectiveness. Everyone gets a chance to talk. Everyone listens. Rounds are often the first tool from sociocracy that a group starts using.

Rounds are simple: the facilitator gives the prompt, and calls on one person to speak. After that person has spoken, the person next to the first speaker has a turn, until everyone has spoken. Depending on the nature of the topic and the group size, one round might take 20 seconds or 20 minutes or anything in between.

We know that for some people rounds take some time to get used to. If people argue that rounds are "constraining", "artificial" and or they prefer "natural" flow, consider:

- What is "natural" is highly debatable. For example, there are/were times and cultures where it was unthinkable for a child to speak during family dinner without being asked. People then probably assumed their style of family dinner was the "natural" order of things.
- Rounds have been practiced in some cultures for hundreds if not thousands of years. Rounds become second nature fairly quickly.
- It is very likely that internalized power patterns shape how we show up in a meeting with "natural" flow. This means the cultural biases we might not even be aware of might give one group of people more time to talk than other groups. This may be based on class, race, gender or other categories. The same biases even distort our perception of how long and how often people from different groups speak. Our perception of what is "equal" might not be accurate.

How rounds support everyone to speak

Not having any format in a meeting typically turns discussions into debates. In debate style conversations, whoever speaks up will be heard, and heard again if they repeat themselves. This works well for people who have an easy time with this kind of format. It does not work for people who don't enjoy having to overtalk people to contribute. Some people are more likely to engage in overtalking than others. We favor more extroverted or privileged people if we choose to talk in debate style. Since debate style is what we resort to in the absence of a format, *not* being intentional about how we talk with each other will favor *some* voices and ignore others. It is crucial to understand that *not making the choice to talk in rounds is still a choice we make with its own implications*.

When we talk in rounds, we know that we will have our turn to talk. We don't have to sit in a discussion wondering how to get our contribution heard, and how to get a turn. We can relax and know that the group will get a chance to hear our input.

How rounds support everyone to listen

In debate style, everybody loses. Just because someone is less likely to speak up in a heated discussion, does not mean their contribution is less valuable. This means that if we choose to skip rounds, we lose out on valuable information.

Rounds change the dynamics of a conversation. When it is other people's turn, we can sit back and listen. And by that we mean: really listen. I don't have to wait for a good moment to jump in and interrupt. I don't have to think about how to prove the other person wrong. I can just listen and take in the other circle members' experience.

In debate style, we often tend to try and convince people of our viewpoint. When some express different views, others may repeat their own views again, just louder. With rounds, it feels more like everyone brings their ideas, perspectives and experiences to the table. It is more like an offering to the group because it is not targeted at anyone.

We can only be a group when we are sure that everyone in the circle is included. Talking in rounds gives everyone the confidence that their voice matters. What we each bring individually becomes the group's. The group wisdom starts growing in the middle of the circle. It is deeply satisfying when that happens, and rounds make it much more likely.

In debate style, our "task" is to win. In rounds, we spend more time listening than speaking. We each have access to only our view of the world. After taking in the experience of a number of people in a row without even considering saying something for myself, it becomes obvious how my own experience is just *one* way to see things. One way among many others.

How rounds save time

When people start out learning about rounds, their first judgment is often that rounds will be lengthy and not time efficient. It takes a bit of practice and experience to see how the opposite is true. There are several ways in which rounds support effectiveness.

- In debate style, people feel compelled to re-state their contribution so they can be sure they can be heard. Rounds slow down conversations enough so every contribution can be taken in and valued. Statements typically do not need to be repeated. We all have been in discussions where the same thing was said by the same person multiple times. Rounds reduce the amount of redundancy because we can be sure we hear it the first time.
- In rounds, as much information as possible is heard early in the process. That means we as a group (or, more precisely, a subset of the group) don't run into one direction just to find out it was a dead end. We move more slowly, taking into account a wider number of aspects and viewpoints. That way, we don't have to change direction as many times. Slow and steady!
- There is a subtle but powerful effect of rounds: rounds help us stay on track. When we start a round, we all start with the same prompt. That means, everyone having their turn after the first person to speak has options: refer back to the prompt and increase the variety of opinions in the group and to see an issue from different angles. The other option is to reflect on what other people have already said and let statements build on each other with increasing information in the group. Ideally, people do both, share their initial reaction and their reflections on what has been stated before them. In an ideal world, people are transparent about that

and build their statements according to the pattern *"My first reaction/idea was..., and then I heard Eduardo speak, and I learned that..., and now I think that..."* Rounds give us the maximum input, both from individuals and for building group wisdom.

- When everyone is part of a decision, it increases the accountability and buy-in of everyone involved. Everyone in the group owns the decision. If members are heard and fully contribute to a decision, no one will undermine carrying out the plans we made together.

5.5.2   What kinds of rounds are there?

Although all rounds are very similar, these are some differences in the nature of a round, depending on where in the decision process they take place (see 179 and 180).

Rounds	Desired outcome
Clarifying question round	Making sure everyone understands a report, a proposal or an idea.
Reaction round	Giving feedback, exploring ideas, suggesting amendments.
Consent round	Finding out whether there are objections to a proposal.

179: Different rounds and their uses

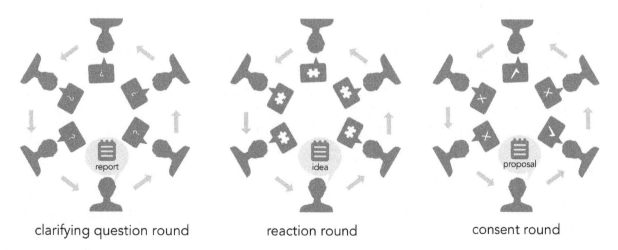

clarifying question round   reaction round   consent round

180: We respond to prompts in different kinds of rounds.

Clarifying questions rounds

A clarifying questions round is called whenever there has been a proposal, a statement or idea that needs to be understood *before* the circle members form or state their opinions. This could be a policy proposal, or a report, but it could also be a complex objection. We are transparent about the nature of the round: *"Let's make sure we understand the proposal/objection before we talk about it more. Now is the time to ask the questions you need to have answered before moving forward."*

Questions can either be gathered in a round and then answered by a knowledgeable person in the room, or they can be answered one by one as they come up. When answers are simple and short, answer them right away. When answers are complex or involve a dialog with the questioners, collect them and respond at the end of the round. Avoid breaking the spirit of a round – don't get into a lengthy discussion on one question in the middle of a round.

There might not be a perfect way to do it, but the facilitator can decide *when* questions are going to be answered. If there are many questions, the facilitator can initiate a second round because new information might also have triggered new questions. Do not forget – the overall aim of this step is to make sure everyone understands the original proposal or presentation. We only move to the next step when everyone is ready.

Sometimes the facilitator will need to work with a circle member to tease out a real question that is mixed in with the member's opinions. Reflecting back a question is a wonderful skill for any facilitator and it can sound like *"so, what I hear you say is that you would like to have clarity on. . . ."*

A challenge in the clarifying questions round is that sometimes people will jump ahead and give an opinion. Or they may express their negative judgment about the proposal through a biased question. A "question" (with potentially a lot of subtext) like *"why don't you just. . . "* is probably going down that path! If someone expresses an opinion, the facilitator can say things like:

- *"Thank you for sharing your opinion. Is there a question you would like to ask in order to understand the proposal as it is written?"*
- *"What I'd like to do right now is to understand the proposal on the table. We'd be happy to hear your ideas for improvement in just a bit. Would you note it down so it won't be lost?"*
- (a more directive version) *"I'd really like you to hold your opinions for now because in this moment, all I want is to make sure everyone in the room gets a chance to understand the proposal thoroughly. You will be able to share your opinion in a bit."*

Encourage *everyone* in the round to speak and to either confirm they understood or raise a question. They can use one of the two options: *"I understand the proposal"* or *"What I need to understand the proposal is. . . "*. This step helps everyone have ownership in the process.

Reaction rounds (generative rounds)

Reaction rounds are a way to get a feel for where the group is at and to gather input from a group. Reaction rounds can be used in very different contexts:

- Reactions to a report, for example a report from a helping circle.
  - *"Thanks for this report. I suggest considering. . . "*
  - *"I find it interesting that Membership Circle seems to. . . "*

- Reactions to a proposal, within the consent process.
  - *"I like the proposal because it creates clarity on. . . "*
  - *"I would like to suggest a small amendment. We don't seem to mention a term end for this policy and I suggest 6 months."*

- Reactions to a question, for example a question around next steps.
  - *"I think this is a good place to create a role to deal with this on an ongoing basis . . . "*
  - *"I don't really have a good idea but I am curious what others have to say."*

- Reactions to an objection.
  - *"I understand the objection. To me, the risk is small and I'd like to see what we can learn by trying what's proposed."*
  - *"Now that I understand the objection better, I agree we need to amend the proposal. I have an idea. . . "*
  - *"I am persuaded. I don't see how we can move forward to towards our aim if we were to consent to this proposal."*
  - *"I have a hard time relating to this objection and will listen. Come back to me please."*

A reaction round can be reflecting on what comes up for circle members, or it can have a concrete prompt (like *"what do you think could be done about this issue?"*). Do not restrict this phase to only one round *if* what people contribute seems rich and productive and contributions seem to build on each other. (For reactions to proposals in the consent process see section 3.3.2.) The facilitator can end the round asking if there is anything anyone wants to add. *"We did two rounds now and we heard a lot of good input. Is there anything that still needs to be said before we move on?"*

Time and attention span are often concerns in meetings. To introduce a quick reaction round the facilitator can say, *"Let's do a quick reaction on that. And by quick reaction, I mean five sentences or less."* Some groups will find it supportive to use a talking stick and/or a timer to keep things moving in a round. Avoid repeating redundant information. One way to save time overall is to give everyone time to quietly write down what they would like to say *before* the round starts. That way, everyone can be concise in their contribution.

Whenever there is some new information, let the circle take responsibility for it by calling for a round. The facilitator is only facilitating – making process easier, "facile". The facilitator is not supposed to be the savior of a group. A sociocratic meeting should feel like ping pong: there comes the ball and the facilitator bounces it back into the group. At the end, we do not even know who contributed what – it was all co-created. If we smash the ball every single time, we might win but the game will consist of people picking up the ball and there will be no flow.

Consent rounds

Consent rounds are very brief. They give only two options.

- *"I consent/I have no objections."*
- *"I have an objection (because. . .)"*

In the case of an objection, we can give a one-phrase statement about the objection, for example *"I have an objection to the time frame of this."*

Note that in consent decision making there is no third option of standing aside or passing. (See more on that in section 3.2.5 on page 88).

We can get consent, especially on uncontroversial decisions (like for example a non-controversial agenda) in a non-verbal way. In that case, the facilitator has to make an effort to get brief eye contact with everyone in the group. In virtual meetings, non-verbal consent can be given by showing our thumbs up.

What makes consent rounds different from reaction rounds is that after every explicit consent round, if there are no objections, a decision is made. We are not asking if people *would* consent (which would be asking for a reaction) but we're asking whether they *hereby* consent.

A consent round is a special speech act; everyone has to be aware that we are not simply providing information but we are declaring a decision made. The facilitator has to be explicit about this – have you been to meetings where afterward, there were different opinions on whether a decision was just considered or made? That's the difference we are talking about here. Be clear! Say something like *"So, the proposal is that . . . , and I will now ask you for your consent. Do you consent to this proposal?"*

5.5.3   Facilitating rounds

Do we always have to talk in rounds?

We recommend it. Below are some occasions when we break from our habit of talking in rounds:

- For clarifying questions if it seems to be safe to assume that there will not be many questions, or if there is a large group. In that case, just ask *"are there any questions?"*
- When we are asking for input (picture forming or proposal shaping) from a large group. We break large groups into small groups so they can do rounds effectively.
- In a group that seems emotionally safe, we sometimes back off from rounds and allow cross-talk for a while. It is best to be intentional about this, however. Once people are "conditioned" to only talking when it is their turn, they might remain silent in a free flow discussion. For that reason, it is important to be explicit: *"I propose we spend the next 10 minutes in free flow conversation and see if that brings up any new ideas."* End your free flow time with a round to re-establish equivalence and to understand where the circle is at as a whole.

We encourage groups to make rounds their default and to be intentional about deviating from that default. However, it is also a matter of practice – and the more a group practices, the better they will get at it.

Can people pass?

Passing in a round depends on the context. It's ok to pass in:

- Clarifying questions rounds. We can briefly confirm that we don't have a question.
- Other reaction rounds that serve a gathering of ideas or brainstorming: fine to pass. For the sake of transparency, give a short explanation and make sure to express whether we request taking our turn at the end of the round:
  - *"I'd like to pass for now. I was distracted and do not know what exactly is expected of me right now. Can I talk at the end of the round, please?"*
  - *"I'll pass because I do not really have anything new to add/all I wanted to say has been said."*

We discourage passing in:

- Reaction rounds during the policy process because then the circle does not have enough information. So instead of passing, say *"it looks good to me"* or *"I don't like this proposal for the same reasons Jane gave. Nothing new to add."*
- Nomination rounds (see section 3.6.2 on selection process): no passing. We need everyone's information for a co-created nomination proposal.
- Consent rounds. We need to hear from everyone to make sure we hear all objections. (See more on abstentions in section 3.2.5 on page 88).

Be aware that *having been asked and passing* is very different from *not having been asked*. Hearing everyone's voice in the process, even if they do not have anything new to contribute, works like social glue for any group.

Gaining clarity

A typical situation: the circle talks and talks, and somehow, it remains unclear where the circle is going. This is not always ineffective – great things can emerge out of a muddy phase. However, it is easy to get stuck.

In collaborative decision making, we operate on many different levels.

- We are working toward an aim.
- We are trying to find a good process to achieve that aim.
- We are practicing working with equal power.
- We are getting to know each other.

It can wear on the group morale when no progress is made. The flowchart 181 shows four ways out of blockages, no matter on what level they might lie. More details:

- Make a proposal on content: do not wait until a proposal on your topic forms magically because chances are it won't (or at least within a reasonable amount of time). Instead, after having heard everyone for two rounds, make a proposal and ask for consent. If there are objections, we have just nailed down what the actual controversial issues are. Now we know what to address. This will move the meeting forward.
- Make a proposal on process: if a discussion does not seem to go anywhere, make a proposal on how to make progress. A common strategy is forming a helping circle to generate a proposal

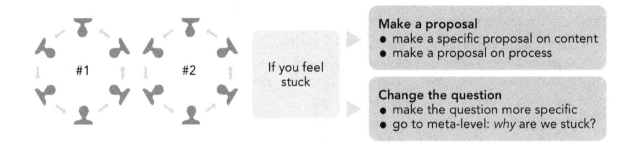

181: 2 flow, then go: after two rounds with no progress, change your strategy.

for the group to decide on next time. This is particularly useful if there is information missing. Make a plan on how to get that information and move forward.

• Make the question more specific: break up the topic into separate parts and do separate rounds on each. Sometimes it is too hard to respond to big topics.

• Move the question to a meta level. For example, if we can't make a decision, we do a round on *why* we think we have a hard time making the decision. If there is an unaddressed issue holding up the discussion, we try to make it easy to bring it up. This can be hard. After all, there is a reason we tip-toe around a topic. But circling forever is not an option either. It might be that our aims are different, that there is some hidden power struggle or that there is caution stemming from a trust issue or from not having enough information about each other. Better to find out!

In general: If we do not know what to do, we do a round! Examples of that are shown in 182.

EXAMPLE
A round on process

The facilitator presented the agenda, and with three big items, the time seemed too short to give justice to each agenda item in an one-hour meeting. One of the agenda items was a selection process for the leader because her term was up. A discussion flared up on whether selections were a waste of time at this point in time. The circle had a deadline just two meetings away, and different people felt very differently about whether to postpone selections.

The facilitator let it flow for a minute or two. Then she called a round: *"What are your thoughts on the priorities of agenda items today?"* Everyone spoke, some wanted elections but did not feel strongly, some wanted to present good results at the deadline. The facilitator proposed to postpone selections until after the deadline and called a consent round. Everyone consented, and they jumped right into content.

They consented based on what they could work with rather than personal preference.

182: Deciding on process together.

More examples on when to ask for input on process:

- The meeting starts and only half (or fewer) of the circle members are present: *"I notice only half of our circle members are present. Let us do a round on how that is affecting our agenda, and how we could deal with that."*
- The group is going off on a tangent that was not on the agenda but seems important (or turns out to be time-sensitive). *"I am noticing that we're not discussing our agenda items right now but that the tangent we're on seems important to people and needs to be dealt with now. Can we do a round to hear if people are ok with talking more about this now? I just want to make sure we're intentional about how we spend our time."*
- The circle is unprepared (did not read a proposal or a supporting document, for whatever reason). *"I get the sense that not everyone got a chance to read the document. Let's do a round on where people are at and what you think can be done in this meeting."*
- You are the facilitator and you do not know what to do. *"I find myself lost right now and I am not sure what is happening. Can we do a round and people just say where they see us in the process right now and what you would suggest?"*

We are never victims of circumstances, but always agents with choices. Example 183 shows what this may sound like with more context.

Not every decision needs to go through the entire consent process. Deciding to take a 10 min break does not justify a 3 minute process of *present proposal, clarifying questions, quick reactions, consent*. The most informal way we practice is saying the proposal, waiting a few seconds for questions and reactions, and having eye contact with everyone, one by one, to check whether there are objections. Shared power relies on trust, and trust needs to be earned in a hundred little steps. The reward for staying in an egalitarian frame all of the time will be a healthy culture in our organization that we can rely on for harder decisions.

If a circle member gets upset during a meeting

What can a circle do if one member of the circle gets too upset to continue the meeting? This might show in uncooperative disruptive behavior, displays of anger, like yelling or getting up from the chair. Ways to respond depend on (1) the capacity of that circle member in that moment to be self-responsible and (2) the time, resource and willingness of the other circle members to take time off the meeting to hear the underlying needs. Do not assume you need to interrupt the work of the meeting to deal with emotional reactivity. Consider the circumstances and be intentional. Options:

- Do a reaction round.
- Invite the person to speak, followed by a request. *"Do you want to share what is going on for you? Do you have a request of us?"* Do a reaction round of reflective listening or empathy before hearing the focus person again.
- Ask a circle member to support the upset circle member outside of the meeting while the meeting continues or after the meeting ends.
- Take a 5min break or a minute of silence.
- Any combination of these options.

If we decide to do a round, we put the person who is most affected emotionally in the middle of

Example: a member calling a round on process

The circle is amending a proposal during the quick-reaction round and gets carried away making changes.

Hope	Excuse me, can we do a quick round on process here? I feel like we are making too many changes and I am losing track of what version we are actually talking about.
Baha	Sure. Thank you for suggesting that. Hye, would you start?
Hye	I am glad you are bringing this up because I felt the same. I think we could just give it to the author and discuss it next time.
Karl	I don't really want to wait until next time but I don't really know what to do now. I do hear that people are feeling confused about what changes we are actually making to the proposal.
Bassim	How about we take a 5 minute break and Hye and I look through the changes we think we made? We could print the current version in the office and bring it back. If people still feel rushed, we will bring it back to the next meeting.
Baha	I like that idea of taking a break.
Hope	I like that too.
Baha	Ok, let's make a quick consent decision on Bassim's idea. Any objections? *(Facilitator looks around, making sure to have eye contact with everyone.)* Great!

183: A member calls for a process round

the round (like in example 184) so they have enough time to get back on their feet but are not the "problem person" speaking at the end. Doing so will be a manifestation of everyone's voice mattering: those with strong feelings and everyone else. We embody the principle that everyone can take responsibility for their feelings and behavior.

Cross-talk

Crosstalk, if it happens too often, can be harmful to the group.

- People might be silently resenting that someone is talking out of turn. They might not say so but virtually no one enjoys being interrupted or sitting through inefficient meetings.
- People might be getting cautious about what they say in fear of being interrupted or criticized – this is important to keep in mind because the impact can be invisible.
- The group misses out on "group magic". The flow of forming and building a thought or a proposal is a wonderful and connecting experience.

Example
Responding to someone who is upset

Context: Circle member Mike is upset and has made comments in a circle meeting that most would interpret as extremely sarkastic.

Anne   Ok, I notice I am very triggered right now and I am guessing many here are. I don't think we can just continue. I'd like to take a moment of silence, 30 seconds, and then I'd like to do a reaction round so we can all express where we are at right now.

(30 seconds of silence)
Thank you. Let's start with Yagi.

Yagi   Wow, that was quite a statement from Mike just now. I guess I am... sad? Confused and not quite sure what just happened. I don't quite know where this just came from. I am interested to hear what others are thinking.

Anke   Yes, me too. I am reminded of a similar discussion that we have had before. I also wonder what this is about. Where I am now is... *(pauses, looks at feelings/needs list and thinks)*...I am confused but also upset. I don't want to have a meeting where people have to watch what they're saying because someone might put them down. Complete.

Mike   This is a tough topic for me. It does not seem like people are even interested in hearing what is going on for me. This agenda item just gets dumped here and I don't want to keep dealing with it. I hear that the way I said what I said does not feel emotionally safe for people and I want to say that I can take some responsibility for that. But I also feel frustrated that my opinion was not being taken seriously.

Anne   It felt good to hear some background just now about where this was coming from. I now understand the context better. As for me right this moment, I am feeling a bit better. But I don't like when stuff like this happens when I am facilitator. I feel extra responsible and don't really know what to do.

Basti   I'd like to give Mike a couple of minutes to express what is upsetting about this topic and then we could maybe do another round about where to go next?

Anne   That's a good idea. Let me check in with Mike. Would that work for you?

Mike   No, I think I am ok. Sorry I interrupted the meeting. Can we just start off where we stopped?

Anne   Any objections to continuing the meeting? *(pause)* Seeing none. I think we were talking about....

184: Example: responding to feelings

It depends on the group – sometimes speaking out of turn adds some clarity or clears up a misunderstanding. But there is such a thing as too much. People who tend to engage in cross-talk have to be educated on the impact of their behavior. One way to address this in a meeting is feedback during the evaluation round at the closing of any sociocratic meeting. Chances are that we will have someone in the group who feels constrained by rounds, and we will have people in a group who get triggered when there is cross-talk. It helps to be open and respectful with each other and find the balance that seems right for the group.

To address cross-talk while it is happening, simply say something like *"I want to hear what you have to say. Please hold that thought or write it down. Let's get back to the round."*

Here are some other blame-free phrases one can use to help live up to the discipline of rounds. Some even work in non-sociocratic contexts.

- *"I have things to say but I am noticing that I would have to over-talk other people to speak and I don't enjoy that. Can we do rounds so we don't have to over-talk each other?"*
- *"I am noticing a lot of cross-talk. I would prefer to go back to our round."*
- *"I'd like to give everyone a minute to explain their viewpoint. That way we could gather all the expertise in the room."*

Running out of time, and adjusting the agenda

It is not unusual to run out of time. If the agenda we consented to at the beginning of the meeting contained some time information, it will be easy to track how close we are to our plan. Once it is clear that the timing of items is impossible to stick to, be proactive.

Make a decision *together*. It is not the facilitator's job to "discipline" the group. Every circle member is responsible for keeping to the schedule, not only the facilitator. A consent decision puts the responsibility into everyone's hands. Below are a few examples of what this might sound like.

- *"I propose we take 10 minute off the last agenda item and continue the discussion on this item now."*
- *"We're running out of time. I propose that we postpone this agenda item until next time. Any objections?"*
- *"We are going overtime on this topic. I propose we drop the last item on the agenda and continue with this for 15 more minutes. Any objections?"*
- *"I propose that we talk more about this topic. Does anyone object to taking 15 extra minutes – which would take us over time for the meeting as a whole?"*

It is fine to adjust plans. Plans are there to support us, not to bind us. And it is better to make an informed and intentional decision before the meeting gets too rushed.

In this example, we make sure the circle makes a decision to get the information and a plan on how the training can be scheduled between meetings. For example, we can have the group consent with a condition.

> Proposal: the training is approved by the circle if and only if the training can still be paid for during the current fiscal year.

We do not have to postpone our agenda item altogether. Instead, we encourage facilitators to be fierce on always making a next step. We cannot consent now? Ok, let's make a plan on how we get the missing information and consent now to a conditional proposal. The rule of thumb is that we do not want to hit the same wall again. What can we do now so we are in a better position at the next meeting? Missing information can be gathered, a piece of writing can be given to a helping circle. This requires flexibility and some creativity.

Even if an agenda item does not go anywhere, *"make a proposal to drop it or to postpone it for 6 months"*. That way, we are making an intentional decision that creates clarity. We are not putting the same agenda item on the agenda repeatedly without progress. There *has* to be a next step, some outcome from every agenda item, even if that outcome is different from the one we planned.

Counter-proposals

It is very tempting to bring up a counter-proposal in a quick reaction round. *"Instead of this proposal, why don't we just . . . ?"* In addition to dismissing the thoughts that already went into the original proposal, counter-proposals put the group into a very awkward situation: they are tempted to consider a new proposal in the middle of the consent process on the original proposal. It is hard to compare two proposals in real time. The complexity, both around process and on content-level, increases immediately as soon as a counter-proposal is on the table, and we have seen many groups lose their focus in the face of this complexity.

More often than not, counter-proposals lead to confusion: some people in the group might still want to consider and improve the original proposal while others want to switch proposals. Just as often, the new proposal is half-baked and some people get overwhelmed or upset, and the circle finds itself in the middle of a meta-discussion that eats up meeting time and often turns the group dysfunctional. This is exactly what sociocracy is intended to avoid!

For the record, if there are several proposals on the same topic, the formally "correct" way forward is to do a selection process between proposals to decide which proposal to continue with. Over time, improving a weak proposal over time is a better strategy than to jump through a lot of very different proposals without too much thought. Possible options are:

- Work sequentially. Bring the original proposal to consent or object and then do the same with the counter-proposal.
- *If* switching proposals, we would propose an intentional decision to do so. Since we cannot deal with two proposals on the table at the same time (unless we are doing a selection process), formally decide to drop the original proposal. This requires consent from the circle!
- If there is no time pressure, a pragmatic solution is to ask for a re-write of the proposals that could be done by the authors of the original and the counter-proposal, working together. Ideally, they'd go back to the input that was feeding into the original proposal.

  - description of the issue
  - needs statement
  - dimensions
  - and proposal ideas

What we can say or do when someone brings up a counter-proposal:

- *"Right in this moment, I am interested in whether this original proposal is going to do any harm to accomplishing our aim. I am sure we can improve it. For now only let us know your objections – whether you see harm in this proposal."*

- *"Thank you, that could be a great idea. Right now, I don't want to confuse people and I don't want to disregard the thought that went into the original proposal. Can we look at your proposal after we have made a decision on this one even though there are some overlaps and differences?"*

- *"This is too complicated now. I suggest we form a helping circle of the two people who seem to have strong opinions. Maybe the two of you could meet and come back to us with one proposal? It does not seem worth the meeting time for all 7 of us right now. So, I hereby propose we form a helping circle to re-write this proposal given the ideas we got from the counter-proposal. Are there any objections to this process?"*

More tips for better rounds

- Passing. In generative rounds, we pass when we have nothing to say. *"I have nothing new to add. I pass."* Taming our ego and supporting a group process by saving time and redundancy requires maturity but people will be grateful. If we *do* have something to say, it is vital to speak our truth whenever possible!

- Asking for more time. It's all about balance. Sometimes some more time to think and listen pays off. Used in the right moment, this is a way to enhance your contribution to the group. We could say *"it is my turn now but I'd rather think more about what I want to say and hear some more from others first. Would you come back to me?"* For the facilitator, it might be hard to track who who passed and needs a turn at the end, but a friendly reminder is easy to do if the facilitator forgets.

- We sometimes write notes of what we want to say. One has to make sure the note-taking does not interfere with the listening but note-taking serves three purposes:

  - Managing one's own impatience by writing instead of talking out of turn.
  - Preparing one's own contribution, making it denser and more to the point.
  - An unexpected effect: people who take notes might talk less. Typically, something feels urgent and burning the moment it is written down. A few minutes later when the turn to speak comes, half of the ideas seem less critical.

- We want to avoid redundancy but we also want to understand where everyone is coming from. If something has been said a few times that we agree with, just passing would be a loss of information. As a temperature check, it is helpful to know *how many* people in a group agree with something. Just saying *"I agree with what Manu said"* might not be specific enough because not everyone might remember what Manu said. Give the highlights or keywords, in your own words. *"I agree with Manu about environmental impact and re-using instead of buying new"* for example. Don't explain it again but give the essence. As people learn to trust that they will be heard in rounds, we might find that their turns speaking get shorter.

- Not knowing. In a generative round, it is perfectly fine to say, *"I hear this side because..., and I hear the other side because...."* We don't have to know. The group decides. Let it build over time.

- Timing rounds. Rounds do not *have* to be timed but if we are running out of meeting time or if we'd like to keep airtime more or less the same for everyone, timing people is a good idea. Facilitators can do it themselves or appoint a timekeeper. We might want to explain in a blame-free way that timekeeping is helpful for everyone, for example by saying something like *"let's time ourselves so we all have an easier time to stay within the time set for this item."* Use a friendly sound that everyone can hear. Don't get too tense when someone goes over time. Some people consider a timer something like a final whistle ending the turn, which it is not. It is *feedback*, or information, that a certain time frame is up. We can make it easier for others to listen if we acknowledge that by saying something like *"I heard the timer go off but it is important to me to add that..."*

- Rounds are best if they are short. Try to split up rounds into smaller pieces whenever possible. In small, controlled moves we can move forward and make sure all group members are still on the same page. Investing time in ensuring a group stays on track together is time-efficient. The solid companionship of knowing where we are is also connecting and satisfying.

- Separate member voice from facilitator voice. The facilitator is at the same time facilitator and member of the circle. As circle members, facilitators are entitled to having an opinion of their own. A facilitator in sociocracy is *not* expected to be impartial. It is not realistic for anyone to be impartial. The goal is to be self-governed. We want members to share the responsibility of managing the meeting. This requires the facilitator to separate clearly their own member voice from their facilitator voice in order to be transparent about potential bias. There are a few tools that help do that.

  - We avoid putting ourselves at the beginning or end of a round. If we do speak first, try to be transparent (by saying something like *"I'd like to speak first to model the response I am looking for"*). That way, it is clear whether we are speaking as a member or as the facilitator.
  - It's helpful to be explicit on which "hat" we are wearing. *"Speaking as a circle member, my preference is clearly to ..."*, or *"Speaking in my role as facilitator right now, I am proposing we do a round on..."*
  - Own your role and be transparent. There is some power in the facilitator's role. Being open about the fact that this is the case helps take the edge off. For example, say *"I am aware that I as the facilitator now have the privilege of deciding whether I accept this friendly amendment, and I will (not) do so because ..."*
  - Be mindful of your own bias. The facilitator does not have to be the one to make a proposal. The facilitator only has to make sure it happens. For example, if the faciliator's spouse is being nominated quite a bit in an election process, that facilitator can ask another circle member to make a proposal, and may gain credibility.

- In virtual meetings, rounds are even more important. Since we lack the visual cue of sitting in a round, it is not obvious whose turn it is. It has proven helpful for the facilitator to call on the next person and the person after that. *"So, next we will hear Kim and then Diego."* That way, Diego can start thinking ahead about what to say, start to unmute his microphone etc. After Kim has completed, the facilitator can call *"Thank you Kim. Let's hear Diego and then Ana."*

- Say when you are complete: Sometimes we take short pauses when we formulate our thoughts. It has become a habit of ours to add a marker that signals the end of our turn in a round. This could be to say *check* or *"I'm complete"* or to explicitly make eye-contact with the person who has a turn after us. That way, we know for sure that we are not cutting anyone off, and we avoid the awkward silence that happens when someone takes a moment to think and we are uncertain whether they are still thinking or done speaking.

5.5.4   Free Flow and popcorn

Free flow is a format where people speak as they want to speak, like during a dinner conversation. There are different variations of free flow.

- Free flow with a facilitator. If there are too many people to manage themselves in talking turns, free flow might require a facilitator. People raise their hand and speak as the facilitator picks whose turn is next. We can build stacks (ordered list of speakers) on a flip chart. We can introduce talking sticks. Those techniques organize who speaks next so only one person speaks at a time.
- What we call "popcorn" is a little different because like a "pop", a talking turn here will be short, just one phrase or a short sentence. Popcorn works well for picture-forming or similar phases where we are gathering short ideas.

The nature of free flow is that people who want to talk more get to talk more, especially those who are used to being in power. It is also easy to run out of time and easy to have a conversation that turns into a *debate* where we are not offering our perspective but try to convince others of our perspective. Any phase of free flow should be closed with a complete round so everyone can be heard again.

5.5.5   Turn and talk

"Turn and talk" is a technique where we let two people (or a small group) turn to each other to talk. This can be very useful if emotions are high, the topic is complex and/or the group is large. Turn and talk benefits from being limited to a certain duration, like one minute for each person in the pair.

With a turn and talk, a circle member has more time and space to think out loud about the topic before sharing an opinion in a round. Having done a turn and talk, circle members are able to state their opinion more clearly and are more relaxed about listening to others.

5.6 Virtual meetings

We find that sociocratic facilitation is particularly useful in virtual meetings. For the authors, the majority of the sociocratic meetings we attend are virtual meetings!

5.6.1 Synchronous virtual meetings

In synchronous virtual meetings, we hold a meeting in a video conference. The meeting is online but everyone is there at the same time. The advantages of sociocratic meetings for online contexts are:

- Clarity of talking turns. Especially rounds work well in virtual meetings. Most people can mute their microphone until their turn comes. Since we do not want to engage in cross-talk, being on a muted computer actually supports rounds. Rounds even make it doable to have meetings where some are online, some are in a room together. We do not risk leaving out the ones on the screen because they have their turn in the round.
- It is easier to show real-time notes in a virtual meeting. We always have two windows on our screen during video conferences; one window shows the people, the other shows the agenda and real-time minute-taking. That way, if a circle develops content or someone makes a proposal during a meeting, that content will be visible to everyone. We always have full transparency and full access to information. We find ourselves missing that option in offline meetings! (One might choose to use a projector to show the real-time notes in an in-person meeting but then people are looking at a screen instead of each other.)
- We also find that rounds make it fairly easy to be present with each other in virtual meetings even with reduced information. We might not be able to read the other people's energy as easily as in an in-person meeting but rounds slow down and condense the meeting enough that we can work confidently with the cues we are getting.

One side note: when having a meeting with members in different time zones, the easiest thing to do is to keep the time information on the agenda as neutral as possible. We always start the meeting information with zero because we work in conference calls with people in different time zones – 0:00 marks the beginning of the meeting, whatever time it might be for individual members in their time zone. We can see at a glimpse how many minutes into the meeting we are at any moment. Also, it helps for not putting the facilitator's time zone as the "standard".

5.6.2 Asynchronous decisions

Asynchronous decision making is very different from synchronous virtual meetings. Asynchronous decision making is when a proposal is approved by each circle member consenting to it at a different time. This can happen, for example, by email, or on given online platforms.

Our experience with asynchronous decision making is mixed and we avoid it and only use it for very defined decisions in circles that know each other well.

Before addressing this, let us review the distinction between (policy) decision making, operational decisions and giving feedback. Policy decisions are made by consent and we need everyone's consent in the circle. Feedback is just content that might be input for a decision in the future. Operational decisions are small decisions that apply to a particular situation.

- It is very easy to give input in an asynchronous way. For example, we would ask everyone in a circle (or beyond a circle) to give their input on an issue, a needs statement, a proposal draft or similar content. People can add their information over time, and they might build on each other's input (if it is visible to everyone what others have already written).
- Operational decisions can be made very easily in an asynchronous context if we have a good sense of who needs to be asked/informed.
- It can be hard to make a good consent decision asynchronously, especially when the decision is complex. For consent, we need to hear from everyone. We want deliberation to happen. Deliberation by email or in online platforms often turns into "decisions by those who spend the most time writing on their computer". Asynchronous decision making can work but it can very easily miss out on the advantages of consent decision making that create and nourish connection: equivalence (for example, how much we hear from every circle member), dialogue and deliberation, moving forward as a group, working through objections while being connected. All the advantages that rounds and connection bring to decision making can be lost in asynchronous decision making if we do not design and use it with a lot of care.

Chapter 6

Implementing Sociocracy

How can we not only *run* an organization in line with our values, but also *implement* sociocracy in a way that is in line with our values? The one principle that stands out is the following: change cannot happen top-down only. A change in power structure has to have both elements of *bottom-up* and *top-down*. Ideally, both the top management and the staff would welcome a change toward shared power. Introducing shared power *top-down* – even done with the best intentions – uses power-over. That will not only lead to skepticism, it also starts off the idea of shared power on the wrong foot. We often work with people who are enthusiastic about sociocracy and who would love to wave the magic wand and get everyone on board, because, after all, it is for their good, right?

Introducing shared power brings along an inherent dilemma. *If you are the one who is in power, by forcing shared power on all members of an organization you would violate one of the basic principles of sociocracy, consent! If you are not in power, you would have to ask someone who is in power to give up power.* Implementing sociocracy requires an organization to be equally willing to step into power and to give up power on every level of the organization.

6.1 Thoughts about introducing sociocracy

6.1.1 Assume consent as decision-making method

In a sociocratic mindset, we are all equals. We cannot start a sociocratic implementation coming from a place of righteousness because dividing up the world into "right" and "wrong" is not going to be effective. That means, the implementation of sociocracy starts even before we say the first word about sociocracy. It starts *in our minds*. Will we be able to hear people's fear with an open heart and with willingness to work with their objections?

We have seen people burning for sociocracy and encountering nothing but resistance – and it seemed like the resistance came *because* they were so enthusiastic. One reason for that is that some people hear criticism as soon as we bring up the possibility of any new system. We can say *"there is this cool way of decision making called consent"*, and people *hear "what you are doing now is wrong"*. There is no point in going there. Other forms of governance are not wrong. Chances are they are less effective or less focused on equivalence. If we notice in ourselves the urge to prove someone wrong, it is probably time to back off and center ourselves. We cannot end "right and wrong" thinking with "right and wrong" thinking. In this spirit, here is what we have found helpful.

- We aim to be transparent from day 1 on. No power games to implement sociocracy.
- We try to work *with* people's objections, just as if we were already a sociocratic organization. Every conversation about people's concerns about sociocracy turns into a way for everyone to practice their listening skills and their ability to work with objections. We can ask questions: what are others afraid of? There are probably valid concerns like *"how will we find the resources to train everyone"* or *"what is the board going to say?"* How can we work with those objections and address them?
- No one has to convince anyone to use all tools of sociocracy right away. One can try a next step or a small-scale experiment that seems safe enough for everyone.

Ideally, consent is formally introduced as the decision-making method as early as possible so there is certainty on *how* the organization makes decisions. Assume consent in your own mind even before it has been formally accepted. Assuming consent means you'll have the mindset of doing-with others as equals instead to doing-to or doing-for.

6.1.2   Find companionship

Find companions as early as possible. For our training, we always encourage people to bring a second person, for the simple reason that this will make it easier for the organization to hear the input. A second person will be able to complement the information shared, and the journey will be shared from the beginning.

A second person in a training (or any kind of learning journey) has the same effect as a double-link: information flows better, and power dynamics are lessened.

Remember not to let the organization fall into camps. We want to overcome the distinction between those in power and those without. Everyone wants to have a say in matters that concern them. Everyone wants to be able to contribute to what is important to them. Everyone wants to be more connected to their co-workers. This is true both for workers and managers. This is not something we have to "sell". We assume that everyone carries that longing already because it comes from universal needs. In our experience, we all agree that change is needed. However, not all of us have hope that positive change can be done. More and more people are ready to do things differently. We start from the assumption that we already have shared interests. We celebrate when we *all* step into our power together.

6.1.3   Persist, lovingly

Change does not come easily. Predictability, ease and comfort are universal human needs. For some of us, at times, the dream of something better is enough of a motivator. For some of us, at times, we need to feel pain to a breaking point before we are willing to risk change. When one person tells you about sociocracy, you might think, *"oh, that is interesting"*, and promptly forget it. When the third person from different parts of your life tell you about sociocracy, you might think, *"hmm, maybe there is something here I should pay attention to"*. At some point, each of us opens to change. When the window opens, be there. Don't break the window.

6.2 How to introduce sociocracy

There are so many ways sociocracy may be introduced to organizations. From the inside or the outside. In a start-up or in an established organization. To an organization that is working well and wants to work even more in line with its values or to an organization that is in deep pain with its finances, its interpersonal dynamics, and its productivity. We start here with a step-by-step approach to introducing sociocracy to an established organization. The sequence of steps is not strict, and many of the steps are repeated in different ways or different levels. This list is framed from the perspective of someone inside the organization and is intended to give you a sense of scope and strategy for the process of introducing sociocracy. We are going to present mostly the same list to you in two formats because different people think in different ways (even the co-authors!). The first list is framed in phases and the second list is 27 steps, one by one.

6.2.1 Introducing sociocracy to an established organization - phases

- Phase 1: Understand. Connecting and educating.

    - Find your allies inside the organization: identify key people who share your concerns about the state of governance and introduce them to sociocracy.
    - Connect your allies with others outside of your organization. Potential ways of doing that: bring some of the early adopters to a training, connect with other sociocratic practitioners in your industry/sector, visit a sociocratic organization. SoFA can help you connect with people in the same region/language/sector.

- Phase 2: Explore. Building a home base and experimenting.

    - Create an implementation team and operate it sociocratically. Encourage implementation team members to educate themselves more by attending webinars, signing up for mailing lists, etc. Frame the challenges of the present governance system and reasons for switching to sociocracy.
    - Introduce elements of sociocracy (rounds, policy term dates, selection process) wherever they are compatible with your current structure. You can run experiments in individuals units of the organization.
    - Understand and engage with the possible concerns about sociocracy in the organization.

- Phase 3: Decide. Solidifying your governance proposal and putting it in place.

    - Write a first draft of the governance agreement, adapting the sociocratic framework to your unique organization. Design the organizational circle structure proposal.
    - Present the governance agreements draft and proposed circle structure and invite feedback. Revise. Repeat as many times as necessary.
    - Make a formal proposal. Work through objections. Consent to governance proposal.

6.2.2   Introducing sociocracy to an established organization - 27 steps

1. List what you see as the challenges of the present governance system and why you are motivated to consider a switch to sociocracy.
2. Identify key people who share your concerns about the state of governance in the organization.
3. Introduce your potential allies to sociocracy. Share videos and articles/handouts, and discuss. Share with them case studies and existing templates (decision making sheet, organizational structure diagrams, governance agreement, table of aims and domains, this book).
4. Bring some of your allies with you to sociocracy workshops and webinars.
5. Have people report to the organization about their experience in the workshops.
6. Gather interested people for informal conversations about sociocracy in the organization.
7. Invite an outside person to do a brief sociocracy intro and answer open questions with parts or the whole of the organization.
8. Create an Ad Hoc Sociocracy Exploratory Circle and operate it sociocratically – this will be your home base from which all energy radiates, so it is not a solo project.
9. More formally frame the challenges of the present governance system and reasons for sociocracy. Share with others and get feedback.
10. Invite key people to participate in study circles and workshops.
11. Introduce elements of sociocracy (rounds, policy term dates, selection to leadership, double-linking, etc.) wherever you can in the existing structure.
12. Find a team or unit that is willing to experiment with making decisions sociocratically.
13. Have people visit an organization that is running sociocratically and report on their visit.
14. Write a first draft of "Governance Agreements" adapting the sociocratic framework to your unique organization. Pay particular attention to legal structure, by-laws, and financial issues.
15. Begin designing the organizational circle structure.
16. Identify both leaders who may be early supporters and people who are most likely to be resistant or wary towards sociocracy and start talking to them one on one.
17. Offer trainings in sociocracy in your organization to build the knowledge base and familiarity.
18. Present the draft Governance Agreements and circle structure, especially to the Board.
19. Revise and revise the draft Governance Agreements and Circle Structure.
20. Identify where every member stands and connect with them to move supporters into leadership, neutrals into supporters, opposers into neutral. Keep emphasizing that sociocracy is flexible and would be adapted based on experience. That after an initial period there would be an evaluation and improvements made based on that evaluation.
21. Repeat the key phrases: egalitarian, effective, safe enough to try, good enough for now.
22. Listen to and take seriously people's concerns.
23. Present the circle structure to key committee meetings.
24. Revise the draft Governance Agreements and Circle Structure.
25. Make a formal proposal to adopt sociocracy, to the Board at minimum and to the whole organization if possible.
26. Work through objections and try again! And again!
27. Launch implementation of accepted proposal!

6.3 Starting a new organization

An organization begins with an idea. Begin with the aim in mind. The founders imagine a product they could make or a service they could deliver. That is the aim. And why would we make or deliver that? Answer and you have your mission, for example to end homelessness by building houses for and with the homeless in this region of this country. (See more on mission and aims in section 2.2 on page 17.) To (mission) by (aim). The mission plus aim is the invitation. You can now call for people to join you as volunteers or as paid staff. They know what they would be doing and why. Next, make your aims ever more specific. One product or service or many. Who are the customers? Design the *input – transformation – output* workflow doing picture forming and proposal shaping. To get to the desired output, what resources (people, skills, raw materials, tools, funding, etc.) will you need? How will you organize the work? What roles and subcircles do you need? Who will fill them?

The first circle will have as input the *aim* and *domain* of the circle, its members, and its resources. In order to function well, we need to define process and operational roles and fill them. Not all of those steps have to be completed in the first meeting, but over time, each needs to be addressed. For securing the input, make sure everyone understands the aim and domain. Consent (or object and resolve) to the initial circle members. Consent to the leader who was appointed by the parent circle or if no formal leader exists, select one. Select people into the roles of facilitator, secretary and delegate. That completes the basic sociocratic structure of the circle. Then it is time to operationalize the aim of the circle: define the workflow that will get the work done, set policies that will give both freedom and limits to how the work gets done, and define and fill operational roles. The output should be a circle that is ready to start.

6.4 Implementing sociocracy in start-up organizations

With success, a simple start-up organization can grow in complexity quickly. Suddenly, we need a website, a social media outlet, a logo, design guidelines, an HR department, accounting … and it never stops. The step from a beginning organization to a running organization is huge. That is why we recommend starting sociocratic governance right away. The easiest way to implement sociocracy is in a start-up. The easiest way to grow is with sociocracy or related, dynamic, decentralized systems.

A sociocratic organization grows from one small circle to a full-fledged structure with many circles. (See section 6.4.1 on sociocracy in growing organizations.) Starting sociocracy in a new organization means one will have to convince fewer people in the beginning when introducing sociocracy because there are not as many decision-makers yet. In this context, it is important to be open and transparent about your governance system. For some young organizations, the effort of onboarding new members is significant, given that it is unlikely that new members come with experience in sociocracy. One can have the best implementation in the world but if trained members are outnumbered by new members who do not know enough about it to care, the organization will slowly drift back toward the mainstream culture. It takes intention and action to keep a new governance system alive.

6.4.1 Structures for small groups

It's possible to start an organization with one circle of members that share the work. There is no necessity to have a full circle structure in the beginning. As the need arises, the groups will differentiate. For example, the group will notice what topics are only affecting some in the group. They might also, quite naturally, outsource tasks that are best done by an individual or a pair in an operational role, for example bookkeeping or maintenance of a specific machine.

If there is just one circle, is that a work circle, or the General Circle? At the early stage, there is no difference. Think of it in terms of domains. The General Circle is the "super"-circle for all the work circles and "owns" the overall domain for the overall aim. When the time is right, we create sub-circles and pass part of the general circle aims/domains to them.

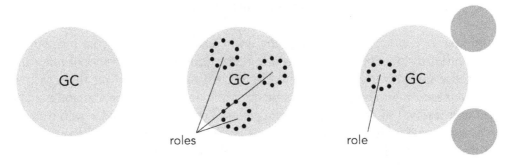

(a) Everyone decides on policy   (b) Everyone decides on policy level;   (c) Differentiation on policy level;
level; everyone does everything   differentiation on operational level   differentiation on operational level

185: Early life cycle of a young organization starting with a work group

The figures in 185 show how an organization can start out as one circle. This, for example, is the scenario of 6 people getting together, forming a group and deciding to start a business. At first, they might all more or less do the same tasks. Quickly, however, they will each have their work area of preference or expertise. One does marketing, one builds the website, one writes pitches to find investors, two build the product. They might still make all the policy decisions together. *"Should they pay for ads, should they build the website themselves or hire it out? Who needs to be asked before someone can spend money?"* On the governance end, this means they all still hold all the domains together, they just define *"ok, you go ahead and carry out our marketing plan"* or *"ok, you go and find someone who will build our website and make sure it happens."* They might decide together *how* they are going to go about interviewing potential customers to find out what their needs are, but only one or two of them are going to work on it. The policy is made together in the whole group, while the operations are "packaged" into roles and assigned to individuals who fill those roles.

The next step is to distribute authority. This is often a painful step because we have to let go of power. For example, the Marketing Circle will now make all the decisions on marketing and does not require approval from the General Circle. Many groups fail because they are not able to take the step of delegating. If founding members still want to keep their fingers in everything, they will run into the typical "founders syndrome." Founders have to let go or they will inhibit growth. The organization in 185 successfully forms department circles with aims (subsets of the aims of

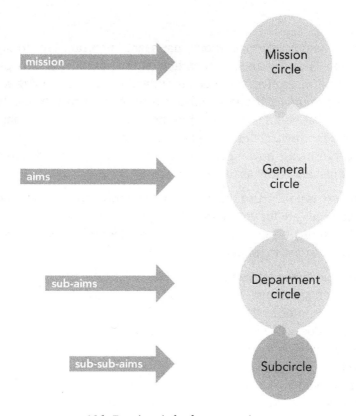

186: Forming circles from your aims

the whole organization) and domains (activities and policy areas they are responsible for). We encourage groups to distribute full power as soon as possible.

6.4.2 Designing a new organizational structure

If you are designing an organization structure, we recommend finding the design of a sociocratic organization that is already doing something that is similar to what you are planning to do. (See our website www.sociocracyforall.org/resources for examples and for a contact form to ask SoFA about existing related sociocratic organizations.)

If you start from scratch then begin with the aim in mind. What are the products the organization will produce? What are the services it will deliver? If we build in a lack of clarity at the birth of the organization, it may struggle with that conflict for the rest of the organization's life because that conflict will be rooted in the personal aims and expectations of members (see section 6.10.4). From the overall organization's aim, we go to sub-aims. What are the different elements of what needs doing, so we can work toward that overall aim? Each aim translates into a department circle. We do not start to draw a circle structure until we can write down a rough draft of the circles' aims. Groups new to sociocracy sometimes struggle to generate an appropriate circle structure.

Typical pitfalls:

- Some groups over-emphasize operations that seem important but do not need much policy work (for example IT and finances, depending on the nature of your organization).

- Some groups orient themselves too much to individuals that are doing work (or are planning to do work). For example, if one member currently does task A and task B, this does not necessarily mean that both tasks would fall into the same domain. That individual may end up being a member of two circles in the new structure.

- Some groups overestimate how much work can be done – which will stretch a group too thin. Better to start small and grow as the need arises.

Organizational structure is policy. Use the proposal generation process (see chapter 3 on page 79). Understand what the needs are for your particular organization and then what the dimensions are. What are the considerations for a circle structure? Readers might add more for their particular context, but this is what comes to mind on a generic level:

- Aims and Domains - how they can be subdivided?
- Operations and policy-making - how much of each expected?
- Number of workers (informs the number of circles)?
- Hand-offs - where does one circle's work ends and another's begin?
- What, in a circle, to delegate to a role?
- What, in a circle, to delegate to a sub-circle?
- Who are our stakeholders, and do we include them in our mission circle?
- What kind of outside experts, if any, do we want on our mission circle?
- What are ways that our products and services can be organized? By type of product or service? By geographical area served?

6.4.3   Generating the mission circle

In the early stages of a start-up, or forming an organization, the workers might be at the same time the members of the general circle and the mission circle. How can we form an MC without stretching ourselves too thin? There are different options.

1. The same members of the GC will be members of the MC. This can work, however, one will have to make sure the group spends enough time on big-picture thinking. Strategies are (illustrations in diagram 187a):

   - Scheduling a separate, extra meeting. This might be the best option. The potential downside is over-burdening leaders and delegates. In the start-up/beginning phase, leaders will have their hands full. Attending the general circle is already an extra meeting outside of their core work as circle leaders.

   - Separating out 30 min (or any other time frame that makes sense to the group) for overall planning in every general circle meeting – the circle will probably have to protect that time well because what urgent day-to-day matters tend to over-ride the less pressing future planning. Those 30 min have to be reserved for MC thinking!

- Making every fourth (third, second,. . .) general circle meeting a mission circle meeting. Disadvantage: too much time between meetings and therefore no flow within the mission circle topics – and missing out on one general circle meeting turn.

2. Adding just one or two more external members to the general circle. The advantages are that it is more likely that the mission circle topics will not be over-ridden by the general circle topics – the GC members will not talk about general circle business if the mission circle member carved out the time to join them for a mission circle meeting. The mission circle member, an external member, will keep the GC "on good behavior". John Buck says it is like "inviting a guest for dinner and seeing how well your kids can behave". In our personal experience, we have made use of that in a very early start-up phase. The external member will be able to provide some outside perspective. When the trees right in front of us make it hard to see the forest, the external mission circle members' perspectives might help. (See diagram 187b.)

3. Another hybrid option: sending more than one delegate from the general circle to the mission circle. This can seem safe to a group from a very horizontal context where there is skepticism on whether the mission circle would be operating in the organization's interest or whether the MC would drift into a power-over attitude. (See diagram 187c.)

4. The fourth option is the standard solution: a mission circle separated out from the general circle and double-linked. The leader of the general circle is the top-down link, and a delegate from the general circle is the bottom-up link to the mission circle. (See diagram 187.)

5. Mission circle members may also include delegates from stakeholder circles (parent for a school, customers of a product, funders for a non-profit, see section. 2.5.3 on page 56.

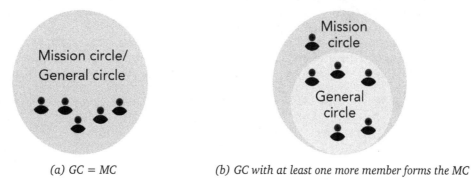

(a) GC = MC   (b) GC with at least one more member forms the MC

187: Early life of a young organization starting with one work group I

If an organization starts out from a board/mission circle: In some cases, it might be the mission circle starting an organization. They would mandate the leader of the general circle (ED or CEO, depending on the type of organization) to form a work team. This is what is shown in diagram 189a.

If the organization grows, the general circle would create department circles, assign them aims and domains and appoint leaders. As soon as the work circles are established, those department circles send delegates back to the general circle. The general circle will send a delegate to the mission circle.

Find more information on implementation in new organizations in section 6.4 on page 225.

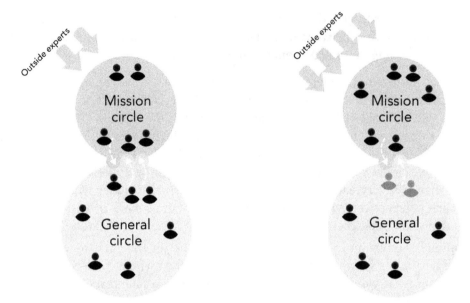

(c) GC and MC are linked with a triple link   *(d) GC and the MC are separate and double-linked*

187: Early life of a young organization starting with one work group II

Every circle needs an aim. Typically the aim is defined by the parent circle. Yet, taking an Open Space approach can enable a company to leverage the innovative power of all people. Everyone in the company is invited at any time to suggest an aim for a new circle - the only constraint is that the aim has to fit within the aim of an existing circle, which then becomes the parent circle. If enough people self-select to work as a circle member on that aim, this new circle is established. If nobody is interested in working on that aim, the circle will not be established. This way a company empowers everyone to follow their passion within the scope of the company's strategy.

(Jutta Eckstein and John Buck)

188: What others say

6.4.4   Partial implementations

Some organizations only implement some elements of sociocracy. While there is nothing wrong with that, the advantage of implementing sociocracy more holistically is coherence. Some features and tools in sociocracy depend on each other. For example, we can only have a general circle if we have leaders and delegates. Having a delegate only makes sense if there is a general circle, and all of those features only work if there is a circle structure. Having a working circle structure only works when circles actually have authority in their domains. (Otherwise they would only prepare proposals for a different decision-making body to decide.)

A huge factor in implementation is training. Everybody has to understand the new governance system

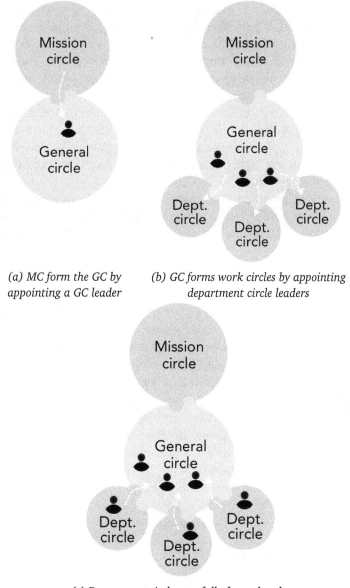

(a) MC form the GC by
appointing a GC leader

(b) GC forms work circles by appointing
department circle leaders

(c) Department circles are fully formed and
link back to the GC

189: Early life cycle of a young organization starting from a mission circle

enough to operate in it. Ideally, training comes before the moment of implementation so everything and
everyone is ready to go. There is some level of chaos that comes with any organizational change.

- Not all "standard" pieces of sociocracy are being used in the organization. One can use consensus
  decision making or even majority vote within a sociocratic circle structure. One could use consent
  for selection processes but not for other decisions. Any piece one leaves out, without a comparable

tool in its place, will be missed. As in a human body, every system has its purpose. For example, an otherwise fully sociocratic organization that never does performance reviews might miss out on improvements on an individual level. An organization that is sociocratic but does not have a board or any equivalent mission circle might miss direction for its long-term trajectory. An organization that never does check-ins at the beginning of a meeting might experience their own meetings as impersonal, without the sense of connection and belonging that improves performance.

- Only some departments or units in the organization are running sociocratically. This might work well if those units' aims and domains are well-defined and well-linked with the rest of the organization. The inherent risk of implementing sociocracy in one unit or division of a larger organizations is that changes in leadership at higher levels of the organization can force a return to the command and control form of management.

- The implementation is incremental. The intention over time is to add more sociocratic elements and tools. The challenge here is that it is hard to find a linear order of features that provide a coherent set. Sociocratic practices are like puzzle pieces that build on each other.

At the core, two things must be in place for any sociocratic organization: a clear aim and a commitment to equivalence, regardless of whether an organization ends up being "purely" sociocratic or borrows from related frameworks or invents an even better version of governance. From a shared aim and a shared process, one can continue a sociocratic journey by choosing tools: consent, linked circles, sociocratic elections. Rounds are a good strategy for including everyone's voice early. Having at least agreement on who will be the facilitator for the initial processes will solve the initial chicken-egg problem of any implementation (as in, who will facilitate the selection process to select the first facilitator?).

Chart 190 on page 233 shows how sociocratic processes and tools build on each other - the related puzzle pieces. The flowchart assumes that existing organizations will have facilitators, aims and a decision-making method in place. Note: the flowchart is *not* a recommended map for implementation.

There is a danger in partial and incremental implementations. Some people may become disillusioned with a partial or incremental implementation when the benefits of sociocracy are not quickly observable or existing organizational problems are not quickly resolved - they may then conclude that sociocracy doesn't work. In those cases, listen with care and remind people of the potential benefits of adopting sociocracy more thoroughly.

6.5   Volunteer organizations

Both in paid and in volunteer contexts, working together has to be productive and efficient or we are losing money, energy, or volunteers themselves. Just as paid workers want to have a say in their work environment, volunteers may have a desire for that as well. For governance, there is no difference between a paid and an unpaid environment. Treat your volunteers like paid staff – have a contract that outlines how the organization will benefit the volunteer, how volunteers will benefit the organization, which defines what the rights and responsibilities of volunteers in the organization are. "Pay" volunteers with feedback about the impact of their work, opportunities for learning, and a sense of belonging and connection. Expect volunteers to be accountable to their commitments.

In a mixed paid and volunteer organization, a typical concern is that either or both a paid person filling a role of a volunteer coordinator could have too much power or carry too much of an organizational burden. A sociocratic organization that includes both paid workers and volunteers can work effectively

Commit to basic principles	Adopt sociocratic elements	Begin to implement processes	Add sociocratic detail	Go deeper
Commit to equivalence	Rounds	ADMIN in meetings	Consent to agenda	
		Meeting evaluation	Constructive feedback	Define feedback channels
		Check-ins	Proposal shaping	Needs assessment
		Lead-do-measure	Add measurements in workflow	Picture forming
			Add measurements in policy	
	Consent	Generate proposal together	Educate on helping circles	
		Options for dealing with objections	Educate on measure and shorten term	
		Consent process	Educate on communication skills	
		Add term ends to all decisions	Clarifying questions rounds	
	Sociocratic elections	Quick reaction rounds	Performance reviews	
	Define and fill facilitator role	Define and fill secretary role	Add logbook	Add logbook keeper	Add stakeholder circles
		Define and fill leader role	Form a general circle	Form a mission circle	Add delegate from GC to MC
		Select delegates	Define hand-offs between circles		Add outside members
Create shared vision, mission, aims	Form circles	Define circle links	Education how to form sub-circles	
		Define operational roles		Define process for removal of a member
		Establish defined membership	Consent to all current members	Circle membership by consent

190: How some of the sociocratic features build on each other

to resolve their dilemmas when both share the responsibilities of decision making.

What do we have to keep in mind if we mix paid staff and volunteers in one organization? Again, for the governance aspect, anything works. Sociocracy is about who does what and who decides what, not about who gets paid for their work. Whether or not volunteers in a mixed organization are decision-makers will depend on their level of involvement.

If we can "hire" a volunteer, can we also "fire" them? It follows from the general principles of membership of circles (a circle can choose its members) that we have to be able to remove people from circles (see section 2.2.3). This is true no matter whether that person is paid or not. That means we might be in a situation where we "fire" a volunteer because working with them negatively affects the circle's ability to work toward their aim. Some find that hard to do because we want to be grateful for anyone putting in their volunteer time. However, remember that any organization based on consent requires its members to be accountable and constructive. If someone's behavior is slowing down the circle significantly, it might be better to let that person go.

We can remove someone from a circle or a role and ask them to do other jobs within the same organization. In this case, we are not excluding them as a member – we might even hold them in appreciation as members of the organization while removing them from one particular circle. For example, someone might be the best cook and volunteer coordinator in a soup kitchen but drive people away as a fundraiser. This person might still be part of the meal or volunteer coordination circle but not the fundraising circle.

How can we include new members in a sociocratic system, especially in a volunteer context? It is harder to require training on sociocratic governance for volunteers because their involvement might be lower and more fluid. Someone told us about volunteers in a community garden, *"the people don't want to be trained in decision making, they are here to dig in the dirt."* Our response was: *"Well, someone still has to make the decisions, and if they want to make them for themselves, they will need a framework to do it in."* Volunteers work within the context of the organization's policies. Organizations need to be clear in their policies about which level of volunteering qualifies for decision making and which levels of volunteering welcome feedback but no decision-making rights. If volunteers have decision-making rights, then they need training and education about sociocracy just like any paid staff member.

Another way to include volunteers in an organization is as a stakeholder group. Volunteers have a stake in the well-being and effectiveness of the organization they contribute their time to. They have in interested in their work having meaning and they have an interest in how they are treated as volunteers. A circle of volunteers representing the interests of volunteers can be double linked with the Mission Circle. The leader of the Mission Circle (or other selected person) would serve as the leader of the Volunteer Circle and one or more delegates selected by the Volunteer Circle would serve on the Mission Circle,.Alternatively, a Volunteer Circle could be a sub-circle of the General Circle or any other organizational circle. In that context the Volunteer Circle would have its own aim and domain and relevant activity and authority like any other circle of the organization.

6.6   Sociocracy in tiny groups

Some people assume that sociocracy is something for medium-sized groups only. What about very small groups, like groups of 4-5 people? Does a circle structure here create too much overhead? It depends.

There is some truth in the assumption that a very small group will not benefit from a circle structure as much as a larger group will. However, sometimes the advantages of establishing circles will outweigh the effort. The considerations:

- The desire to *focus attention to one particular part of the overall aim*. The aim drives the entire organization. Often, even in a small group, members get overwhelmed. Topics start falling through the cracks.
- The desire to have differentiation of who does what. Having a circle structure might give clarity on what the authorities are. It makes a difference whether a group is a general circle that holds the entire domain together or whether that group is a general circle of "circles of one". In other words, does everyone know who has authority to act on what?
- The desire to have all agenda items be always relevant for everyone in the GC. Is everyone doing exactly the same work and therefore interested in the same topics? If not, one might benefit from a circle structure, even in a small organization.

Let's say one has a group of seven people who are part of a climate action group. The overall aim might be *"Supporting climate awareness in Madison county"*. Four people are interested in promoting permaculture as an inspiring alternative to the practices that generate harmful climate change. Three are interested in doing public education events. One manages the website and the mailing list. The aim of three of the members is to collect and write articles and make them available on social media. If, at a meeting, the circle talks about event planning and strategy around their event series, the website manager might be bored. Conversations about permaculture might not be relevant to the event planners.

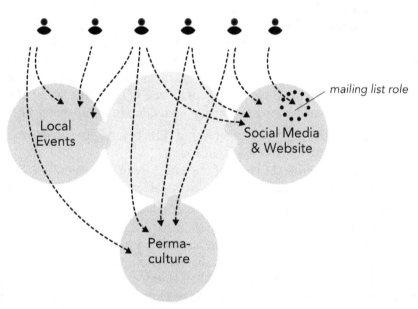

191: A tiny organization: a small number people spread out into several circles

The advantage of breaking up into circles is to keep every meeting relevant and to make policy in a group that actually carries out that piece of work. Also, we can be sure that each of the sub-aims gets the attention it needs. The general circle might only meet from time to time, as the real work happens in the work circles, and this is what those people are actually burning for.

Here is another very subtle advantage of having the clarity of domains and aims and who holds which domain: it is easier to recruit prospective members if they have a clear choice about where to put their energy. The question to them is not: *"do you want to join a group that does events, social media, a mailing*

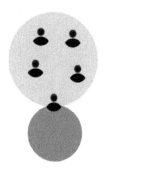

the circle's domain
(policy & operations)

the sub-circle's domain
(policy & operations)

192: Only one member in sub-circle

list and permaculture?" The question becomes *"do you want to help us organize a monthly event? We'll show you who else is connected to us and how it all comes together."* Volunteer workers are sometimes intimidated by unclear structure because we all know that volunteer work can easily be "dumped" on the first one who does not say *no*. In a structure with complete clarity, this will be less the case and people feel more confident to join.

In tiny organizations, there is a tendency to have circles that only have one member. There is a problem here: what about double-linking? A circle of one, in our view, is more a transitional solution because it lacks the sparring partner, the other perspective. In a small start-up situation, one might assign one person to do marketing. That person might at the same time be the one who oversees all marketing activities (most likely because he or she is the only one doing it), and he or she makes all policy decisions. By default, the circle member of a circle of one is the leader of the circle.

In that temporary set-up, we have to pay more attention to transparency than usual.

- Make sure, the leader (and only member) of this circle of one attends the circle meetings of the next higher circle and reports on a regular basis.
- Make it a priority to grow the circle of one into a more stable position, by adding members or by finding a better place for the domain, for example by merging it with another domain/circle.

What is the difference between a circle of one and a person who holds a role in a circle? The general answer is that circles make policy whereas roles carry out policy. But the difference can get blurry. A circle of one with a narrow aim and domain may not be much different than a person in a role with a broad aim and domain of decision making that in other circles or organizations would be considered policy. In the end, what is significant is not the identity as circle of one or as role filler but how well values of effectiveness and egalitarianism are being served by the way we conceptualize the identity.

6.7   Organizations with few workers and many members

Sociocratic circle structures scale very easily. It is easy to split up into more and more layers of specificity by adding sub-circles and sub-sub-circles that structure domains and aims in which workers make decisions together.

Things get tricky if there are many members of an organization who are not part of decision making on the policy level. For example, this can be true for food coops (many member-owners, only a few workers in the store), platform cooperatives (many contributors, only few platform stewards) and towns (many citizens, only few involved in governance). Sociocracy is designed to let workers make decisions about their own work. Especially in cases where many people contribute but are not formally organized in circles where they can have a say, sociocracy falls short.

Option 1: Many, many circles This is the option that has served organizations like the neighborhood parliaments in India where hundreds of thousands of families are connected in linked circles. Each member, by being part of a forum that is small enough so everyone can be heard, has a voice and can request help and support. A lot of power rests on the grassroots level of such an organization. Organizing many people in this way requires a huge community organizing effort.

Option 2: More distance but also more feedback A different situation is what we have in platform cooperatives. Think, for example, a social media platform like Twitter being replaced by a sociocratically run (and cooperatively owned) alternative. There simply aren't as many decisions to be made, and tasks to be performed as there are members. A platform cooperative has a group of contributors who greatly outnumber the decision-makers for policy. Here are some thoughts about this dilemma:

- It does not have to be an issue if even a large number of contributors are not part of decision making, as long as they have the *option* of being heard by the decision-makers and there is clarity about the criteria for becoming a decision-maker. (For example, a certain threshold for work contribution could be required to become a circle member.)
- Be intentional about the feedback lines in both directions: decision-makers in the organization have to proactively ask for, and members need to know how to give feedback.
- Stewardship of an organization requires attention – more attention than an ordinary member can give in passing. Sociocracy is about protecting working groups; defined membership for decision-making circles is an essential requirement of consent decision making.

Separate intentional, intensive use of well-defined feedback from decision making. We can hear many perspectives throughout the whole process of generating proposals, and we can hear many people leading up to a review process of a policy. In our view, this is the best way to include many voices and still benefit from small and solid groups of decision-makers. (See also section 4.4.3 on page 162.)

A sociocratic IT business we are aware of created a transparent system of including all employees over time by replacing circle members with new members on a defined term so that every 2-3 years, every member has been part of a circle. This is a useful idea to give more people the experience of being in a circle, understanding how the decisions are made. This option can be combined with the two other options. It requires trust, transparency and a clear way of how to include the voices of the employees who are not currently circle members.

6.8 Legal issues

Some people rule out sociocracy for legal reasons, for example because their legal form seems to determine what options they have in how they are governed. For example, individual schools in the United States public school system are limited in their capacity to choose self-governance. For non-profits, sometimes the funding sources limit how they govern themselves. We urge groups not to give up too fast. Most organizations have more leeway than they think, and there are a number of workarounds.

Since the legal side of organizations depends on the type of organization and your location. We will only give a few examples. Below are some examples of stumbling blocks with very easy solutions:

- For example, we sometimes hear *"but we're legally required to have a vote"*. Consider that consent is everyone saying they are willing to go with a proposal. We are therefore simply increasing the majority rule from 51% to 100%. There is no legal issue there.
- The requirement to have board decisions can be dealt with the general circle forming the official board, confirming decisions made in circles.
- Any legal body like a board that only represents a part of the organization can be integrated into a circle structure. For example, a Condominium Homeowner Association Board (HOA) legally only represents the people whose names are on the property deeds. But a community is larger than a set of homeowners. A community might include many people whose names are not on the deed – renters, lovers, relatives. If we want equivalence in a community, the organizational structure needs to be inclusive. We have seen and supported implementations in cohousing and other intentional communities where the HOA Board was a sub-circle of a department circle. If we look at it that way, the domain of an HOA is just a small piece of the decisions that need to be made in a community. Be creative!

6.9   Sociocracy, ownership and control

Owners of for-profit organizations usually have control of their organizations by direct ownership or by majority vote of the shareholders and/or their Boards of Directors. Nonprofit organizations and volunteer associations are usually controlled by majority vote of their Board of Directors. Sociocratic organizations are not owned and controlled by anyone because of decision making by consent and the double-linking circular organizational structure. The sociocratic organization owns itself. Without the fear of power-over control, investors can be welcomed because they bring needed funds to the organization. Hostile takeovers or unwelcome moves of operations overseas are no longer possible. In nonprofit contexts where funders replace investors, funders are welcome as partners rather than dominant or absent outsiders, and the measure of effectiveness includes both the well-being of workers and the degree of positive impact on society. A sociocratic organization needs to have sociocratic principles and practices stated in the organization's articles of incorporation, partnership agreements, by-laws and/or any other documents that define the legal entity. A sample set of bylaws for your purpose may be found online. However legal advice is beyond the scope of this book.

6.9.1   Sociocracy and the distribution of profits, salaries and wages

Here are three aspects to keep in mind:

- Transparency: financial information including salaries and profit distribution is open to all members of the organization. They do not have to be open to the public (although they could be).
- We can put any policy around remuneration in place, we just have to do it by consent. If we want to decide by consent that only the webmaster is paid, we can do that. If we decide by consent that your operational leader earns twenty times as much as everyone else, that is your choice. The tendency, however, is that organizations with transparent pay will not have as big of a pay gap as intransparent organizations that keep pay opaque, and we hope that every sociocratic organization

will strive for more equality in pay as well.

- In a sociocratic organization adopting the model of shared ownership, investors get a fixed rate of return, as with a loan, and they get a share of short and long-term profits. The workers get a fixed rate of return for their labor (their salaries or wages) and also get a share of the short and long-term profits. Therefore all share an interest in the well-being of the organization and all its members.

Consideration of formulas for the division of profits among investors and workers is beyond the scope of this book. For a more extensive discussion on those topics see "We the People," "BossaNova" and the writings of Gerard Endenburg (for references see section 7.3.1 in the appendix).

6.10 Typical pitfalls in implementations

Learning *about* sociocracy is very different from running a sociocratic organization. And *implementing* sociocracy is very different from having a well-running governance system in place. At any stage of the implementation, there can be pitfalls that are unexpected for the novice. After seeing many organizations implement sociocracy and sometimes struggle, we can identify some typical pitfalls. After all, offering this manual poses a risk for its authors: the risk that people take this book, implement sociocracy in an organization, fail, and then broadcast a claim that "sociocracy does not work".

We have seen sociocracy work and many others have too. But like a perfect human body sometimes needs help, organizations are organisms with a lot of complexity that might need support. Organizations are self-repairing, but only in the ideal case of everyone having full expertise and perfect awareness (i.e. no blind spots of their own). Reading through this manual so far is like reading a book about biology – now it is time for some first aid education! We want to tell readers the typical symptoms of an "ill" organization to enable them to self-diagnose. Depending on the gravity of an issue, practitioners might be able to "treat" the issue themselves, or they might consult with governance "doctors".

What are the most common diseases? The tricky thing is that one symptom of stuck governance is that we get triggered, for example we get stressed, overwhelmed, upset, overworked or burned out, maybe scared. That might interfere with your ability to say *"oh, that's a governance issue. We have been giving the general circle too much power and that's why we feel this way"*. Many typical struggles that upset people are governance issues: people who talk too long, lack of accountability, people stepping on each other's toes, tasks falling through the cracks – the list is long. Remember how feelings are pointers to met or unmet needs? (See section 4.1.3.) Whenever someone gets upset in the context of an organization, consider that there might be a governance issue one could address. Did someone give feedback? How can similar issues be prevented next time?

If we could wave a magic wand, we would have readers review this chapter on a regular basis. Practitioners would read it every few months in a new implementation, or they would read it every year to make sure they are still on track. Some of these "diseases" develop slowly over time. Once they are chronic, it gets harder to treat them. Groups can decide to check in with a "governance doctor" on a regular basis (i.e., a retainer arrangement), like a yearly physical for the health of your organization and the well-being of its members. An organization's governance is part of the organizational culture and the interpersonal relationships, which are a core asset of any organization.

6.10.1   Issues that the organization had before

Sociocracy can support member involvement and effectiveness (potentially leading to a more stable financial situation), ideally leading to a self-governed organization that can identify weak spots. It will be resilient and innovative, and heal itself. However, implementing sociocracy does *not* solve issues that are outside of the scope of governance. If the business plan is not viable, or funding is not solid, then a sociocratic organization will fail just as any traditionally governed organization. If communication skills are low, then those need to be addressed, or the organization may fail.

Sociocracy will not help if an organization is already having very deep issues. It is not a magic bullet. To stay in the metaphor of diseases: surgery can be life-saving. However, when a patient is very weak, the life-saving surgery can be too much and can kill the patient earlier than he would have died without surgery. Or, as a colleague said, in reference to our analogy of learning how to swim, "when someone is drowning, it is not the time to teach how to swim". Changing the governance system in times of crisis can add another level of complication that brings the organization over the edge.

When implementing sociocracy, it's good to ask whether this is a good time or whether there are other serious issues not related to governance that need to be addressed. If one ignores other serious issues, the implementation will fail just as fast as the organization will.

We know from experience that struggling organizations often have more than one chronic issue. We *can*, with outside help, identify areas where tools from sociocracy might be helpful. Training facilitators in sociocracy, for example, can give a lot of benefits with only little investment or change.

6.10.2   Power struggles

Sociocracy shifts the power-structures in organizations. Some have to give up power, some have to step into power and leadership. In consensus organizations, some individuals often have disproportionate power over the group. Since sociocracy equalizes power, these individuals may resist, oppose, or try to undermine the implementation of sociocracy. The combination of individualism and victim mindset can be toxic for community and for sociocracy. In majority rule organizations, different factions may be accustomed to manipulating for control of power and they may see sociocracy as another system to be manipulated. In for-profit organizations, the distrust based on the historical management-labor divide may be quite a barrier to overcome.

The case of trial periods

Some organizations implementing sociocracy start with a trial period. They want to try out sociocracy for 6 months and then evaluate. This sounds like a good idea, and sounds even very much aligned with sociocracy – try out a proposal for a certain time frame, evaluate and then decide how to proceed.

There is a subtle difference between ordinary proposals in a sociocratic organization and implementing sociocracy in a trial version. Since with sociocracy, we also change the method used for decision making, it has to be very clear what the decision making is, with which we decide whether or not to extend or end the trial. What does the organization fall back into? Imagine a consensus-run organization implementing sociocracy for half a year. What decision-making method do they use to decide whether they are continuing – consensus or consent? How are we going to treat objections to using sociocracy as a governance method? Especially in a consensus situation where some people might still be attached to the powerful position of the minority, one can end up in a position where those who feel threatened by the concept of consent decision making will undermine the trial period, making it impossible to experience how consent *could* be, and then using it against sociocracy's case when the time for evaluation has come. In a way, even if we wished it were different (given that short-time experiments are our favorite tool for dealing with objections!), we have come to the conclusion that there is no trial for governance systems like sociocracy.

Instead of a trial period, do a proposal like figure 193. This is something we have learned from

Example implementation proposal

We adopt sociocract as our governance method. In 6/12/18 months, we will evaluate how effective our implementation has been and generate an improvement plan.

193: Example implementation proposal.

experience. Referring back to the preconditions of consent: sociocracy requires willingness to talk until objections are integrated. In a trial period, we are leaving a back door open. We will *not* be truly open to working things out which means the organization's members are going to engage in a self-fulfilling prophecy of "consent does not work". Putting an entire organization through a yes/no trial period may not provide realistic data. Consent only works when we accept that working things out as equals and with honest curiosity is the only way of relating to each other. If the group is not ready to accept that, one might have to find the small-scale experiment that the group *can* say "yes" to. It will provide the data that is needed so everyone can say "yes" to consent decision making for the whole organization.

Hidden power structures

Implementing sociocracy has to be aligned with the values of sociocracy. One of them is that circles need authority over their domain. What is meant by that is *full* authority. The circle needs to be the only and ultimate decision-maker in their domain. Imagine a sociocratically run department in a big corporation that itself is *not* run sociocratically. They might be able to *pretend* to be in power but they do not have ultimate decision-power. The corporation can close down the experiment, or the company sold, without the department having any say.

Sociocratic organizations own themselves. As long as *anyone else* has power over the organization, it cannot own itself. Shifting power is not cosmetic, and in our world, it is not just a fad for squeezing more productivity out of happier employees. This is not (only) about productivity. It is about deep change, and not all environments might be suitable for it at first. We do not discourage sociocratic experiments in corporate departments or in non-profits where the board – or the founder – is not buying in on the governance system. We are just aware of the experiment's vulnerability and ask departments to protect themselves from that uncertainty. In our view, this is also true if a single owner has the power to install (and therefore also to withdraw) a governance method.

6.10.3   Lack of defined membership

In sociocracy, circle membership has to be clearly defined. We have to know who is in and who is out. If we do not, we will have people dropping in and out of circles. For decision-making groups, this is a problem. If we do not know who is a member and who is not, we also do not know who needs to consent, which means we won't be able to hear all the objections or we will be distracted by objections from people who are not members.

There is more: we will not know who has access, for example to money in the circle's budget. Lack of defined membership makes it hard to be transparent (we do not know what they are thinking because they are not there, and they do not know what we are thinking), effective (we risk waiting for them because we think they might come back) and to speak with equal consideration. We cannot make a decision with every circle member in mind if some of the circle members are frequently absent – to an extent that we do not know whether they still consider themselves a member.

Lack of defined membership is a problem mainly for volunteer organizations. In paid contexts, often, people are hired to fill a role which automatically puts them into a certain circle. However, the following scenario can happen almost anywhere. Imagine a circle that has worked on a proposal, with one circle member being absent (unexcused, maybe) for three meetings. The circle is led to believe that this member has dropped out but lacked the intentionality to follow up to hear what is going on. Now the proposal is ready to be consented to, and our missing circle member shows up, still considering herself a member – and objects to the proposal. This can be frustrating and disheartening and can easily lead to volunteers losing their interest in working in the organization. In short, defined circle membership is a must for all decision-making groups.

Excusing absences and follow-ups if someone missed a meeting has to be part of the organization's culture. The person to follow up on this will be the circle leader and the person who missed the meeting. A circle can decide to put a circle member on leave. (In that case, they might stay informed but not have consent rights for that time period), for example for health reasons or extended travel. Intentionality and clarity: we have to *know* what our agreements are and who our members are.

6.10.4   Clarity of domains/aims

If a group keeps struggling around the same questions, it might be because they do not share the same aim. Imagine a situation where we share the aim of having a cohousing community in Toronto. If we find ourselves continually arguing about location, it may turn out that some want a community on the east side and some on the west side. If we have clarity about our aim, we may realize we have two groups with distinct aims – the east side and the west side groups.

This can be subtle – for example, we can share parts of the aim but we might prioritize them differently.

> Let us look at the example of a social enterprise that produces fair trade chocolate and lobbies for fair trade. One aim is to create more opportunity for workers in the fair trade industry, one is to produce chocolate. Those two aims are not in conflict with each other; we can do both. But if we have a surplus to re-invest – does this go into extending the production, or does it go into education around fair trade?

We are not stuck in conflict forever *if* we see that a divergence on the aim is what is going on. If we realize the reason underlying the struggle, we have a choice of re-stating our aim or to split into two organizations, each with its own distinct aim. For example, one organization's aim of producing fair trade chocolate and the other's to lobby for fair trade. Either solution might be better than to spin our wheels and to wear out fighting the battle and hitting the same wall again and again.

In a similar way, domains benefit from clarity. In section 2.2.2, we described how two domains should neither have overlap nor gaps between them.

> Imagine a fridge in a bakery café. Does the Front Desk Circle maintain the baked goods in the front desk fridge, or the circle that produces the baked goods?

Imagine nobody doing it – then we'd have baked goods out of date in the fridge. Imagine *both* are assuming that they are in charge. Then they would step on each other's toes. This would either lead to resentment and frustration around doubled work, or un-doing each other's efforts. Obviously, neither is a desirable outcome. Most likely, everyone would be willing to define the domain without gaps. The trick is to remember what the effects of lack of clarity about domains and aims looks like, so we can respond with intentionality.

The signal for both lack of clarity of domain and for lack of congruency of the aim is the same: the same issue keeps coming up in different ways. If there are recurring issues about the same topic, it is time to get curious. What might be underlying these recurring struggles? Might it be related to how each member understands the aims or domains? Change can then come from a place of understanding and acceptance.

6.10.5 Paying too little attention

A new governance method requires some attention. We have seen organizations declare sociocracy hoping for easy transition. We do not see this work. This section outlines the typical areas that require attention.

Underestimating the prevailing culture

Sociocracy means culture change. Especially in existing, hierarchical organizations this cannot be underestimated. That culture change includes questions of identity, power-over and power-under. There is a huge learning to do for everyone as we question how we have been doing things, who we are, and what is driving us. Be prepared, eyes wide open, for intense feelings around topics of power!

There are some judgements that are held as truths very widely and that make it hard to accept sociocracy as an option.

- Judgment: *"People do not want to/cannot take on responsibility."*
  Although it is true that some people find peace in not having too much responsibility from time to time, it is easy in sociocracy to keep the scope of responsibility at a level that works for members. We disagree with the original statement in that we assume that everyone wants power in their world, even this "world" is just a piece of the organization. It is about the hat we wear: while I might be executive director in my day job, I might want to just hammer nails in my volunteer work, without shouldering too much responsibility. That is fine. We tend to think of some people as "natural" leaders but it not realistic for every "natural leader" to be leader in all their organizations and contexts. At the same time, an organization needs more than "natural leadership". Through the layers of circles, everyone can operate at the level of abstractness or specificity that works

for them at that moment and in that part of their life. It is also possible to wear multiple hats. In our own community, we hold roles as cartwright (very specific) and cleaning windows of the community building. We also have very abstract jobs, such as member of the General Circle or as leader of the Governance Improvement Circle. In the role as window-cleaner, I do not want to have the well-being of the community over the next 5 years on my mind – I am cleaning windows so all I think about is how to clean them, as service to my community.

Roles and circles give us a more fine-grained, dynamic way of working together. We can be flexible in our personal development. We can start small and grow into leadership, or we can let go of responsibilities. Our commitment and the specificity of work we choose will fluctuate over time, making it possible to give up responsibility when life pulls us in a different direction for a while. This commitment can be shaped according to our needs and the needs of the organization. A dynamic organization lets us be flexible. This flexibility is the strength of the dynamic governance system, and it makes it uniquely human as well.

- Judgment: *"We need experts to decide this."*
  We consider this half true. We can rely on input and data from experts but we have to strive to make an informed decision about matters that affect us. Just a good, compassionate doctor will help us make an informed but empowered decision about our health, "experts" on any topic can be asked for their input – sociocracy does not limit flow of information. The decision still remains in the circle.

- Judgment: *"Hearing everyone is slow and tedious."*
  This might be true in the moment – an autocratic decision is always the fastest decision, in the short run. But it is not the most sustainable one. This concern comes up most often in organizations that tend to make decisions in large groups. In small groups rounds increase clarity and reduce debates. Just learning rounds, some find it hard at first, and then they fall in love with the level of insights it gives them into other people's perspectives. Over time, people appreciate the input we gain from hearing from everyone, and how it makes decisions better over time. The mutual respect leads to a more pleasant organizational culture which pays back over time.

- Judgment: *"Too much process/too artificial/too constrained."*
  Some people are turned off by the presence of structure. It can be a problem if people are slowed down because they are monitoring everything they say to see whether it is "right process". Typically, however, this is a matter of practice and gets much easier very quickly. We can support this by offering more education on a continuing basis. Let us consider the alternative: no process – "absence" of power. But power is never absent, not in a world where people have grown up in a system of power. The tyranny of structurelessness is real. We want to think of power as something positive. With intentionality, this power can be harvested, shared and steered, to everyone's benefit.

Internalized patterns of inequality

Consent is not a guarantee for shared power. There are always power dynamics: privileges of all kinds are either on the surface or very close to it. We all carry our experience of power. Most people, especially those who have had less-than-average access to privilege, carry internalized powerlessness. It is hard to work through that and impossible to just "strip it off". We can start noticing it. For example, there are circle members who, in a round, will add preambles or postscripts to their contributions: *"well, I do not know, my ideas are always not as good as yours"*, or *"yeah, that's just what I think, this was probably not useful for you"*. A combination of awareness, communication skills and practicing equivalence can do a lot. If we hear circle members making their own contribution small, we often speak up and let them know how we appreciate their contributions. That is probably not going to change their internalized patterns immediately but it might be a step toward awareness.

The opposite is true as well. If we notice that someone is speaking with a sense of superiority, it might be useful to bring it up. Some people are not aware of it and might be grateful for that to be brought to their attention. In general, we find that most people *want* to talk with a sense of equivalence but they lack the awareness or skills to do so.

Sociocracy requires people to claim their power. Sociocracy does not address directly internalized experiences of privilege! A way to address that is by doing personal work on awareness of privilege and power. What sociocracy does is to provide space so everyone can speak as equals. Rounds are crucial here because rounds embody the sense of everyone's voice mattering. As we get to know each other more, stereotypes and power-over/power-under patterns recede. (See "Power Under" in references on page 258.)

Anecdotally, sociocratic elections seem to run counter to the mainstream patterns at least to some extent. We have seen numerous elections where the person elected was not the typical leader – at least in comparison with majority vote.

Sociocracy is not free of bias!

There are a few biases that seem to be baked into sociocracy, and we are aware of it:

- Sociocracy is biased toward people who speak compellingly.
- Sociocracy is biased toward people who can form and express ideas with little preparation.
- Sociocracy is biased toward people who are able and willing to follow formats.

We can be aware of these biases and try to work around them. For example, a good facilitator can summarize what someone has said to make sure the group can harvest the wisdom in it. Circle members may request to go last in a round because it takes them a while to think something through. If we own and acknowledge these challenges, we can be allies to those who have a harder time expressing themselves and find creative solutions together. Another creative solution we have found. If there is someone who prefers having time to think before speaking, start a round by a minute of silence for everyone, and during that time everyone plans what they are going to say. Over a round of 6 people each speaking for 1-2 minutes, we can easily save time by taking a minute for people to sort their thoughts.

The last bias, the advantage of people who are able and willing to follow a format, we address with support, charts, posters on the wall and clear prompts. Rounds are useful to harvest people's ideas and seem to neutralize (not marginalize) people whose contributions do not seem constructive. But if someone is "off" very often, it is hard to include their voice. There have been experiments with substitutes. For example, the actual circle member is not at the meeting but someone else takes their viewpoint and speaks for them. We know it can be done – but it takes quite some effort to do so.

Not letting go of power – and not taking on power

Holding on to power is a mistake that is very easy to make. We have seen it many times in superficial implementations. What people forget is that power has to be passed on to the work/department circles as much as possible.

- Flat organizations shifting to sociocracy sometimes have issues around giving trust to small circles. Everyone wants to involved in deciding everything. They create a structure where the general circle has many members (with many first-level department circles). We have seen new implementations with 7 department circles represented in the general circle. That makes 15 people in one circle – leaders and delegates from 7 department circles plus a leader or 14 people if a general circle member is selected leader of that general circle. With that many people in the room, it is hard to hear everyone because every round is long. It also becomes almost impossible for the general circle to attend to every sub-circle. Decision making will be slow and the benefits of small circles of decision-makers lost. These groups have to be reminded that the magic is to *separate decision making from giving input*. A small circle can get feedback from as many people as is reasonable, possibly the whole organization. Being able to be heard on a decision does not mean having to have consent rights. Being transparent means being forthcoming with information and proactively asking for input.
- Hierarchical organizations are used to having a top-down structure. They want circles to do their work, but they often want to have a finger on it. This is understandable and might happen with best intentions. But it undermines the purpose of distributed leadership and will grow resentment in the work circles. The ones who have the knowledge and do the work in any given domain have to be the ones to make decisions in that domain. The main concern is that we deprive the work circles of the opportunity to fully step into power, action and leadership.

  The antidote is awareness. Everyone in the organization has to embrace decision making power distributed out to the most specific level possible. One has to ask the question – is it that the general circle wants to hold onto power, or is it that work circles are shying away from power? One might have to train the circles on how to make policy. Depending on your context, there might be hesitancy to take full charge of policy. Once a group successfully unleashes the power in the most specific circles, they will notice the difference.

The irony of this pattern is that both very flat and very hierarchical organizations can be equally stuck in the paradigm of centralized power. What we can do:

- Define the domain of circles and ensure that circles (and holder of roles) actually act on their authority.
- Educate about how holding on to power slows down the organization. Educate about the difference between feedback and decision making and about how trust is earned and decisions made better by feedback.
- If it is still hard for an organization to let go of a centralized notion of power, run a small-scale experiment. Ask for permission for a circle to hold a certain domain for a certain time period with some defined requirements for getting feedback. (Readers might recognize it: this is the standard approach to deal with objections – making it smaller and specific enough so a decision-making body feels comfortable about giving consent: *"Let's give this circle the authority to make decisions about their internal budget and on this particular project for 6 months and have them track their progress. We are asking for a monthly report by email and a follow-up meeting in 6 months where we evaluate what it was like to pass authority to that circle."*

Not enough education about governance

We have seen implementations struggle when only a small fraction of the people were trained. Only when everyone (or a significant fraction) feels empowered through understanding the governance structure, can we reach equality.

Education has to be available over time (see section 6.11 for continuous education), and it has to include not only *how* we do things but also *why* we do things. People are busy doing their work, and it is the aim, not the governance method, that drives the work. They might not hold the information on the how and why of processes because it is not in their focus. That is why we explain "in the moment" and educate only on what is relevant to people. For example, the more the members of an organization know about *why* we do elections the way we do them, the more likely they are to stick to a format. They will be more willing to teach it to each other. They will be more skilled in adapting processes to their context because they will know which pieces are important and why.

If we fail on educating enough members on governance, this can lead into power struggles when the group falls into camps (those who know and those who do not) which can lead into those who do not feel comfortable in the process fighting the new governance system. We will then find ourselves in the same difficult situation of people questioning processes and slowing things down. It can cost an incredible amount of energy to be dealing with that kind of disruption.

We sometimes observe a victim mentality around governance – as if one was constrained and "at the mercy" of the governance system. The governance system is *for* the members, offering tools and options to harness the power we have.

It has to be clear to people that processes are not there to constrain them but to *free* them. Education has to be stating the positive: The reason for doing rounds is not to constrain people. We do rounds so we can support each other in speaking and listening. The language we use in explaining processes is extremely important because it can either support victim mentality (*"That's how it's done. Just accept it, it's the rule."*) or empowering (*"This is a useful idea for us because it helps us..."*).

The importance of education is not because sociocracy is hard to understand or to learn. It is because it is easy to slip back into unexamined and unchallenged old habitual patterns. Culture change requires intentionality, practice and some effort. Here is an example from one of our organizations.

> I found a note in a room taken care of by a certain circle. The note was a complaint about something in the room. The member was not well familiar with the circle structure and certainly left the note with best intentions. However, it is unclear whether this note will ever be seen by the circle that is in charge. The more effective way would have been to send an email to the circle leader.

This example shows how information about the governance system and how it works can either empower people or leave them voiceless. The voice of the person leaving the note cannot be heard as well as the person who knows the best way to contact decision-makers. Knowledge is power, once more.

Rigidity

In new implementations, what happens here and there is that groups get into arguments over what is "right" process. Instead of focusing on content, there is obsession with how to do things the "proper" way. The important thing to understand here is that if it is rigid, it is not sociocratic! The *intention* behind the tools and patterns is to ensure effectiveness while making sure no one is ignored. The tools and methodologies, almost everything in this book, are just good practices that we and the global sociocratic community have seen work well for everyone who values effectiveness and equivalence. We recommend staying close to those best practices until there is enough experience to experiment. Diverting from best practices when groups are inexperienced often leads to trouble that could have been avoided. On the other hand, it's good to keep your eyes wide open right from the beginning – groups might have to tweak and adapt from the first moment on.

We integrate effectiveness and equivalence. The time-efficient solution may compromise on equivalence. The "formally accurate" process may mean to compromise on effectiveness.

For example, if a group seems to want a second change round after the regular change round in a selection process, there is no law that they could not do that. *Every group is free to choose their own process in every moment.* There is no right and wrong, there are just more effective and less effective strategies to integrate effectiveness and equivalence. What's hard is if there is no intentional shared decision.

The metaphor of steering works well here. Steering is not fully predictable, as there might be bumps in the road. Steering is also never just going straight. We might have to adjust a little left and right even when we are driving straight. We need a sense of direction that is our "best practice" but we also need to be able to react to our circumstances – otherwise we might crash despite doing everything "straight".

If there is an argument over process and it is a matter of personal preference, the facilitator decides. If there is still resistance, switch to curiosity: what might they, "the governance police", be feeling? They might be anxious, concerned, or overwhelmed. They might be needing ease, effectiveness, acknowledgment. They are certainly acting the way they are with best intentions. Get curious. Ask them. Listen to them.

The sociocratic processes are not rules. They are best practices. They are the best way we know to do things. If some people in your group hear them as rules, keep your focus on the intention. *"I understand that you want to do things right and stay true to our values of equivalence and effectiveness. I am looking to tweak things here and adjust so we can move forward – all without compromising those values."*

Shying away from giving and inviting feedback

We have already talked a lot about feedback in Chapter 4. Getting to a point where most of the people in an organization feel comfortable with feedback can take a long time. We have heard of groups who implement sociocracy and get rid of all the elements around feedback, even meeting evaluations. Especially in volunteer organizations, performance reviews are often dropped, because of the fear that is associated with feedback. Those organizations are not only missing out on an opportunity to improve, but also risk getting stuck.

"Disruptive" behavior': feedback as superpower   We have heard many times from struggling organizations that do not work effectively because there is this person who always... (fill in the blank). There is a standard question we ask in response: *"Have you told them about the impact this behavior has on you?"* More often than not, people had not engaged in an honest conversation. How can we expect people to change without feedback? Feedback is the magic power we all have, and it can shift us from finger-pointing to stepping into responsibility. The world opens up when we get to a point where we realize that we have power in our world because we have the option of giving feedback. We are shifting from a fixed, blaming mindset (*"This is never going to work because of her."*) to a growth mindset: *"There is something I can do."*

This cannot be said enough: everyone has to give feedback about what is going on. The vast majority of struggles can be dealt with. It is silence and sometimes willful looking the other way that keeps organizations from moving forward. We are aware that some people might not change, even with kind and specific feedback. Still, feedback can provide a lot of opportunities for positive change.

When someone's behavior makes it impossible to carry out the aim of the organization or circle, they have to be removed. There will hopefully be a number of (defined) steps and a lot of feedback, one-on-ones and similar measures before that step. We can engage, be curious, be transparent and explicit about our own needs and the other people's impact on us.

Introducing and improving meeting evaluations   If an organization does not do meeting evaluations, start doing them. If we do superficial meeting evaluations of the "good meeting" kind, it can help to model making them more specific. *"When you made that proposal, my mind went completely blank because I had the judgment that you were trying to undo all we had worked for in the past 3 months. I am sure that's not what you are trying to do but I honestly have no idea where that proposal was coming from. I'd appreciate if you could explain what led you to make that proposal because I feel a little irritated here leaving the meeting. I regret not speaking up earlier; it took me a while to get back on my feet."*

Introducing performance reviews   If an organization is not doing performance reviews, depending on the nature of an organization, we can introduce them by modeling ourselves. *"Hey, can we take 10 minutes in this meeting and look at my contribution to this circle? I have been wondering about how you perceive me in this group, and I'd love to hear what you think."* We can then do the simple format of understand/explore. Ideally, this will be enlightening and might inspire people to do the same. Of course, putting in a proposal that performance reviews be done every year might be another approach. Another idea is to attach it to elections. When someone (or you) is selected to fill a role, request that a performance review be done half-way through your term. *"I am excited about being facilitator but I am also wondering whether my style works for people here and I want to learn more about facilitation. Can we put in the backlog or on the calendar that half-way through my term, we do a quick round where we talk about how my facilitation is working for me and for you? That would give me enough time to learn on the job and you some time to experience me in this role. Then I'd have the second half of my term to make adjustments. I'd be grateful for that."*

Giving and receiving feedback, even positive feedback, can be very uncomfortable. But being completely stuck as an organization, that is also uncomfortable. Better be uncomfortable and growing than be uncomfortable and stuck!

6.10.6   Logistics

Managing the just-right level of information

Circles have to find the "just-right" level of information to be transparent. If people are overwhelmed by information, they will not even read the most important email anymore. If your office kitchen is full of signs and reminders, people will likely not read them all. If we send out requests for feedback too rarely, we might be missing out on good information. It is always a balance.

We also have to find a mix that works with regard to the channel and frequency we use to spread information. Do we send out emails, make announcements in meetings, invite public hearings, a newsletter, social media, posters, a file system? Do we invite feedback by direct contact, online surveys, paper

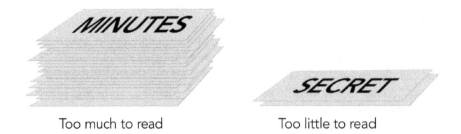

Too much to read   Too little to read

194: Too much information overwhelms people; too little information does not provide enough

etc? Most people have experienced that the just right level of information depends on the context, it depends on what people are used to, how tight-knit the community is, and many other factors. It seems important to use more than one channel. Some people respond to emails, some people tend to read signs. What works well is to put information as close as possible to the situation we are regulating. The circle made a policy about how to use the community garden hose? Laminate a short version and hang it next to the garden hose. The circle made a policy on how to clean up after renting a room? Include the policy (short and in understandable language) in every rental confirmation email, or automatically send it out to people on the day they are renting. If people tend to use too much dishwasher detergent, put a spoon into the detergent that has the capacity of detergent you want people to use. If you want people to use unscented detergent in the laundry machines, a sign on a door might be ignored – it might be good feedback to put the sign right where the detergent goes. Information is not enough, one needs to say it in the right way, with the right timing and location. It helps to be a little creative here.

The most important thought to remember: As the policy-maker in that domain, your priority is to be helpful. Do not operate from *"well, I am right because we made the policy, and you are wrong because you did not follow it."* If people are not being accountable, we can try to think what we can do as a circle so that it will be easier for others to be accountable. Think of the users of your domain as your customers, even if they are your co-workers, family members or neighbors.

One can also gamify it – making it fun to follow a policy. There is a famous example of public toilets and with stickers in the shape of flies that opened my eyes to this aspect of accountability. It was observed that men peeing miss the toilet – sitting in resentment and righteousness did not change anything. There was a brilliant experiment of putting little stickers in the shape of a fly into the toilets, visible for everyone peeing while standing up. People were playful and had the urge to pee on the fly. The side-effect of aiming better was less clean-up. Those stickers were much more effective than any sign or system of punishment.

A very helpful change we made in our own community was to offer the full minutes of a circle meeting in our online logbook, and to only send out a brief email containing the circle name, members, date, and a summary of decisions with a link to full minutes. Everyone can skim a user-friendly 6-line email. Most people trust the other circles, so as long as nothing unexpected happens, all is good and easy. If there is a new policy and a circle is expecting some reactions, they will put a draft into the minutes and direct people's attention to it.

It is the people's job to take information in, but it is your responsibility as a circle to get information out in a way that can be taken in.

Not enough care for sub-circles

One job of a parent circle is to take care of their sub-circles. Calling it "parent" circle is completely on point here! The child-circle reports to the parent circle, but the parent circle has to listen and reach out. When the child circle stops reporting because the circle fell apart, the parent circle has to notice.

A very simple system to support circle care is to keep a list of sub-circles and to check on them at least every other meeting. This can be a quick "all is well", or it can be longer, depending on your context. Ideally, we will have the leader and the delegate of every child circle present, so there should always be someone present to give a status report. If the child circle falls apart, all responsibility falls back on the parent circle. (For example, the parent circle could then appoint a new leader.)

> SoFA supported an organization with geographic circles nationwide in the US. Local groups were connected, forming regional groups, and regional groups into a national general circle. One of the regional groups had collapsed. The general circle was too busy with strategic thinking and was not paying attention to all of its department circles. The issue was not discovered for quite a while.

When circles turn dysfunctional, they often go silent. Although it is the circle's responsibility to reach out for help and let the parent circle know, it is *also* the parents' circle responsibility to check on the child circle.

"Too-many-meetings" and "too-many-circles" syndrome

Another typical pitfall is starting an organization with too many circles (and too many meetings). The organization has to be developed according to the work that needs to be done (and the people available to do that work), not around wishful thinking. The danger is that we stretch ourselves too thin. We can only populate as many circles as we can populate. Work circles are formed to focus our attention to a certain domain, so the equation has to include (1) the number of people to do the work (2) the amount of work to do.

Instead of starting a new circle, we can define an operational role (see section 2.3.2 on page 42) and leave policy-making in the circle. Operations can be taken care of by one or two (pair) members. That way, work and attention are taken off the plate for the circle, but there is no new circle to be sustained. That also reduces the time spent in meetings.

Another misconception is that every meeting has to happen with all circle members every time. This is certainly true for policy meetings but not for for operational meetings. Often, delegates do not need to attend operational meetings. Policy requires the whole circle's consent. We can work with subsets of that group for other meetings, whenever it makes sense. Form helping circles with only part of the circle as often as possible to reduce the amount of time everyone has to sit through a meeting.

Also, the circle decides how often policy meetings are. Nothing is set in stone – it is helpful to be on a regular schedule because it is easier to track but meetings don't have to happen with the same frequency all the time. One circle might meet weekly, another one monthly, another one monthly in summer and twice a month in winter. Whatever makes sense in a context will guide our decision.

6.11 Continuing education

Governance is not something one learns in one day or in one-weekend workshop. Neither is it something one can learn *just* by doing it. We need some shared language and some explicit training so we can make good choices and discuss them.

A group might do some intensive training before and during implementing sociocracy in their organization. But there is ongoing tweaking, refreshing and reminding to do.

- People do not take in everything during an initial training. If one teaches everything at once, they either reach overload from too much information, or they have gaps because you answered a question that they had not asked yet. Bottom-line: one needs to review, more than once. It is best to do some intensive training, let people experiment and then review parts bit by bit as they are using it.
- One needs to do some adjusting. People might remember some of what they learned, and they will fill the rest in "creatively". They might come up with their own style which may or may not be effective and might benefit from some feedback.
- Many people focus on the how-to in the beginning. The *why* might not be in their focus. In the long run, they need both, which means one has to review the *why* of processes. To us, the *why* is just as important as the *how* because only when we know why we do something, we will honor the process and be able to adjust it and make it better.

See section 7.3 for more resources.

•

6.11.1 An easy way to keep learning: live commentary

How can a group keep learning, without spending too much time on it? One way is to schedule extra training where individual topics are covered. Another way is to do a refresher class once every two years.

There is a low-maintenance way, however, that we highly recommend: train your facilitators to give a *live commentary* during meetings. For example, if we have an election, it is helpful if the facilitator gives some explanations on what is happening. See the example in Figure 195, with all *live commentaries* in bold.

In an inexperienced group, this style would be very helpful. Every piece of information is delivered right when it is needed. It will also train newcomers right away!

6.11.2 How to educate new members: onboarding

If we are about to join a sociocratic organization, there might be a process already, a basic training everyone might have to go through to become a member.

If an organization expects new members to just be trained on the fly, they might be in for an unpleasant surprise. Imagine only half of the members being trained well enough to be active promoters of the governance system (after all, we join an organization because of its mission or aim, not because of its governance method). If the membership increases by 50%, the people who are trained and active supporters will only be a third of the members. Some circles may even wind up without any members well-trained in sociocracy. They will probably just "go and do" instead of asking for training because they might not be aware that sociocratic self-governance is in parts significantly different from traditional systems. It is very unlikely that the unintentional changes coming from lack of attention to

---

Example: "live commentary"

So, we want to fill the role of the delegate here. Yuong is our delegate at the moment, and we selected him two years ago. **We select for a time frame so that we don't get stuck in our ways and have an opportunity to reconsider and either re-elect the same person or fill the role with someone else.** I suggest that we select for a time frame of two years again. **We can always change that later if we see the need.**

Since we have done this a few times already and the role has not changed, I assume that we do not have to define the role or the qualifications. Are there any questions or reactions on that? *(pause)*
Ok, seeing none, let us go to nominations. We do a nomination round, and everyone writes down their nomination. **That way, we can be sure that we get everyone's original ideas. We as a group do not want to get narrow minded too soon, and it's really valuable to hear people's original ideas.** We will then share who we nominated and why. Remember you can nominate yourself, **and that's not volunteering, just input for the group that you consider yourself qualified for the job...**

195: A selection process with some elements of "live commentary" for educational purposes

governance will be in favor of both effectiveness and equivalence. Things might get stream-lined for effectiveness, compromising on equivalence, or they might tread water because they don't know how to integrate effectiveness into egalitarian organizations.

New members will feel more connected and empowered through training as they understand how the governance system works. Here are some ways of bringing new members up to speed. Most of these ideas can be combined to find the mix that works for a given context, and including "old" members in this does not hurt:

- open Q&A for governance questions
- training during all-member meetings
- sharing short training videos
- study group whenever there is a new group of people
- an in-house library with books like this manual or *"We the People"*
- posters and charts in the meeting room (see resources)
- a buddy system
- a written overview of your governance system
- your own in-house video about sociocracy and your specific implementation (ask SoFA for resources)
- making a training mandatory for onboarding new members
- a list of recommended videos for onboarding new members
- webinars like the ones offered by Sociocracy For All
- New members come 15min early and/or stay 15 minutes after every meeting to be briefed on process before the meeting, and can ask questions after the meeting.
- Integrate governance education into the general orientation to the organization.

Chapter 7

Appendix

7.1 About Sociocracy For All (SoFA)

Sometimes we can feel it when the insight sinks in for people. It tends to happen when training participants experience the sociocratic circle structure with their own bodies, standing in linked circles. They experience how sociocracy embodies interdependence. How it ensures transparency. How no one can be overpowered anymore. How sociocracy requires self-responsibility. Some training participants get silent, while their minds and hearts are taking in what they see and feel. Sometimes they say things like "...but...that's...big" – expressing how deep and how wonderful of a change sociocracy would mean to their company, their community or their volunteer organization. They become filled with hope and excitement. A few get tense or sad, as they lack confidence that their own organization might ever embrace a system like sociocracy.

We all have had our share of experiencing oppression. Our extractive and divisive system hurts everyone. That's why, in sociocracy training, there is never just practice. The power structures that are out there in the world are ingrained in us and therefore they are always in the room, very close to the surface, and with it our pain, sadness, fear, hope and longing.

Sociocracy is not a superficial tool to make workers *feel* like they have more power so they gladly put in more effort into a system built on power-over. It's not another management method. It's deep change. It's real. To us, sociocracy is a tool so powerful it can be the operating system for a new paradigm and economy: based on connection, consideration and care. In boardrooms and in living rooms. In classrooms and in community buildings. Our vision is a world outside of the paradigm of right and wrong, winners and losers. All of us know that a more beautiful world is possible, we feel it and we long for it. We are equipped with what it takes to live it. AND we need to create an environment that brings out those strengths. Systems that allow us to work *from* the longing for connection instead of stuffing it. Systems that are built on trust, instead of systems that reward divisiveness and ridicule or outlaw consideration.

Pretty words won't make it happen. Good intentions won't be enough, and neither will awareness or individual action. Taking on a system ingrained in mainstream culture requires more than that. More people need to know that there are options. More people need to have access to skills and information about those options. People who already know about the tools and use them need to find each other so we can be companions for each other. To troubleshoot together and to celebrate together. Since there

254

are still so few of us, we need each other so we can be support if one or some of us struggle and deals with disappointing setbacks. Culture change requires places where we can recharge our batteries.

In Gandhi's model for social change, we need political action (intervening where there is injustice), personal transformation, and a constructive program. We see sociocracy in the constructive program, showing what the alternative for governance could look like. A good model and relevant skills. That's the area that we're most invested in. Superficial sociocracy won't change culture. Talking about it won't. The revolution needs skills in a lot of people so the new paradigm can be a lived reality everywhere. The ultimate goal will be to put trainers out of business – because every child learns how to listen, speak and collaborate. Until sociocracy is the new normal there will be need for learners to build the skills and experience it takes to use sociocracy in the real world.

That's where SoFA comes in. SoFA was founded in 2016 by the authors of this book, after years of previous experience with sociocracy, with the mission of spreading sociocracy widely so everyone – *everyone!* – benefits. Our current circle structure is shown in 196.

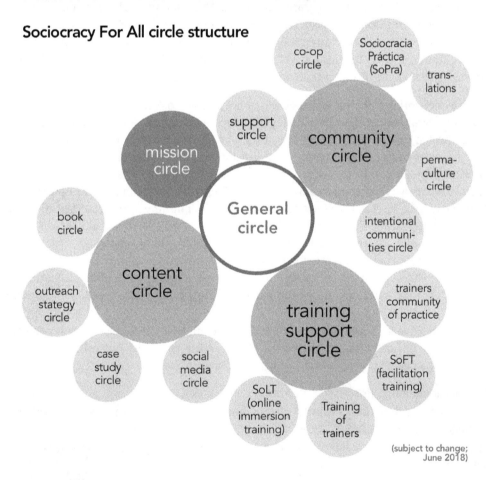

196: SoFA's organizational structure (as of early June 2018). Note that especially on sub-circle level, there continue to be changes as we continue to incorporate new people and projects, and adjust the structure to best meet our needs.

SoFA members have a lot of ideas and projects in the pipeline that we're already working on as you are reading this manual. So if you have an idea or something you're wishing for, chances are there are others wanting to join in with you. How can we make onboarding easier? How can SoFA collaborate with research more? How can sociocracy benefit families and children, how can towns be governed sociocratically? What's needed for social change towards more egalitarian societies? (Please note that membership in SoFA requires some experience with sociocracy because it is a working organization.)

- Content Circle produces accessible resources and creates opportunities for people to engage with those resources; this includes webinars, twitter feed, Facebook page, medium articles and youtube channel. Everything we say or write, we try to make accessible to everyone, so the next wave of people can be inspired by the hope that better systems are possible and available.
- Community Network Circle makes sure people using sociocracy in similar contexts can find each other and exchange their experiences or create content that works for their particular sector. We are working in the areas of cooperatives, permaculture, intentional communities and we have an ambitious project of bringing sociocracy more comprehensively to Spanish-speakers.
- Training Support Circle holds attention for training, training formats, training of trainers and evolution of training. This includes a study group curriculum (Empowered Learning Circles, ELC), the Sociocracy Leadership Training SoLT and advanced training programs.

SoFA is also a network of like-minded people. Many come to SoFA for training and want to make sociocracy an integral part of their lives. They also become members for the companionship – many of us share the chronic experience of having been the naively hopeful person in a broken system, looking for meaningful ways to find more alignment of our longing and our lives. Many of us have looked for fellow travelers for a long time, drawing hope from the deep intuition that there can be better ways. To us, our members are our dear companions, our tribe. They turn social change into pleasure.

SoFA can be a place for you if you are able and willing to put time into sociocracy, to use it, to spread it, to teach it and improve it. And of course SoFA is a place to get resources and help. SoFA is primarily a volunteer organization. If you want to contribute to this effort, let us know!

If you are part of a sociocratic organization, you are invited to contact us! That way, we can understand how we can support practitioners better. We can support each other in learning more. See www.sociocracyforall.org/sofa to see our current circle structure and membership processes.

Support SoFA   SoFA is a US based non-profit and we see ourselves as a movement service organization. Our funding is based mostly on fee for service. If you are inspired by our mission and would like to contribute to SoFA's capacity, we are inviting you to donate to SoFA.

- Click on the donation link on our website.
- You can send us donation checks to our mailing address. (Sociocracy For All, Unit 8, 120 Pulpit Hill Road, Amherst MA 01002, USA)
- If you consider making a major donation and/or contributing in the form of stock or bequests, please contact us.

7.2   About the authors

Ted   I was born in 1979 and raised in Germany with German and British parents and 3 siblings. I studied linguistics, literature and history, in Tübingen and Bologna, graduating with the counterpart of a PhD in linguistics for work on syntax and semantics.

What does linguistics have to do with sociocracy? Linguistics studies how the human mind works. Language and communication are humbling and complex – and still we are able to form sentences no one has ever formed before us. For linguists, it takes considerable effort to understand something that our mind seems to do so effortlessly. It is intriguing to think of group decision-making as an extension of language processing and how we can think together. How can we practice mutual understanding and shared decision-making so that it feels just as effortless?

To me, there is a social mission in linguistics. Linguistics is not grammar-police: linguistics studies how people speak, not how *some* people *think* they should speak. Everyone's voice matters – and anything we say is always a perfect expression of the human mind. My mind loves concepts, and even more I love switching back and forth from concrete examples to the level of concepts, and back again.

I moved into a cohousing community in 2012 as this community had just adopted sociocracy (they refer to it as Dynamic Governance). I soon became interested and involved. It was sociocracy that brought Jerry and me together, and together we founded *Sociocracy For All* (SoFA). Within SoFA, I currently hold several roles, mostly around content production, tech and networking.

The cohousing community is home to my children, Helena, Sophia, Antonia, Julia and Emilia. They grow up knowing their 70 neighbors and being known and loved by them. Although not all of my children can even pronounce the word *sociocracy*, every dinner conversation involves at least one round of highlights and lowlights from their day.

Jerry   Love is the only resource without limit, endlessly renewable. Yet so many experience shortages. It is like water. There is plenty of it. But there are distribution problems. And there are contamination problems. The sadness that human beings are more clever than they are wise. We do have answers to all our problems. Except we have not yet figured out how to work together consistently and effectively. That is what has attracted me to sociocracy and Non-Violent Communication.

I was born in Cuba and moved with my family to New York City in 1961 when I was 8 years old. From my parents, I got the love of nature and love of mind. What I learned outside the classroom as a young adult was that there was hope that we could model community living in a way that demonstrated healthy relationships with other humans and the land. What most influenced me was my 12-year involvement with Movement for a New Society (MNS). We were a network of small groups dedicated to revolutionary nonviolence, which meant seeking to help build a just and joyful world through direct action to challenge whatever systems were generating pain, through training activists in all the skills needed, and through valuing the sense of community in how we lived.

The reality of trying to live these ideals is humbling. What I can say for myself is that I am still trying. And the gift has been the sharing of this journey with the principal author of this book, Ted, and the amazing energy and capacity Ted has brought into creating *Sociocracy For All*. The gift is also now being part of the world-wide weaving of so many threads seeking to live the understanding that all people are one and that everyone's needs matter.

7.3   Resources

7.3.1   Literature

- Buck, John and Sharon Villines (2017). We the People: Consenting to a Deeper Democracy. Second edition. Sociocracy.info.
- Eckstein, Jutta and John Buck (2018). Company-wide Agility with Beyond Budgeting, Open Space & Sociocracy: Survive and Thrive on Disruption. See `https://leanpub.com/bossanova`
- Charest, Gilles (2007). La démocratie se meurt, vive la sociocratie! Edizioni esserci. (French)
- Endenburg, Gerard (1998). Sociocracy as Social Design: Its Characteristics and Course of Development, as Theoretical Design and Practical Project. Eburon, Rotterdam.
- Endenburg, Gerard (1998). Sociocracy: The Organization of Decision Making. "No objection" as the Principle of Sociocracy. Eburon, Rotterdam.
- Romme, Georges (2016). The Quest for Professionalism: The Case of Management and Entrepreneurship. Oxford: Oxford University Press.
- Romme, A. Georges L. and Gerard Endenburg (2006). Construction principles and design rules in the case of circular design. Organization Science, 17: 287-297.
- Romme, A. Georges L. (1999). Domination, self-determination and circular organizing. Organization Studies, 20: 801-832.
- Romme, Georges L, Jan Broekgaarden, Carien Huijzer, Annewiek Reijmer and Rob van der Eyden (2018). From competition and collusion to consent-based collaboration: A case study of local democracy. International Journal of Public Administration, 41: 246-255.
- Rosenberg, Marshall (2003). Nonviolent Communication: A Language of Life. 2nd edition. PuddleDancer Press.
- Wineman, Steven (2003). Power Under. Trauma and nonviolent social change.
  (See `http://www.traumaandnonviolence.com`)

7.3.2   Other ways to learn

You want to learn more! Great!

Since the sociocratic landscape is changing and evolving all the time – as it should! The most current information will always be online. Globally, there are more and more sociocratic consultants and trainers, communities and parts of the movement.

- Sociocracy For All. `http://www.sociocracyforall.org`. A non-profit committed to spread sociocracy and make it accessible to everyone. Resources, networking, training, consulting.
- The Sociocracy Group. `http://www.thesociocracygroup.com/`. A consulting group focused on sociocracy, mostly in Europe.
- The Sociocracy Consulting Group. `http://www.sociocracyconsulting.com/`. A consulting group focused on sociocracy, based in N. America, Australia and Canada.
- Governance Alive. `http://www.governancealive.com/`
- Sociocracy 3.0. `http://www.sociocracy30.org/`

We invite you to explore how you could *do* sociocracy instead of learning *about* sociocracy. What can you do that is a small step toward implementing some of the ideas and tools? How can you become a more experienced facilitator? Where could you take this to make it come alive? Could it be, for instance, an online class on facilitation to become more familiar and to bring more positive change to your immediate community?

Join a community of practice, within SoFA or outside of SoFA. The list serve in `sociocracy.groups.io` is a popular place for ongoing discussion of sociocracy and is open to new members. SoFA's Facebook group (`www.facebook.com/groups/SociocracyForAll/`) is another place where you can post questions and meet people. Sign up for the SoFA mailing list and you will receive several emails a month with references to new articles and videos, and upcoming webinars and training. Check out the SoFA youtube channel (`www.youtube.com/c/sociocracyforall`) and the SoFA website `sociocracyforall.org` for a virtual library of videos, articles, visuals and sample documents – most valuable for download free with creative commons license. We have a study group curriculum that you can use to try out sociocracy formats.

7.3.3 Charts and templates

The reason we decided to write a book is that we wanted all the information in context and in one place. We try to update our materials while staying aligned with terminology and basic patterns to remain our content coherent and accessible.

The materials that are or will become available with this book are:

- The meeting sheet (see page 262) in high resolution and with translations into different languages.
- Links to translations of parts and entire versions of the book – talk to us if your language is missing and you would like to help out. For SoFA, accessibility also means offering as many resources as possible in people's own languages.
- Digital versions of the feelings list and needs list (see page 260).
- In planning stage, as of June 2018: governance agreements repository (a collection of governance agreements, by-laws etc.), videos of the skits in this book etc.

Please see `www.manyvoicesonesong.com` to access these resources.

Universal feelings list (partial)

When needs are met

adventurous	engaged	loving
affectionate	excited	moved
alive	fascinated	peaceful
calm	friendly	playful
confident	glad	relaxed
content	happy	satisfied
curious	hopeful	tender
delighted	interested	thrilled
energetic	joyful	warm

When needs are not met

agitated	embarrassed	nervous
alarmed	exasperated	overwhelmed
ambivalent	flustered	protective
angry	grief	sad
annoyed	heartbroken	scared
anxious	helpless	stressed
confused	hopeless	suspicious
despairing	impatient	tense
devastated	irritated	terrified
disconnected	lonely	torn
discouraged	longing	troubled

Universal needs list (partial)

Connection
Acceptance
Affection
Clarity
Communication
Confirmation
Compassion
Intimacy
Understanding
Love

Autonomy
Choice Space
Spontaneity

Peace
Beauty
Ease
Harmony
Order
Wholeness

Interconnection
Belonging
Consideration
Community
Cooperation
Dignity
Mutuality
Support
Trust

Meaning
Contribution
Creativity
Hope
Inspiration
Purpose

Celebration
Joy
Mourning
Play

Competence
Effectiveness
Efficiency
Growth
Learning
Power

Honesty
Authenticity
Integrity

Basic Survival
Shelter
Food & Water
Rest
Safety
Security
Touch

2018 sociocracyforall.org
newenglandNVC.org

197: Feelings and needs list. Get a high-resolution image on our website under www.manyvoicesonesong.com

Feedback form (practice sheet)

Pick an incident that triggered you in some way. What happened? Do you notice your judgments and interpretations mixed in with your observations of what happened? Start with stating what you observed without adding in judments and continue with the fill-in-the-blank form below.

When I see/hear/notice...
one observation without judgment

I feel...
one or two feelings, rather than a projection or a thought

Because I need/value/care about....
one or two universal needs, not strategies

Would you be willing to ...
specific, stated in positive & doable?

Giving feedback

You can use this sheet as a basis for reaching out to give feedback to a someone in your organization.

- [ ] Process what happened with the help of this sheet and maybe with another person.
- [ ] Check if there is willingness to receive feedback.
- [ ] Find a good channel/time/context to deliver feedback

Sociocracy For All
2018 sociocracyforall.org
newenglandNVC.org

198: A sample version of a feedback form. Get a high-resolution image on our website under www.manyvoicesonesong.com

Sociocracy For All
resources, videos, training, consulting, community, advocacy for shared power

sociocracyforall.org 2018

MEETING SHEET FOR FACILITATORS

basic patterns

under-stand	1. report clarifying questions measure: all understand
explore	2. prompt reaction round measure: all ideas gathered
decide	3. proposal consent round measure: decision made

standard meeting format

Opening	Check-in ADMIN	attendance, duration, minutes, infomation, next meeting time
Content	Consent to agenda	
	report/feedback decision read back notes	understand (explore) ((decide))
	update backlog	
Closing	Check-out	content, process, interpersonal

operational meeting

Opening	brief check-in ADMIN
Content	List of projects
	for each project:	understand status (explore ideas) decide, assign
	update backlog
Closing	brief check-out

performance review

under-stand	review documents achievement round improvement round
explore	improvement areas improvement plan ideas write up plan
decide	consent to plan schedule follow-up document
	follow-up

	UNDERSTAND			EXPLORE		DECIDE		
Generate policy	understand context	explore underlying needs	synthesize issue/needs	picture forming (scope?)	explore proposal ideas	synthesize ideas into proposal		
Policy review	understand current policy	review data/feed-back	synthesize status of policy			Consent process		
Objections	understand objections	explore needs/relation-ship to aim	synthesize objection	understand scope of amendments	explore amendment ideas	synthesize amendments into proposal	amendments: o modify proposal o shorten term o measure concern	
Consent process	understand proposal	explore reactions	synthesize reactions	re-state proposal	consent round	acknowlege consent/objection	plan publication	prepare materials	publish
Selection process	understand role	explore term/quali-fications	consent to list of quali-fications	write down nomination	nomination round	change round	propose candidate	consent round	publish decision

Universal needs list (partial)

Connection
Acceptance
Affection
Clarity
Communication
Confirmation
Compassion
Intimacy
Understanding
Love

Autonomy
Choice Space
Spontaneity

Peace
Beauty
Ease
Harmony
Order
Wholeness

Interconnection
Belonging
Consideration
Community
Cooperation
Dignity
Mutuality
Support
Trust

Meaning
Contribution
Creativity
Hope
Inspiration
Purpose

Celebration
Joy
Mourning
Play

Competence
Effectiveness
Efficiency
Growth
Learning
Power

Honesty
Authenticity
Integrity

Basic Survival
Shelter
Food & Water
Rest
Safety
Security
Touch

First aid kit: options for facilitation
o adjust/postpone/modify agenda items
o round "what do we do now?"
o changing desired outcome for items
o time limit during rounds
o creating helping circle for lengthy topic
o take a break to address issue
o take a break away from the issue
o make a proposal (content/process)
o ....

creating a role
☐ tasks/aim
☐ authority/domain

proposals
☐ complete wording?
☐ term?
☐ dimensions covered?
☐ (measurement?)
☐ (feedback plan?)
☐ (needs statement?)

forming an agenda
☐ topics
☐ order/timing for each item
☐ desired outcomes for topic

creating a (sub/helping) circle
☐ aim
☐ domain
☐ leader
☐ (members)

199: Meeting sheet for facilitators. Get a high-resolution image on our website under www.manyvoicesonesong.com

Selection process

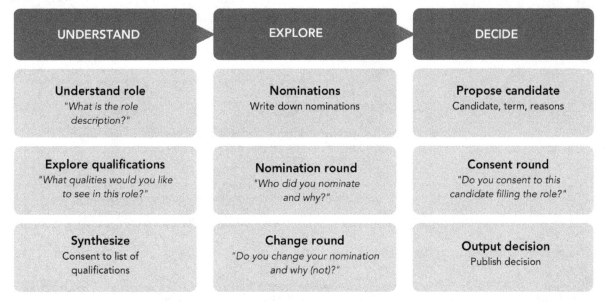

200: 3x3 matrix for the selection process: In this matrix, you can see each step used in the selection process in the context of input–tranformation–output and understand – explore – decide. Each step has a quote to make more tangible what is entailed in each step.

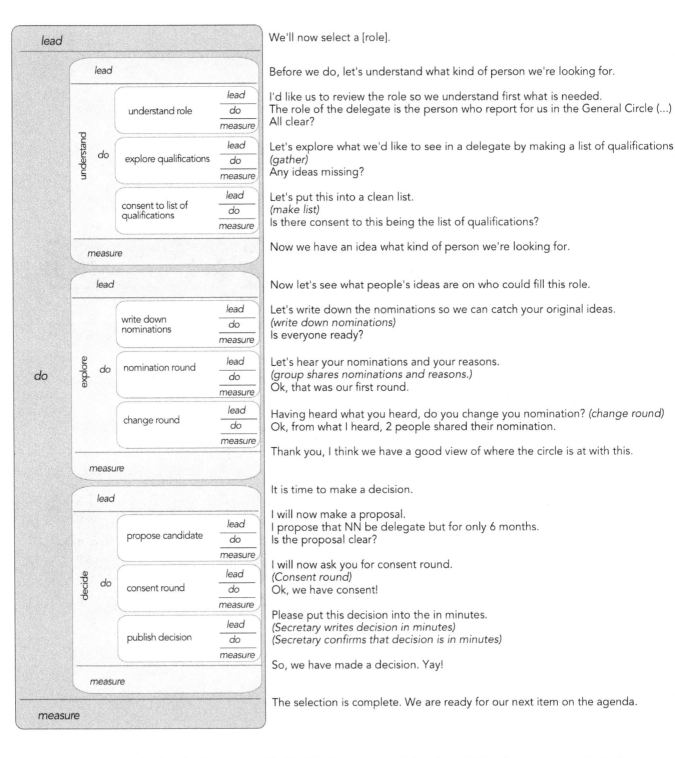

				We'll now select a [role].
lead				
				Before we do, let's understand what kind of person we're looking for.
do	lead			
	understand	do	understand role	lead
				do
				measure
				I'd like us to review the role so we understand first what is needed. The role of the delegate is the person who report for us in the General Circle (...) All clear?
			explore qualifications	lead
				do
				measure
				Let's explore what we'd like to see in a delegate by making a list of qualifications (gather) Any ideas missing?
			consent to list of qualifications	lead
				do
				measure
				Let's put this into a clean list. (make list) Is there consent to this being the list of qualifications?
		measure		
				Now we have an idea what kind of person we're looking for.

We'll now select a [role].

Before we do, let's understand what kind of person we're looking for.

I'd like us to review the role so we understand first what is needed.
The role of the delegate is the person who report for us in the General Circle (...)
All clear?

Let's explore what we'd like to see in a delegate by making a list of qualifications (gather)
Any ideas missing?

Let's put this into a clean list.
(make list)
Is there consent to this being the list of qualifications?

Now we have an idea what kind of person we're looking for.

explore

lead

Now let's see what people's ideas are on who could fill this role.

write down nominations — lead / do / measure

Let's write down the nominations so we can catch your original ideas.
(write down nominations)
Is everyone ready?

nomination round — lead / do / measure

Let's hear your nominations and your reasons.
(group shares nominations and reasons.)
Ok, that was our first round.

change round — lead / do / measure

Having heard what you heard, do you change you nomination? (change round)
Ok, from what I heard, 2 people shared their nomination.

Thank you, I think we have a good view of where the circle is at with this.

measure

decide

lead

It is time to make a decision.

propose candidate — lead / do / measure

I will now make a proposal.
I propose that NN be delegate but for only 6 months.
Is the proposal clear?

consent round — lead / do / measure

I will now ask you for consent round.
(Consent round)
Ok, we have consent!

publish decision — lead / do / measure

Please put this decision into the in minutes.
(Secretary writes decision in minutes)
(Secretary confirms that decision is in minutes)

So, we have made a decision. Yay!

measure

measure

The selection is complete. We are ready for our next item on the agenda.

201: 3x9 Matrix for the selection process with skit: This is a more detailed version of 200 – the most reasonable level of detail for the selection process. The columns in 200 are now arranged vertically to allow the reading flow. Each step in 200 now falls into three steps (lead-do-measure). We also added the framing statements for each part as they would sound like in natural language.

Policy process

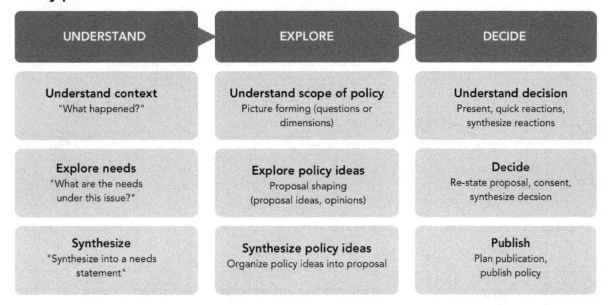

202: 3x3 matrix for the policy process: In this matrix, you can see each step used in the policy generation and decision process. 203 is the more detailed chart of the last third of this chart.

Consent process

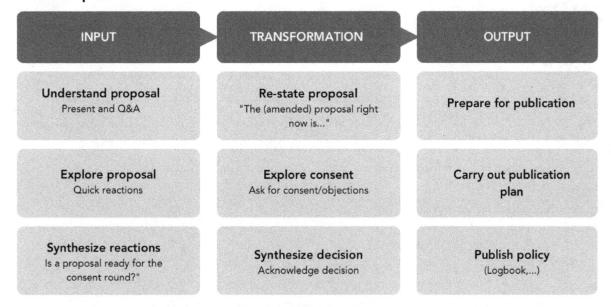

203: 3x3 matrix for the consent process: In this matrix, you can see each step used in the policy generation and decision process. This is the more detailed version of the last third of 202.

lead

Box	Skit text
	We'll now make policy round....

input (do)

lead

understand trigger/ issue — lead / do / measure	Before we do, let's understand the need for this policy.
	Let's hear a description of the issue that triggered this. *(report of issue)* Clarifying questions?
explore underlying needs — lead / do / measure	Let's explore what we see as the needs here. *(gather needs)* Any needs missing?
synthesize issue/needs — lead / do / measure	Let's put this into a clean list so we know what problem we want to solve. *(make needs statement/driver statement)* Is there consent to this being the the list of needs?

measure

Now we have an understanding of what we want to solve.

transformation (do)

lead

Now let's see what we can do about the issue.

picture forming (understand scope) — lead / do / measure	Let's write down what questions/areas would a policy have to cover. *(write down dimensions)* Let's consent to this being our list of dimensions.
explore policy ideas (proposal shaping) — lead / do / measure	Let's hear your opinions and proposal ideas for those dimensions. *(group shares proposal ideas and reasons in as many rounds as needed.)* Ok, now we have a list of proposal ideas.
synthesize policy ideas into proposal — lead / do / measure	Let's sort these ideas into a proposal draft. *(organize into proposal)* Great, now we organized all our ideas.

measure

The proposal is ready for the next step.

output (do)

lead

It is time to make a decision on the proposal.

understand proposal — lead / do / measure	This is the proposal. Are there any questions? (answer questions) What are your quick reactions? (hear quick reactions) From what I hear, people seem to like the proposal. overall except....
make decision — lead / do / measure	I am amending the proposal. *(Present)* Do you consent to this proposal? *(Consent round)* Ok, we have consent!
publish decision — lead / do / measure	Please put this decision into the in minutes. (Secretary writes decision in minutes) (Secretary confirms that decision is in minutes)

measure

So, we have made a decision. Great job!

measure

If no one else has anything to share, it looks like we're done.

204: 3x9 Matrix for the policy process with skit: this is the flow of understanding the need, generating policy and decision about policy. The last third, the decision process, is shown in more detail in 205 on page 267.

					It is time to make a decision on the proposal.

lead

lead

understand proposal	lead
	do
	measure

This is the proposal. Are there any questions?
(answer questions)
I think we have answered all questions.

explore quick reactions	lead
	do
	measure

What are your quick reactions?
(hear quick reactions)
Thank you for your reactions.

synthesize reactions	lead
	do
	measure

I will now make small amendments to the proposal.
The amended proposal is....
So, there are a few small modifications here.

input do

measure — We have a proposal ready for a decision.

Let's make sure everyone understands the proposal.

---

lead — Let's move on to the consent round.

re-state proposal	lead
	do
	measure

Let me re-state the proposal.
(re-states proposal)
I hope all is clear.

consent round	lead
	do
	measure

Let's do a consent round. Do you have objections to this proposal?
(consent round)
Looks like there are no objections (in case of objections, go to objection chart)

consent given?	lead
	do
	measure

Is the decision written down and could you read it back to us?
(Secretary nods and reads decision.)
Great, that all sounds correct. thank you.

do transformation

measure — The decision is made.

---

lead — Let's make sure this policy can go public.

prepare publication	lead
	do
	measure

Who do we want to inform, and how can we best do that?
(Circle makes a plan)
Does this sound good to everyone?

make materials	lead
	do
	measure

Let's make sure the policy is written well in the notes.
(Secretary puts policy into minutes.)
Would you read to us what is going out public? *(Secretary reads back minutes)*

publish decision	lead
	do
	measure

(Secretary coordinates with logbook keeper to add to policy/policy material.)
(Logbook keeper puts policy in logbook.)
(Logbook keeper confirms with secretary.)

output

measure — *(Confirmation to circle/leader that policy is public)*

measure — *(Policy is made and published.)*

205: 3x9 Matrix for the policy process with skit: This is the more detailed version of the last third of 204. Note the level of detail needed in the decision-making process. The output phase might be much simpler in a small organization.

Integrating objections

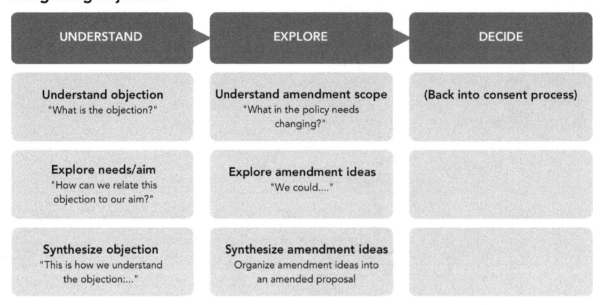

206: 3x3 matrix for the dealing with objections.

Reviewing policy

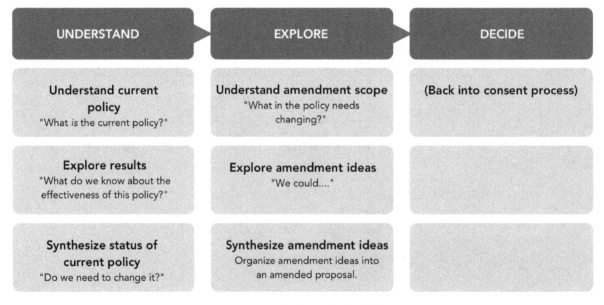

207: 3x3 matrix for reviewing policy.

Index

CPSIA information can be obtained
at www.ICGtesting.com
Printed in the USA
BVHW092020070720
583174BV00002B/86